Blair's community

MANCHESTER
1824

Manchester University Press

To Jim, with thanks for everything

Blair's community

Communitarian thought and New Labour

Sarah Hale

Manchester University Press

Manchester and New York

distributed exclusively in the USA by Palgrave

Published by Manchester University Press
Oxford Road, Manchester M13 9NR, UK
and Room 400, 175 Fifth Avenue, New York, NY 10010, USA
www.manchesteruniversitypress.co.uk

Distributed exclusively in the USA by
Palgrave, 175 Fifth Avenue, New York,
NY 10010, USA

Distributed exclusively in Canada by
UBC Press, University of British Columbia, 2029 West Mall,
Vancouver, BC, Canada V6T 1Z2

British Library Cataloguing-in-Publication Data
A catalogue record for this book is available from the British Library
Library of Congress Cataloging-in-Publication Data applied for

ISBN   0 7190 7412 6   *hardback*
EAN   9780 7190 7412 7

15 14 13 12 11 10 09 08 07 06   10 9 8 7 6 5 4 3 2 1

First published 2006

Edited and typeset by
Frances Hackeson Freelance Publishing Services, Brinscall, Lancs
Printed in Great Britain by CPI, Bath

Contents

Acknowledgements

The book grew out of my DPhil at the University of Sussex, where I spent, in total, nine very happy years and amassed intellectual debts too numerous to mention. Two deserve special thanks: Andrew Chitty, who first sparked my interest in political theory and introduced me to the joys of intellectual activity, and, above all, Luke Martell, whose support and encouragement have been unfailing and unstinting.

Part I

New Labour

Introduction

This book is about communitarianism and New Labour; in particular, about communitarianism and Tony Blair. It is not, unlike most work on the topic, about New Labour's, or Blair's, communitarianism. It concludes, in fact, that there is no such thing; that Blair and New Labour are not and never have been communitarian, despite frequent references and appeals to community, despite consorting with known communitarians, and despite the adoption of language and even whole discourses used by communitarians.

The book traces how the myth of New Labour's communitarianism developed and gained currency, and shows why it is just a myth, by examining the party's policies and utterances,[1] both in and out of government, and comparing these with the work of the established communitarians who are so widely supposed to have influenced it. It examines how suitable conditions emerged for the myth to take root, the factors that enabled it to grow and become widespread, and the desire of politicians, commentators and even academics to believe it.

When Tony Blair became leader of the Labour Party in July 1994, the modernisation process begun by Neil Kinnock gained renewed momentum and became the focus of public attention, culminating with the rewriting, in 1995, of Clause IV of the party's constitution to remove the commitment to common ownership of the means of production. While Blair has consistently argued that the broad aims and goals of his party remain unchanged, and while it is largely accepted that the mainstream Labour Party has never been a bastion of socialism, this was certainly an enormous symbolic shift, important because it was seen by many to leave an ideas vacuum at the heart of the party; a void where ideology should reside.

Both within and outside the party there was a feeling that such a void needed to be filled. There is a perceived danger that a party without ideology will be seen as being without principles (indeed, the two are often not clearly differentiated), and as opportunistic rather than merely pragmatic. This view was reflected in the spring of 2002, when a Labour backbencher, intending to be helpful, asked Tony Blair for 'a brief characterisation of the political philosophy which he espouses and which underlies his policies' on the basis that Blair had in the past been 'subject to rather unflattering or even malevolent descriptions of his motivation'.[2] The fact that Blair's reply, which related to investment in public services and a specific scheme to bring overseas specialists into the NHS, merely seemed to underline his lack of a philosophy is less important than the question's demonstration that, even after a full term of New Labour government, parties and their leaders are still expected to have a philosophy. The desire of the party to be seen as more than simply an electoral force is evident in Blair's frequent appeals to the idea of values, frequently in the abstract and in isolation from reference to specific policies.[3]

In the absence of an explicit New Labour philosophy, political correspondents and academics set about identifying an implicit one. Where there were no prima facie ideological imperatives behind policy, commentators set out to construct explanatory ones. Within the party itself, an attempt was made to meet the perceived lack by developing the 'Third Way'. The Third Way's starting point was its definition in terms of what it was not: neither Thatcherite neo-liberalism nor state socialism. But this was only a starting point. Academics and think tanks were explicitly invited to flesh it out with positive content, the most high profile of the former being Anthony Giddens of the LSE; of the latter, Demos, the New Labour-inspired (and inspiring) think tank established by Geoff Mulgan. Tony Blair himself published a pamphlet entitled *The Third Way: New Politics for the New Century* under the auspices of the Fabian Society. The origins and content of the Third Way are an area of extensive academic research in their own right, which this book barely touches upon,[4] but the ideas which came to be associated with the Third Way had to come from somewhere, and to be defined in certain ways.

One of the most important ideas associated with New Labour, either as part of the Third Way, or as an alternative source of ideas to it (and on some accounts predating it), is communitarianism. It is not, however, the only one. Other ideas, ideologies, philosophies, theories or sets of principles linked with varying degrees of plausibility to the development of New Labour include the American New Right writers Charles Murray[5] and Lawrence Mead,[6] whether or not mediated through the lessons famously learned from Clinton's Democrat Party;[7] also Murray's views on dependency culture mediated through former welfare minister Frank Field; the British New Right,[8] in particular its conception of citizenship;

Thatcherism, in particular the idea that the Thatcher governments changed forever the context of British politics;[9] traditional conservative philosophy such as the work of David Selbourne; a continuation of the themes of previous Conservative governments;[10] the concept of citizenship[11] in some of its various forms, particularly the European tradition; the European tradition of focusing on social inclusion, interpreting inclusion as largely being through paid employment;[12] previous British political and social movements including Fabianism,[13] ethical socialism,[14] Christian socialism, radical liberalism and the New Liberalism[15] of the early part of the twentieth century; the British Socialist tradition,[16] the popular philosopher (and Christian Socialist) of the 1930s John Macmurray;[17] Anthony Giddens and his developing theory of the Third Way,[18] and the influence of the relatively new phenomenon of think tanks.[19] In addition to this, there are also claims that the New Labour government does not have any guiding principles or philosophy at all.[20]

Most of these suggestions were either short-lived, or very much minority views. Communitarianism on the other hand retained a remarkably durable and broadly based profile, to some extent subsuming ideas about inclusion and citizenship under its umbrella. Communitarianism itself, cited as a characteristic of New Labour's approach, cropped up consistently from 1994 onwards, as Chapter 1 describes.

All this presupposes that there is one definable entity called communitarianism, but any but the most cursory look at the attribution of communitarianism to New Labour shows that there is no single understanding of what the concept means; indeed, there is such an enormous range of frequently conflicting conceptions of communitarianism as to render the term highly problematic as a means of describing the party or its policies. Compounding the problems this presents, commentators rarely acknowledge (or even seem to be aware) that the particular conception of communitarianism which they are employing is not the sole, universally understood one. Some commentators do of course recognise the existence of various 'types' of communitarianism (Elizabeth Frazer[21] and Stephen Driver and Luke Martell,[22] for example, develop explicit typologies), but this does not necessarily solve the problem.

Even those accounts which recognise the variety of communitarian positions tend to go on to compare New Labour policy and rhetoric with generalised, abstracted or constructed accounts of communitarianism. This is the case even when the names of particular communitarian writers are invoked. It is this generic communitarianism which is then held up against New Labour policy and found to match. But this raises new problems for the understanding and analysis of policy.

Generic communitarianism may represent a 'lowest common denominator' form of communitarianism, which contains only those features that all communitarian writers and doctrines have in common; for example, the use of the term 'community'.[23] This inevitably leaves out much more than it includes from all articulations of communitarianism, and will have more features in common with many other positions than with other communitarianisms. Because communitarian positions are so diverse any common thread would be thin indeed; too thin to hang a comparative analysis with New Labour on. Worse, commentators rarely acknowledge that they are working with such a thinly spread understanding of communitarianism, frequently invoking the name of one or more specific writers in the context of a very generalised understanding of the doctrine.

Alternatively, commentators may 'mix-and-match' different aspects of various writers' communitarianism which the writers do not have in common, picking out from each only those aspects which do coincide with New Labour positions. This equally produces a broad and vague conception of communitarianism, which generally takes as its starting point a New Labour position and then calls upon coincident but incomplete accounts of communitarianism drawn from more than one source with which it can then easily be matched. Again, this results in a conception of communitarianism which is too wide and indistinct to be useful as a descriptive or analytical tool.

Many existing accounts of New Labour's communitarianism do not mention specific communitarian thinkers; where they do, most do not engage deeply with their work. Many commentators take for granted that the meaning of communitarianism is understood; some, particularly on the academic side, attempt explicitly to define it, but almost every commentary is working with either a different definition/understanding or none at all. When concepts are understood as broadly as this it is relatively easy to find points at which they overlap with policy.

This book dispenses with such generalised and constructed understandings of communitarianism, and compares New Labour policy and rhetoric directly with of a range of *specific*, articulated communitarian positions – including those of the writers most frequently cited as a communitarian influence on the party, as well as those whose significance lies in the fact that they offer alternative conceptions of communitarianism. It considers and compares their respective understandings and presentation of central concepts (such as community and duty), of the best ways of promoting those concepts, and their priorities in terms of what *should* be promoted.

On the New Labour side, the analysis focuses upon speeches (particularly those of Tony Blair, but also of Gordon Brown and other leading members) and Labour Party policy documents from 1994 onwards, and government White and Green Papers from 1997, also taking into account more minor sources, including newspaper articles published in the name of leading New Labour politicians, and radio and press interviews with them.

The analysis of communitarian writers focuses on published texts. Where a writer has produced explicitly communitarian work, this is the main focus. Where communitarianism has been 'read into' a writer's work a wider range of their output is considered. A wider range is also examined from those authors who have been cited by commentators as having influenced New Labour's communitarianism. In part this is to avoid the trap which commentators have previously fallen into; namely that of considering the work too selectively. It could of course be suggested that this book itself is selective in the material which it uses to reach its conclusions, but such an accusation would be unfair: it is selective only to the extent of highlighting the clearest examples in a detailed examination of each writer which focuses on the core and most significant aspects of their work, at the same time showing that commentators have frequently based their claims on marginal or misunderstood aspects. Furthermore, while some degree of coincidence does not necessarily show that New Labour *are* communitarian, significant areas of dissonance suggest more strongly that they are not. There is also an element of redressing the balance: aspects of communitarianism which suggest that New Labour *are* communitarian have already been pointed out, in many different ways and in many different forums.

The book is divided into three parts. Part I sets out how and why New Labour have been seen as communitarian, and the influences that have been attributed to them. Chapter 1 establishes the existence and persistence of widespread assumptions about New Labour's communitarianism, drawing on both academic and quality press accounts. It then goes on to examine what is meant by 'communitarianism' and its different forms and variants, establishing that the use of the term has become problematic and tends to obscure more than it illuminates. Chapter 2 begins by looking at the development of 'New' Labour under Blair's leadership, focusing in particular on the policy and rhetoric that came to be seen as demonstrating communitarian influence or reflecting communitarian ideas. It shows that these are open to a number of interpretations and have been used selectively in the past to provide evidence of communitarianism. It then looks at the direct relationship of leading

New Labour politicians with Amitai Etzioni, itself seen as evidence of his influence, and places this in the context of his meetings with all the British party leaders, as well as leading figures in the US, all of whom took something different from the encounter.

In Part II, these putative influences are analysed in detail, alongside relevant aspects of New Labour policy and rhetoric, and two further communitarian writers, Jonathan Boswell and Henry Tam, are introduced; writers who have been noticeable by their absence from the New Labour literature so far. Chapter 3 considers the communitarian political philosophy of Michael Sandel, Alasdair MacIntyre, Charles Taylor and Michael Walzer: work which is cited relatively infrequently, but nonetheless significantly, as an influence on New Labour. In four subsections the chapter sets out the main relevant tenets of each author's work and uses these as a context in which (and tools with which) to examine Blairite policy and discourse, before looking at more generalised accounts of communitarian political theory and the policies which they are said to suggest. The chapter concludes that not only is this philosophy not reflected by New Labour, but that it is well nigh impossible that it could be, given the vastly different and conflicting demands of academic philosophy and political necessity.

Chapter 4 challenges the view that the work of the Scottish moral philosopher John Macmurray, cited by Blair himself as an influence, is congruent with New Labour's position. It sets out the key points of Macmurray's philosophy and compares them with Blair's views as expressed in speeches and written pamphlets, concluding that although as a young new MP Blair expressed views that reflected aspects of Macmurray's philosophy, it has played no part in the making of New Labour under his leadership. Themes which form a substantial part of the New Labour conception of community are completely at odds with the view of Blair's supposed mentor.

Chapter 5 considers Amitai Etzioni, the communitarian writer most frequently cited by commentators as having influenced New Labour. It traces the possible routes of any such influence, then goes on to look closely at Etzioni's communitarian work and compare it with New Labour positions, particularly in the policy areas of welfare and law and order. The chapter demonstrates that Etzioni's work has in the past been read very selectively – the bulk even of his most explicitly communitarian work has largely been ignored – and that he is both implicitly and explicitly critical of New Labour policies.

Chapter 6 introduces two 'forgotten' British political communitarians: Jonathan Boswell and Henry Tam. These writers are rarely, if ever, acknowledged by either politicians or commentators despite writing explicitly for a British policy audience. After setting out their proposals for 'community in the economy' and education and citizenship respectively, it concludes that these writers have been ignored because of the relative (in British terms at least) radicalism of their ideas.

Part III assesses the extent of these influences, concluding that it is negligible.[24] It then sets out a critical analysis of Blair's and New Labour's particular conception of community, and ends by suggesting reasons for the power and endurance of the myth of New Labour communitarianism. Chapter 7 presents an account of the Blairite conception of community as a contractual relationship (albeit one shorn of the ideas of equality and voluntarism embodied in social contract theory). It is this, frequently explicit, contractualism which does most to render the New Labour vision antithetical to both traditional and communitarian conceptions of community. There then follows an assessment of why such discourses were seen as a 'communitarian turn'; why this idea was accepted and promulgated so easily both by journalists (as a simple matter of influence by the ideas of Macmurray and Etzioni) and also, in a more nuanced fashion, by the academic community, who sought to categorise and define New Labour's communitarianism, having accepted the idea of it.

1

New Labour and communitarianism: first impressions last

When, in October 1994, *Guardian* journalist Seumas Milne wrote that 'Tony Blair's New Labour "project" is communitarian to its fingertips',[1] he was both articulating and contributing to an impression of the party which was to endure for a decade and more. Many saw communitarianism not just as an influence on New Labour, or a position expressed by the party, but as a – or even the – defining feature of its 'newness'. While the main argument of this book is that this impression, and the assumptions about communitarianism and about New Labour which underlay it, were mistaken, this chapter shows how widespread and persistent such assumptions were in both the quality press and in academic discourse.

Subsequent chapters deal with references to specific writers; this chapter focuses on generalised claims about communitarianism and the communitarian nature of New Labour, first from the press, and then in academic work. The examples from press and academia are treated slightly differently, reflecting generalised differences in approach. Journalists tend to treat 'New Labour's communitarianism' relatively superficially, and the aim here is to show the range of understandings of communitarianism, both articulated and taken as read, in their work, as well as to establish that such impressions were indeed both widespread and durable. Academic commentators are more likely to undertake an analysis of 'New Labour's communitarianism' – or, sometimes in this case, 'communitarianisms'. Through this we can review some recent thinking about communitarianism and identify a number of potential problems with the ways in communitarianism is identified and interpreted. For reasons that will hopefully become clear as the chapter progresses, this work resists the temptation to offer a definition of communitarianism beyond the very general observation that it is a political or philosophical position that holds that community (variously defined) matters, and that contemporary philosophy, politics and/or society to some extent fails to recognise this sufficiently. Similarly, to provide a typology would be counterproductive, as it would depend upon the sort of hard and fast definitions which, it is being argued here, are unhelpful in understanding how and why communitarianism has been so readily associated with New Labour.

Communitarianism in the news

Prior to the mid-1990s, the term 'communitarianism' was unfamiliar even to people with a keen interest in politics. Its vastly increased profile can largely be credited to the efforts of Amitai Etzioni, of which more later. By the mid-1990s it was cropping up fairly regularly, if not frequently, in the quality and political press (in which are included the magazines the *Economist, New Statesman* and *Spectator*).

Commentators who mentioned communitarianism only to dismiss its significance were very much in the minority. A couple, early on, suggested that communitarianism had been one of a number of ideas which New Labour flirted with but abandoned fairly quickly. One article on the 'Third Way' noted that some have suggested that that term is 'simply the latest buzz phrase' in the search for 'intellectual ballast'. A 'party insider' was quoted as saying: '"first there was 'stakeholding', then there was 'communitarianism', now there is the 'third way'".[2] These are all presented as transient terms used in an attempt to describe Blair's 'political philosophy'. This however was highly atypical of the coverage of communitarianism at this time and subsequently.

The idea that New Labour were communitarian was not a flash in the pan. It began before Blair became leader, and examples continue to emerge in the third term of Labour government. In May 1994, during the leadership election campaign, a leading article in the *Independent* noted that in his first speech since the death of John Smith (the previous Labour leader, who had died earlier that month), Blair used rhetoric which 'highlighted the need to foster communities and repair the social fabric' and saw this as 'an initial attempt to set out a *communitarian Blairism* to replace Thatcherism and become the driving political philosophy of the nineties'. While Blair had been making points like this for some time, his new, higher, profile brought both his views and the idea of communitarianism to the attention of the press and public. Interestingly, the communitarianism espoused by Blair is seen in this article to draw on the ideas of Robert Owen, a name seldom if ever mentioned since.[3] The author also notes that Blair's rhetoric 'sounded comforting, but lacked policy radicalism'.[4]

Unlike other suggested New Labour positions (such as stakeholding) communitarianism was seen not only to survive but to thrive once the party came to government. At the end of their first term, during the 2001 General Election campaign, Mary Riddell wrote (with great certainty) in the *Observer* that '[s]ix years have passed since the first wave of communitarian waffle, peddled by Amitai Etzioni, percolated Labour thinking ... [I]t is certain that the ubiquitous mantra of "rights and responsibilities" tracks back to Etzioni ...'[5] Riddell notes that it did not seem likely at that time that a movement like Etzioni's, with its apparent disregard for civil rights and individual autonomy[6] would 'take root' in the Labour Party, but that it did, and '[a] parliamentary term on, we have an Identikit guru and yesterday's gospel of faith-based communitarianism rehashed for tomorrow's election'.

Press commentators' ideas of what communitarianism is, and the degree of detail in which they describe it, vary greatly. The idea that New Labour is communitarian is sufficiently established that in many cases it is simply mentioned in passing, taken for granted. In what way the party is 'communitarian' is frequently left undiscussed. Sometimes it is linked to the work of a particular writer or writers, but very often it is not. When no particular writer is named, there is often an assumption that the reader is aware of what communitarianism 'is', and by extension, an indication that it is an undifferentiated and uncontroversial ideology, while it actually admits of more, and more conflicting, interpretations than many other political creeds. Some journalists do develop their own ideas of what communitarianism might mean, occasionally using this to criticise New Labour, while others set out what they believe to be its basic values. There is nonetheless a large degree of vagueness as well as disagreement.

Many articles in the quality press simply refer to 'communitarianism' without making explicit what ideas are being taken to characterise it or mentioning any specific writers. A leading article in the *Independent* refers to 'the communitarian movement, which can claim Tony Blair as one of its members ...'[7] Although the Communitarian Movement as an organisation is the creation of Etzioni, this article does not mention him, but paints communitarianism as a doctrine of nostalgic social conservatism apparently independent of any particular thinker. (The alternative interpretation that the writer of this piece assumed that readers would have heard of the Communitarian Movement and know of its association with Etzioni seems less likely.) An article in the *Independent* about family policy refers in passing to 'Tony Blair's communitarian philosophy',[8] which is seen as being consistent with the Conservatives' 'back to basics' campaign, at least on the issue of single-parenthood, and as an aspect of what the article calls 'new social conservatism'. Anthony Barnett, in an article in the *Independent* prior to the 1997 General Election, asks just what sort of change Blair wants and what ideological beliefs underlie that, and concludes that Blair is not a free-marketeer, a Fabian or a liberal, but that his 'political attitudes are communitarian rather than individualist'.[9] An article in the *Economist*, about public spaces, says in passing that '[p]romoting parks and public spaces fits neatly with the communitarian ideas beloved by the Blair government'.[10] A *Times* article about entertainers' withdrawal of support from Labour under Blair suggests that Blair is much more comfortable with a more traditional, even conservative, audience, and lacks appeal to those 'Old Labour ... people who still see the movement as a crusade and who are not entirely at home with Mr. Blair's espousal of Tory economics and slightly cranky communitarianism.'[11]

One of Blair's own few recorded uses of the term 'communitarian' falls into this category of vague usage. In an edited extract from the speech which he made to Rupert Murdoch's News Corp organisation in July 1995, Blair says 'a communitarian philosophy ... applied with common sense, allows us to move beyond the choice between narrow individualism and old-style socialism'.[12] For Blair, 'the Left' is in a unique position, having 'the moral authority to enforce the rules because it sets them within an active and strong community'. This is necessary because, as he says in the opening lines of the speech, '[t]he only way to rebuild social order and stability is through strong values, socially shared, inculcated through individuals and families'. The left needs to treat this seriously, Blair asserts here, because the poor and disadvantaged are 'the first casualties of social breakdown'. He claims that this means that the inculcation of such values does not represent a move towards authoritarianism or 'an attempt to introduce a regressive personal morality', implying that he identifies these potential outcomes solely with elite groups. Blair then, at least in this speech, appears to identify communitarianism with strong, socially homogeneous values, and an application of the 'traditional values of the Left' (of which social justice and mutual respect are mentioned) via rules, within a strong and active community. As with many of Blair's speeches, it is hard to be sure exactly what he is saying, but it seems fairly clear that these ideas are what he takes communitarianism to refer to.

In Andrew Marr's view, it was through this speech that 'Blair formally came out as a communitarian.'[13] Marr however, focuses on the more potentially radical implications of communitarianism; his concern is whether Blair will be able to deliver what he sees as central – the return to citizens of the 'power to affect the world around them', asking 'would [Blair] allow people in Birmingham, Sussex and Cumbria to run schools, drugs projects and urban regeneration schemes in ways he disapproves of?' Clearly Marr believes the answer to this question to be no; but for him,

Blair's 'authoritarian tendencies' (to use the words of the *Economist*) constitute an obstacle to, rather than the realisation of, communitarianism.

According to the *Sunday Times*, the communitarian content of Blair's
News Corp speech was familiar to the Americans present: 'There was a
resonance about his visionary concern for rebuilding the family, about
his "communitarian" middle way between narrow individualism and the
old style politics of the left. They had heard it all before, during the 1992
presidential election ...'[14] The idea that Blair's position reflects that of
Bill Clinton a few years earlier is echoed by the *Economist*, which noted in
a piece on a visit by Blair to the US that 'Mr. Blair's desire to emulate Mr.
Clinton's success is evident in his espousal of Clintonite policies such as
workfare, and his endorsement of communitarianism.'[15] Again, the idea
of communitarianism is not elaborated upon, but Blair's espousal of it is
taken as read.

When Blair raised similar themes to those in the News Corp speech in
his address to the 1996 Labour Party conference, the *Economist* reported
that 'Mr. Blair has evidently decided that blather is the better part of
valour. He made up for lack of substance with a speech that set new
standards in British politics for mawkish sentiment, smug religiosity and
grandiose nonsense.' Although dismissive of Blair's rhetoric, the *Economist* nonetheless concludes that Blair's 'authoritarian communitarian tendencies' are disturbing, and 'will express themselves in the desire to boss
citizens about'.[16] This article in effect recognises two commonly perceived
aspects of political communitarianism: the rhetoric of community and
the possibility of a kind of authoritarianism in which 'shared' values are
enforced to some degree.

This aspect is recognised by Nicholas Deakin who, writing about the
voluntary sector, sees hidden dangers in Labour's apparently
communitarian plans for voluntary sector reform, warning voluntary sector organisations of the risk of 'being wanted for the wrong reasons ...
plunging into the warm bath of communitarian rhetoric and finding
yourselves used as a convenient device for keeping the neighbours in order and educating youth in the civic virtues'.[17] Referring to the sometimes violent protests against individuals identified as paedophiles in the
Paulsgrove area of Portsmouth in the summer of 2000, the *Guardian*
suggests that residents 'are getting together, bonding as a community – if
not in quite the way the prime minister and all his communitarian rhetoric envisaged'.[18] A report of Blair's unsuccessful speech to the Women's
Institute in 2000 put part of the blame for its hostile reception on his
apparent lack of anything new to say, citing 'reheated communitarianism'
as an example.[19]

For other commentators, communitarianism is identified by yet another, different, set of characteristics. Patrick Wintour, writing in the *Guardian* during the 1995 Labour conference, refers to 'the philosophy of communitarianism' as entailing 'taking on civic responsibility in exchange for opportunity'.[20] Wintour perceives this as the result of Blair's looking to Australia and the US for policy ideas, in contrast to John Smith and Neil Kinnock, under whose leadership Labour tended to look more to Europe, and in particular to German social democrats.

A number of articles suggest that New Labour's communitarianism may have its roots in the traditions of English ethical socialism and/or social liberalism. In October 1994 the *Economist* noted, in the light of Blair's speech to the party conference, that the way was open for Labour under his leadership to become a party which promoted meritocracy, but saw the greatest opposition to this as coming from a 'powerful tradition in Labour Party thought, communitarianism'.[21] This article perceives communitarianism as a tradition within the Labour Party, rather than a recent addition to or change of direction for it, and numbers among its proponents William Morris, G.D.H. Cole and R.H. Tawney. On this view, communitarianism is anti-meritocratic because 'for the communitarians, the greatest good is attachment, the greatest evil alienation; and the principal purpose of political activity is to advance the first at the expense of the second', meaning, among other things, that they would seek less rather than more social mobility, and desire 'in short, to recreate the organic certainties of the pre-industrial world'.[22] On this understanding, any communitarian strand in New Labour would be in stark conflict with support for meritocracy, and would tend to lead to the sorts of policies associated with 'old' Labour: 'to give just a little more money to this declining industry, to allow the benefits system to eat more and more of the nation's money, to shirk opportunities and stifle change'.[23]

From a different political perspective, John Gray also identifies communitarianism with the British tradition of ethical socialism, saying in an article in the *Guardian* that economic globalisation has made social democracy redundant, and that '[i]t follows that the core *communitarian values of ethical socialism* cannot be identified with their embodiments in the policies and strategies of any earlier time'.[24] In contrast, Michael Freeden, in a letter to the *Independent*, claims two of the writers – Cole and Tawney – along with H.J. Laski, J.A. Hobson and L.T. Hobhouse, as exemplars of a 'British ideological heritage' which can and should be drawn upon as an *alternative* to importing communitarian ideas which he describes as 'a largely conservative backlash against a humanist individualist tradition'.[25] What these writers of the British left stand for is generally agreed upon by the *Economist*, Gray and Freeden; what the latter disagree upon is what constitutes communitarianism.

In another of his pieces for the *Guardian*, Gray identifies Conservatives of the centre and left, such as Kenneth Clarke and Michael Heseltine, with communitarianism, predicting at the time of John Redwood's challenge for the Tory leadership that in the event of his being successful, '[t]he progressive communitarian conservatism that survived as a tempering force even in the Thatcherite eighties will be wiped out'.[26] Prior to his brief resignation as Conservative leader in the summer of 1995 it was reported that John Major too was seeking to 'associate the Conservatives with communitarian values' with the launch of a scheme to promote volunteering and 'good neighbourliness' – the values with which the idea of communitarianism is here identified.[27]

Although these examples show that communitarianism is not exclusively linked with the Labour Party, let alone with New Labour, the context of the articles suggests that it is Labour who have put the idea on the agenda, with the Conservatives attempting either to co-opt it for their own purposes or 'jump on the bandwagon'. Although it is in many of its variants a doctrine which would appear to sit comfortably with Major-style conservatism, and his government promoted many of the values identified subsequently as communitarian (such as voluntary service), the identification of Conservatives, both by themselves and by sympathetic commentators, as communitarian, has arisen in response to Labour initiatives.

This is explicitly recognised by an article in the *Economist*, which says: 'The Labour Party is not alone in showing renewed interest in the word "community". Several right-wing intellectuals, who would not have let the word pass their lips in the 1980s, have recently discovered that they, too, are communitarians.'[28] Names mentioned include John Gray, David Willetts, David Green of the IEA, and David Selbourne. The article concludes that 'the two parties give different twists to the communitarian argument' but that for both it represents a 'revulsion against the more chaotic aspects of the modern world and a longing for a steadier society'.

While some commentators see communitarianism as part of Labour's traditional heritage, others detect a communitarian influence coming from the US. Amitai Etzioni is the writer most frequently associated in the press with New Labour's perceived communitarianism. Much of this stems from a visit he made to Britain in 1995 to coincide with the UK publication of *The Spirit of Community*. Conservative MP Alan Duncan, and Dominic Hobson state that '[t]he philosophy of Tony Blair is drawn partly from Amitai Etzioni's influential *The Spirit of Community*,[29] quoting Etzioni's desire 'to recreate a "moral, social and public order based on restored communities"'. The Labour Party's new Clause IV, Duncan and Hobson say, 'pulsates with this "communitarian" ethos'. For these authors, on the libertarian right, Etzioni's ideas appeal to 'socialists in search of fresh versions of a bankrupt creed', and communitarianism is basically another manifestation of the socialism of Tawney, William Temple and Beatrice Webb, and as such presents a grave threat to individual freedom and social progress. This offers a contrast to those commentators quoted earlier who believe that the British socialist tradition exemplified by these writers is utterly incompatible with the American communitarianism associated with Etzioni. Duncan and Hobson also mention *The Principle of Duty* by the conservative David Selbourne as another seminal communitarian text, and see this as equally dangerous.

According to Charlotte Raven, in an *Observer* piece about think tanks, Tony Blair has been 'lapping up the "theories" of communitarian guru Amitai Etzioni', whose work Raven dismisses as a 'hotchpotch of homilies and homespun ideas', to plug the gap left by Labour's perceived abandonment of socialism. In this case, 'community' means 'how to hold a street party without worrying your flat is getting robbed': it is seen as a law and order/security issue, and Etzioni's answer is popular because the central notion of personal responsibility 'is one way of teaching the buggers to stop blaming other people, in particular politicians, for whatever straits they find themselves in'.[30] In the *Independent*, Diana Coyle set out to find out how far certain public figures practised what they preached on family and community involvement (not very, was the answer in most cases). Again, she saw Etzioni as being the most significant figure, saying that 'Etzioni is one of the people who have made community and family two of the most fashionable words in today's policy debate', taking as read that such a fashion had been established.[31] Etzioni's influence is frequently perceived as going beyond the British Labour Party. According to the *Economist*, 'Bill Clinton, Al Gore and Helmut Kohl have all acknowledged Mr Etzioni's influence; so have many others from across the political spectrum. Somebody in Britain's new model Labour Party is clearly reading his speeches. In politics, they are all communitarians now.'[32]

Etzioni's perceived influence on Blair is again mentioned in passing in an *Observer* article about divorce reform. The importance of marriage and the nuclear family is, it is said, 'a view associated with the Right, but it attracts support across the political spectrum, especially from those influenced by the communitarian ideas of the social theorist Amitai Etzioni, most notably Tony Blair'.[33]

Nick Cohen claims that 'Blair is reported to be capable of quoting whole chunks' of 'The Parenting Deficit', a chapter from *The Spirit of Community* published as a pamphlet by Demos.[34] In another article, Cohen refers to Demos as 'the communitarian think-tank'.[35] According to Sarah Baxter, 'Demos, the radical think tank ... claims responsibility for introducing Blair to the notion of rights and responsibilities espoused by Amitai Etzioni, the American communitarian.'[36] The *Economist*, in an article about Blair and academia, claims that 'some Labour policy advisers have proved adept at distilling contemporary intellectual ideas into policy proposals. Geoff Mulgan, former head of Demos, a think-tank, plays such a role in Mr Blair's staff: he is close to communitarian thinkers such as Amitai Etzioni'.[37] No less a commentator than Anthony Giddens, in a review of Etzioni's book *The New Golden Rule*, says that 'his ideas have influenced Tony Blair and other European politicians'.[38]

In contrast, Melanie Phillips, herself sometimes considered a populariser of communitarian thought, says that while Etzioni is a 'significant player', it is a misapprehension to believe that he has 'captured' Blair.[39] She introduces the possibility of New Labour having been influenced by communitarian philosophy, citing the name of Alasdair MacIntyre in an article examining 'what the talk of morality and community really means'.[40] Although she conceives of communitarianism in terms very similar to Etzioni's – it 'attempts to forge a new equilibrium between rights and responsibilities' – she does not see Etzioni as a direct influence on New Labour or Blair, (although she does believe that MacIntyre's thought feeds directly into Etzioni's). Rather, she suggests that '[i]t was Gordon Brown who brought the MacIntyre position into the Labour Party' and that this 'chimed with his own Scottish ethical tradition, as it did with Blair's particular Christian perspective' and, again, with the traditions of ethical socialism. Just as Keith Joseph famously handed out reading lists featuring Hayek and Friedman to his civil servants, Phillips suggests that 'maybe Gordon Brown will be handing out ... similarly a list of American philosophers'. Although MacIntyre (who despite doing most of his work in the US is not in fact American) is the only one mentioned by name, it is reasonable to assume that Phillips believed this list would include Michael Sandel, Michael Walzer and possibly the Canadian Charles Taylor.

Communitarian philosophy – the work of Sandel, Walzer, Taylor and MacIntyre – is mentioned in other press articles as a possible source for New Labour thinking. Writing in the *Independent*, Demos director Geoff Mulgan suggests that the communitarian philosophy of these four writers – unusually, he names all four of them – is one of 'several diverse currents' upon which the party's 'shift, towards what can loosely be termed communitarianism, has drawn'.[41] This communitarianism is characterised for Mulgan by the movement of the language of community to centre stage (from the 'margins of Liberal pavement politics') in Britain, and in the US by the communitarian movement's 'programme of self-help and moral education, and for its call for new responsibilities to match the growth of new rights'. Mulgan also recognises in passing a potentially more radical form of communitarianism, espoused by Sir James Goldsmith, which 'crystallised a widespread desire to return to a more localised, more traditional way of life against the depredations of rationalism, high science and free trade'.[42] The trend which Mulgan sees as underlying all these shifts is, he believes, deeper than a simple 'pendulum swing' from right to left, and represents 'a return to clearly articulated principles of right and wrong, and a rejection of the common alibis of recent decades that make it possible for crime to be blamed on society ...' While communitarian philosophy has had 'little direct influence', it has 'given intellectual backbone', in Mulgan's view, to a backlash against both individualism and the insecurity engendered by rapid social change.[43]

Press accounts of New Labour's communitarianism, then, reflect a very broad range of ideas about what constitutes or characterises communitarianism. Sometimes these ideas are made explicit; more often, they are implicit, indicating an assumption that communitarianism is easily understood and already familiar to the reader. In fact, even these few examples reflect a great range of – frequently incompatible – conceptions of communitarianism and ideas about its manifestation by New Labour.

Characteristics of communitarianism are seen to include authoritarianism, the radical devolution of power, rights and duties (with the stress on duties), responsibility in return for opportunity, community development, strong and active communities, volunteering and good neighbourliness, strong socially homogeneous values; social conservatism, traditional socialist values, a substitute for socialism, the rejection of individualism and a middle way between socialism and individualism, and finally, rhetorical blather (possibly as a cover for some other agenda). Many of these conceptions are mutually incompatible; for example, it is seen both as an expression of traditional Labour values, and as antithetical to them; as implying both authoritarianism in the form of government diktat and the radical devolution of power. Many of these are offered as alternatives to New Labour's communitarianism rather than conceptions they have adopted, showing the dangers of referring to 'communitarianism' without further elaboration. For the kinds of communitarianism which New Labour *are* held to have adopted, sources are said to include: communitarian political philosophy, the Communitarian Movement associated with Etzioni, other sources in US politics, Australian politics, and the Labour/socialist/ethical socialist/social liberal tradition.

A great many names are mentioned in connection with New Labour's communitarianism: Robert Owen, Amitai Etzioni, Robert Putnam, Bill Clinton, William Morris, G.D.H. Cole, R.H. Tawney, H.J. Laski, J.A. Hobson, L.T. Hobhouse, Kenneth Clarke, Michael Heseltine, John Major, David Willetts, David Green, David Selbourne, William Temple, Beatrice Webb, Geoff Mulgan, Demos, John Gray, Michael Sandel, Michael Walzer, Charles Taylor, Alasdair MacIntyre, Sir James Goldsmith and Gordon Brown. Clearly some of these names are more serious claimants than others, both to the mantle of communitarianism and the ear of New Labour. Nonetheless, this fairly random listing shows that many of those believed by the British press to have had some connection with New Labour's communitarianism make pretty uneasy bedfellows, and it seems unlikely that they could share a common creed. Even if they have all, in different ways, contributed something to New Labour thinking it is debatable whether the result could be considered a coherent communitarianism.

To expect consistent, well thought-out positions might be too much to demand of the press, however, with their very broad readership and tight deadlines. For a more considered view of New Labour's communitarianism we might expect to turn to academic commentators' accounts and analyses.

Academic accounts of New Labour's communitarianism(s)

Some academic accounts take New Labour's communitarianism as their main theme, and examine it in detail. Others, considered in greater depth at the end of this section, focus on analysing communitarianism itself, albeit in the context of ideas about its manifestation in and implications for policy. However, there are also examples to be found in the academic literature, and, importantly, in politics textbooks, which simply reflect, in the same way as the press accounts, a prevailing and accepted assumption that 'communitarianism has been widely recognised as a key ingredient in New Labour's political philosophy'.[44] As was the case for the press accounts, this does not necessarily imply agreement on what is meant by 'communitarianism'.

Work from across academic disciplines casually refers to New Labour's communitarianism, in various forms and contexts. David Gilbert (a historical geographer), writing in *Renewal*, suggests that New Labour is pursuing a US-centric, abstract communitarianism to the detriment of one rooted in the real communities of Britain. Indeed, he notes, the *idea* of community is becoming popular at just the time when 'real' communities – he refers particularly to mining communities – are dying out.[45] This hints at an alternative communitarianism, although it is one which Gilbert does not see developed in Blair's vision. Gordon Hughes, in what is effectively an attack on Etzioni's communitarianism (referred to as 'moral authoritarian') and a call for the recognition of other types of the doctrine (including 'radical egalitarianism'), identifies New Labour very strongly with the former, saying that 'Etzioni's message has been taken up by ... Tony Blair and ... Jack Straw in a series of well publicised interventions on street incivilities and the "parenting deficit"',[46] and refers to the communitarian manifesto's 'particular influence over Tony Blair's "New" Labour Party'.[47] Some writers have taken a more cautious view; Michael Harris is one of the few writers who mentions communitarianism in the context of New Labour while taking a more wary approach, saying that while '[a]t times there has seemed to be a communitarian flavour to New Labour, and to some of Blair's pronouncements concerning rights and responsibilities', the commitment to social cohesion which this would indicate would appear to be at odds with their endorsement, as Harris sees it, of 'post-Thatcherite individualism'. One solution, he suggests, is that 'New Labour at heart is not communitarian in the proper sense of the concept, though the rhetoric could serve it well.'[48] This still nonetheless assumes that the rhetoric is communitarian, an assumption that does not in the end withstand scrutiny.

Some authors of textbooks have also endorsed the view that the Labour Party has become communitarian under Blair's leadership. This is particularly significant because such sources are likely to influence the beliefs of larger numbers of people than specialist articles or even books. Gillian Peele notes that '[m]any in the Labour Party displayed an interest in the resurgence of communitarian ideas that occurred on both sides of the Atlantic',[49] citing both Etzioni and John Gray. In the same book, the chapter on crime and public order has a subsection entitled 'New Labour's Communitarianism'. The authors of this, John Benyon and Adam Edwards, say that communitarianism appeals to New Labour because 'it could be presented as a radical alternative to both laissez-faire conservatism and "statist" social democracy, attracting disenchanted Conservatives without alienating traditional supporters'.[50] More significant, though, is John Dearlove and Peter Saunders' claim that in contrast to any other period in its history, the current Labour Party is heavily influenced by the ideas of 'intellectuals' and developed a programme based around these which it put into practice upon winning power.[51] These authors refer to the party's 'commitment to the principles of communitarianism and stakeholding',[52] and claim that while Thatcher 'urged a return to "Victorian Values"' and Major 'launched a "Back to Basics" campaign', 'Tony Blair sought to reintegrate society by developing a "Third Way" based on some of the key principles of "communitarianism".'[53] The name which comes up again in connection with this is Etzioni's. After summarising Etzioni's ideas, Dearlove and Saunders concede that they are 'not without their critics' and that 'New Labour, while influenced by them, was not wholly converted.'[54] In a later chapter, however, they say quite definitely that New Labour's approach to the 'problem of community' was 'influenced by recent American writing, and in particular by Etzioni's work on "communitarianism"'.[55]

Most of the above examples could be summed up as 'passing mentions' of New Labour's communitarianism, in work which has something else as its primary focus. They nonetheless have a role in perpetuating and disseminating the impression that communitarianism is an important factor for the party. More significant though, in an academic context, are those writers who have analysed New Labour, communitarianism and the relationship between the two in greater detail. These analyses accept to a greater or lesser degree that there is some link, but disagree on the source(s) and extent of New Labour's communitarianism. Perhaps more significantly, there is no agreement on what communitarianism *is*. Each writer is working with a different – clearly defined but nonetheless competing – definition. That is why this book at no point seeks an overarching definition of communitarianism as such, but rather engages directly with communitarian writing.

Defining communitarianism

Elizabeth Frazer has written extensively about communitarianism and politics, and notes that Blair and other prominent Labour Party members have embraced a rhetoric of 'community'.[56] She places political communitarianism as one of three types, the others being the philosophical communitarianism of Sandel, Taylor, MacIntyre and Walzer, and 'vernacular communitarianism', which refers to the stress on the importance of community building in the discourses of community workers and activists. This last represents a conception of community as a concrete, localised phenomenon, an idea which is occasionally found in New Labour rhetoric.[57] Frazer discerns four 'varieties' of political communitarianism:

that of the British left and centre left; a British conservative variety; the communitarianism of Etzioni's 'Communitarian Movement' and a fourth strain based around the Jewish journal *Tikkun*,[58] which has a longer history and takes a broader view of what constitute threats to community, considering, for example, the abuse of property rights by corporations (in contrast to Etzioni's primary focus on the abuse of, or over-reliance on, individual rights by individuals).[59] New Labour is identified most closely with the 'British left' strain of communitarianism, which has come 'practically to dominate Labour Party and centre-left politics' and Frazer cites extracts from Blair's speeches to illustrate this.[60] On the other hand, Frazer rejects the idea that Etzioni has been a significant factor, noting that 'there is no reason, given Blair's intellectual history, to accept [Etzioni's] claim' to have been an influence upon Blair, particularly with regard to the rewriting of Clause IV.[61] Macmurray, though, as part of the British Christian Socialist tradition, is held to have been a source of communitarian thought, for Blair in particular.[62] Henry Tam is also mentioned, but not fitted into any of Frazer's categories, and his work is not considered in detail.[63]

For Frazer, political communitarianism in all its variants displays three key features. Firstly, it emphasises building upon what is shared,[64] and '[c]ommunitarians insist that on virtually every issue there are shared values, meanings and goals that can be appealed to'. This is reflected in Blairite 'one nation' appeals, and in the idea that community can be rebuilt by rediscovering values shared by all.[65] A second characteristic of communitarianism is its emphasis on participation and community action, which 'forges civic bonds, and promotes individuals' and groups' independence from state bureaucracies'.[66] This aspect of political communitarianism is very clearly apparent in the emphasis upon 'community' solutions to welfare issues, such as moves to encourage 'voluntary' provision in all sorts of areas, from pre-school education to mental health.[67] The third characteristic identified by Frazer is a more inward-looking one: the idea that 'community politics brings politics down to its proper human level – the level of the person, and the human encounter'.[68] Emphasis on the importance of 'human encounter' calls to mind Macmurray's 'personal life',[69] and similar sounding sentiments are to be found in Blairite rhetoric (particularly in his coining of the concept of 'social-ism').[70]

In her emphasis upon community and what it means, Frazer makes it clear that, for her, any coherent notion of communitarianism must, at least implicitly, have roots in some conception of community. In other words, the mere presence of references to, say, rights and duties (a frequent feature of Blair rhetoric), is not sufficient to characterise such talk as communitarian; communitarian rights and duties must relate to intra-community relationships and be understood as so doing. This view is not necessarily shared by other commentators.[71] For a number of press commentators, as well as some academics, any reference to rights and duties, and a particular reciprocal relationship between them, echoing as it does key tenets of Etzioni's work, characterises the source of those references as communitarian.

Although Frazer is concerned primarily with the analysis of political communitarianism and the concept, community, on which it is based, rather than with the study of New Labour, it is apparent that she perceives the party as displaying significant aspects of communitarian thought, mainly that of the British left variety, derived from, or at least chiming with, the party's Christian Socialist traditions.

Plotting 'New Labour's communitarianism'

A particularly in-depth study of New Labour's communitarianisms (the plural is deliberate) is that undertaken by Stephen Driver and Luke Martell. These authors conclude most strongly that New Labour *are* communitarian, primarily because they 'sell community as the hangover cure to the excesses of Conservative individualism'.[72] Driver and Martell adopt a fairly broad view of what constitute 'communitarianisms', and set out to ascertain which of these New Labour has adopted or moved towards, and which, in turn, it may have left behind in a 'shift in Labour thinking from social democracy to a liberal conservatism which celebrates the dynamic market economy and is socially conservative'.[73]

The use of the plural illustrates the authors' view that there are many kinds of communitarianism, which can be charted and upon which the government's position can be plotted. In this way a number of different policies and policy proposals can be described as communitarian while not necessarily having much in common with each other and occasionally being clearly opposed to each other. Furthermore, the possibility remains in this analysis that a number of other positions, not occupied by New Labour, could also be communitarian.

Driver and Martell identify three levels and six dimensions of communitarianism[74] which between them cover a lot of political and philosophical ground. The three levels are sociological, which is essentially a descriptive assertion that 'individuals are shaped by their communities'; ethical, a moral assertion that 'community is a good thing', and meta-ethical, which concerns the basis upon which moral claims are made. In the case of communitarianism this generally means the rejection of universalism in favour of particularism.[75] The six dimensions are: conformist–pluralist, more conditional–less conditional, progressive–conservative, prescriptive–voluntary, and moral–socioeconiomic.

They conclude that the Labour Party under Blair has shifted away from the communitarianisms which are compatible with or characterise social democracy, and towards those communitarianisms which they describe as 'conditional, morally prescriptive, conservative and individual' rather than the 'less conditional and redistributional socioeconomic, progressive and corporate communitarianisms' which are a possible alternative.[76] Labour's communitarian thinking is characterised by three interwoven themes: 'economic efficiency, social cohesion and morality',[77] which ideally form a virtuous circle – the aim of policy – given the right conditions. The evidence for this is drawn from both the policy and rhetorical positions of New Labour, and assumptions are made about the background to, and possible motivation behind, the espousal of these particular values.

For Driver and Martell, in terms of the three 'levels' they identify, New Labour are 'sociologically communitarian' because they draw on the 'communitarian idea of there being a common stock of values, meanings and institutions which give shape and structure to the lives of community members',[78] although in the rhetoric, 'community' is frequently conflated with 'nation'. While Driver and Martell recognise this,[79] for them it does not rule it out as communitarian. Secondly, New Labour espouses 'ethical communitarianism', evidenced by their underlying assumption – sometimes spelt out – that community is 'a good thing'.[80] Finally, on the 'meta-ethical level', it is claimed, New Labour reject the anti-universalism of philosophical communitarianism (such anti-universalism is found most clearly in the work of Walzer), because they claim that 'there is [in policy] a strong moral agenda which transcends communities'.[81]

So far, this does not seem to point to anything which is distinctively New Labour; such positions have been manifested by most if not all British governments and parties. On the sociological level even Thatcher, for all her reputed individualism, undeniably had a strong sense of British identity and of a common culture associated with that (perceived as being under threat from immigration). At the ethical level, writers on the right have sought to defend 'community' against the perceived threat of usurpation by the state, seeing community as having a particular moral role in the provision of welfare.[82] And it would be hard to find anyone, politician or not, who does not subscribe to at least some universal values.

It is in terms of the *dimensions* of communitarianism identified by Driver and Martell that a more distinctive New Labour position begins to emerge.

In those terms, Driver and Martell find that the New Labour government's policies epitomise a more rather than less *conditional* communitarianism,[83] in which the bonds of mutuality which are the communitarian ideal are codified and enforceable. This draws upon 'traditional centre-left themes such as cooperation, fellowship and mutualism'[84] but distances itself from 'old fashioned' social democracy which sought to mediate these virtues and distribute their benefits through the mechanism of the state. In the new model, 'social inclusion' is almost exclusively achieved through the medium of paid work; it has become synonymous with economic inclusion.[85] The government perceives its role in this as to take steps to increase 'job opportunities', although, in contrast to Keynesian social democracy, certainly not by direct intervention. The conditionality enters the equation in that the government's position is that certain duties are owed in return for these 'opportunities' – the main one being availment of them. (For example, when Blair says that 'If we invest so as to give the unemployed person the chance of a job, then they have a responsibility to take it or lose benefit.')[86]

Driver and Martell refer to this as 'assistance and fellowship increasingly requir[ing] reciprocal obligations'[87] – hence the characterisation of it as 'conditional'. However, although it is fair to characterise this as 'more conditional', it is misleading to cast it in terms of reciprocity and mutuality, because these kinds of relationship are generally understood to pertain between individuals or groups of roughly equal power and status, not, as in this case, between the individual and the state. Although the language of 'less conditional communitarianism'[88] is maintained, the substance is not. The question is whether the 'more conditional communitarianism' detailed can usefully be called communitarianism at all, when the reciprocity and conditionality are features of individuals' relationship with the state, rather than deriving directly from their relationship to each other as members of a community. It requires the identification of community not only with the nation, but with the state and the government, which despite being a position explicitly articulated by Blair in referring to 'the Government ... acting as a community',[89] stretches the concept of 'community' to breaking point.

Furthermore, issues raised by the power structures involved need to be considered. While communities can and frequently do have hierarchical structures, the relationships between members are, at least ideally, characterised more by mutuality of concern and respect than by power – if only because of the possibility of ultimate appeal to the state if intra-community power is abused. The power of the state over the individual is undeniably of a different order, and to present the relationship between individual and state as if it were equivalent to that between members of a community is at best disingenuous. While New Labour rarely do this *explicitly*, by presenting the state, and its creation and administration of, for example, a particular kind of welfare policy, as the embodiment or mediation of the relationship of us all to each other as fellow citizens/ members of the national community, it *effectively* does so. This marks a slippage in the use of language appropriate to the discussion of community-type relationships into the arguably inappropriate realm of individuals' relationship to government and state.

Communitarianism has also, Driver and Martell note, opened the door to conservatism on moral issues in the Labour party, by allowing them to endorse one vision of community, as built on traditional family and educational values, and taking the sort of tough line on crime previously associated with the right. Views expressed by leading members of the government in these areas certainly seem on the face of it to chime with the positions advocated by Etzioni, and represent a move away from 'the more progressive ethics of much centre-left thinking,'[90] although Driver and Martell note that some voices within the Labour Party continue to defend these positions.

In asking whether New Labour's communitarianism is of a 'prescriptive' or 'voluntary' variety,[91] Driver and Martell note that 'communitarians generally look to the intermediate institutions of civil society to provide individuals with a bulwark against the state',[92] a view which implies a plurality of such intermediate, 'civil society' institutions, but decide that 'the institutional implications of Labour's moralism look to be *dirigiste*'[93] This leads to the identification of an alternative communitarianism, which has a 'central moral content' which is defined by politicians.[94] However, although the provision of a moral infrastructure is frequently seen – by Etzioni, for example – as a function of communities, on this view it is the small scale, face to face nature of local communities that enables them to be effective in inculcating and reinforcing morality. The very reason communitarians like Etzioni give for promoting communities is that the government cannot fulfil this role. Therefore an attempt on the part of government to take over that role is a challenge to communitarianism rather than a manifestation of it. This again raises the question of whether an 'alternative communitarianism' is helpfully described as communitarianism at all.

Next, Driver and Martell distinguish between communitarianism based on common moral values, and that based upon 'socioeconomic foundations'.[95]

The former is the type found in the work of Etzioni. The evidence for the latter type of communitarianism is extrapolated from '[a]rguments for universal social rights as part of citizenship made by postwar welfare reformers, or socialist arguments for greater material and social equality [which] relate community to socioeconomic conditions'.[96] The 'community' which is key to this conception is 'rooted in shared experiences of education, in common health and welfare provision and in greater material equality'[97] – in other words, unsurprisingly given the sources from which it is drawn, in the vision of the social democratic welfare state. Although there are economic (rather than socioeconomic) aspects to part of Labour's 'communitarianism', in their view of paid work as the primary route to social inclusion, Driver and Martell conclude that it is increasingly of the 'moral' variety – and that this may in fact be in conflict with the government's economic and welfare policy aims.

In their final distinction, between 'individual' and 'corporate' forms of communitarianism, Driver and Martell argue that '[c]ommunitarianism can be applied to different entities – states, trade unions, businesses, professions, individuals etc.'[98] In 'individual' communitarianism, the reciprocal relationship of 'obligations and responsibilities, rights and duties,'[99] taken, on this view, as paradigmatic of communitarianism, is between the individual and society; in the corporate version, between businesses or other corporations and 'the community'. The conclusion here is that the Labour government is assiduous in extracting reciprocal duties from individuals; less so from corporations. The 'stakeholder' ideal which would have held corporations (particularly private sector ones) accountable to the wider community has quietly been abandoned. Overall, Driver and Martell conclude here that 'New Labour's communitarianisms' are part of the party's shift away from social democracy and toward what they term 'liberal conservatism'.

Driver and Martell suggest a broad range of possible sources for New Labour's communitarianism, including Etzioni, MacIntyre, Sandel, Macmurray, Tawney, Hobhouse and T.H. Green.[100] Elsewhere, they refer to the joint 'influence of North American communitarianism and English ethical socialism'.[101] They also suggest reasons why the party has moved in that direction, saying that 'Communitarianism is New Labour's answer to Thatcherism; so too is it Blair's rebuff to Old Labour', enabling the party to distance themselves from 'Old Labour's postwar social democratic record and from the liberal influence on this record' while still offering an alternative to Thatcherite neo-liberalism.[102]

The amorphous nature of communitarianism

Even in academic accounts, then, we see that communitarianism is given a very broad range of meanings, some but not all of which can be matched up with aspects of New Labour policy and rhetoric, but most of which are also compatible with other political traditions and previous governments. A range of communitarian names are cited, each of whom may have supplied some part or aspect of this broadly conceived communitarianism. Although more closely analysed and more clearly articulated, academic accounts of New Labour's communitarianism reflect as broad a range of ideas as the press accounts discussed at the beginning of the chapter, the main difference being that the academic accounts explicitly recognise the diversity of conflicting conceptions. These however can only be understood in terms of the account of communitarianism which each provides; comparing academic accounts of New Labour's communitarianism is hindered by the different dimensions, understandings and emphases each writer brings to their examination.

This book attempts to get round this problem by comparing New Labour policy and rhetoric directly with the positions and prescriptions of selected communitarian writers, including some who are not (or are very infrequently) mentioned in other accounts, alongside those cited most often. This approach makes available a diverse and sometimes conflicting range of clearly articulated (although not always self-styled) and discrete communitarian positions, which can be considered independently rather than being combined (or distilled) into a single 'communitarianism'.

Before proceeding to that analysis, however, the next chapter sticks with the prevailing broader, vaguer, view of communitarianism. It examines the policy and rhetoric which have led New Labour to be labelled as communitarian in so many different ways, and asks how consistent and useful a picture it presents.

2

New Labour and communitarianism: where's the evidence?

Chapter 1 showed that there has been a widespread impression that the Labour Party, in its transformation under Tony Blair's leadership into 'New Labour', has adopted significant aspects of communitarian thinking, and looked at some commentators' accounts of what communitarianism *is*. The aim of this chapter is to examine the roots of those perceptions: on what basis did so many commentators, both journalists and academics, conclude that New Labour has adopted or even been influenced by communitarian ideas? It examines the different sources of 'evidence' called upon, and the form such evidence takes, including key factors which are seen as indicators of communitarianism in policy, and investigates the different conceptions of communitarianism – often not explicitly recognised – implied by these. It then goes on to examine the 'evidence' first hand, calling into question many of the commentators' conclusions, and suggesting alternative interpretations. The chapter concludes that the only meaningful way to examine whether New Labour policy is or has been communitarian is to apply the yardstick of specific, articulated, communitarian positions.

Sources of evidence of communitarianism

Commentators have drawn on three main strands of 'evidence': New Labour rhetoric, New Labour policy in office, and the company seen to be kept by the party's leading members, especially in the mid-1990s. The first of these, rhetoric, is to be found in speeches, interviews and articles by leading party members, particularly Blair himself. These sources are particularly important in relation to the period 1994–97, before New Labour came to power, because there is less concrete policy to examine. Nonetheless, they continue to be highly informative subsequently, when they may be complemented by or set against proposed and enacted policy. Under the heading of rhetoric can be included the wording of the new Clause IV, with its references to community and common endeavour, and to rights and duties.

Policy proposals also properly come under this heading, particularly when they are unofficially 'floated' through speeches, interviews or press releases rather than published as official policy documents. This is a technique that New Labour have used fairly frequently, both to create an impression (say, of being tough on crime) and to test public responses to policy ideas. One notorious example was when Blair used a speech on 'Values and the Power of Community', delivered in Germany to an international audience, to float the rather incongruous idea of drunken louts being marched by police to the nearest ATM to pay an on-the spot-fine.[1] This particular idea was greeted with ridicule in the press and strong objections from the police, and was quickly dropped; but it had by then served the dual purpose of creating an impression of activity on the issue of anti-social behaviour, and testing the reception of a particular measure.

The second source of evidence of communitarianism is the policies formally proposed and enacted by New Labour in government. This includes White and Green Papers, regulations, and official party policy documents. There is some degree of overlap between parts of 'policy' and 'rhetoric' – for example, it is not really clear into which category policy papers presented at Party Conference should fall – but it is not important to differentiate them sharply here, and they are considered in parallel. The remainder of the book looks mainly at these two sources, but as one of the main reasons for New Labour's initial labelling as communitarian was their association with Etzioni and his perceived influence on the party, this third source of evidence will be dealt with first.

Much of the discussion of New Labour's communitarianism appears to have been prompted by Amitai Etzioni's visit to Britain in 1995. This coincided with the UK publication of *The Spirit of Community*, his first overtly communitarian book, and Etzioni took the opportunity to meet a number of leading politicians and spread his message through the British press. This certainly did much to establish the term 'communitarianism' in the vocabulary of British journalists and to raise awareness of Etzioni's ideas, and also, for some commentators, to draw their attention to other communitarian thinkers, activists and ideas.

Chapter 5 demonstrates that Etzioni's communitarian position is not reflected in New Labour policy or rhetoric, so in the light of this he cannot be considered to have influenced the party. Nonetheless, claims of direct influence were made at the time of Etzioni's visit, and they contributed greatly to the persistent impression which is argued against in Chapter 5.

Etzioni himself is certainly happy to be associated with changes in the British Labour Party, drawing attention to the wording of the new Clause

IV and its reference to 'community' in an interview in the *New States-man*.[2] In his preface to the British edition of *The Spirit of Community*, Etzioni says that 'Tony Blair of the Labour Party as well as David Willetts of the Conservative Party, and Paddy Ashdown, head of the Liberal Democrats, often speak communitarian', and goes on to list politicians who do likewise in Germany, France and the US. This actually suggests that they are doing so independently of Etzioni's influence, and indeed, Etzioni goes on, with rather disingenuous modesty, to say this explicitly: 'Communitarians like myself have not implanted these ideas in their heads; they are visionary people who have seen the power of a compelling set of ideas whose time has come.'[3]

When Etzioni visited Britain in 1995 to promote *The Spirit of Community* it was politicians of all parties, not just Labour, who went to hear what he had to say and were happy to be associated with it. However, although again it is impossible to be certain, it does seem likely that even if it did – along with many others – already share many of the concerns articulated by Etzioni (albeit without listening too carefully to his prescriptions), New Labour may at least have picked up on some of his language. Although there is no copyright in the explicit linking of 'rights and responsibilities' in the way that had become most associated with Etzioni, it is notable that Blair began to use this language more heavily around this time, and continues to do so in ways that even Etzioni has explicitly distanced himself from.[4] Such ideas are not in any case the sole preserve of New Labour or of 1990s politicians. It was Margaret Thatcher who said in 1987 that '[p]eople have got entitlements too much in mind, without the obligations.'[5]

If Blair and some of his colleagues picked up on some of the language of Etzioni, then this is as likely to have been through the medium of the London based think tank Demos than via direct contact with the man himself. Demos was founded in 1993 by Geoff Mulgan, later to become a Downing Street policy adviser, and is, in its own words, 'an independent think tank committed to radical thinking on the long-term problems facing the UK and other advanced industrial societies ... [which] aims to develop ideas – both theoretical and practical – to help shape the politics of the twenty-first century'.[6] Mulgan is the key link between Etzioni and Blair, and Demos can claim credit for introducing Etzioni to British policy audiences: they published his pamphlet, *The Parenting Deficit* (extracted from *The Spirit of Community*), in 1993.

While it is nonetheless more likely that similarities between the position of New Labour and Etzioni reflect their common response to a *zeitgeist* which was turning against the perceived selfish individualism and associated irresponsibility of the 1980s, of which Etzioni was simply the most articulate and successful communicator (or exploiter), it is also possible that Blair and others found Etzioni's language attractive and adopted it to describe their position. In one way at least it is fair to credit Etzioni with the spread of communitarianism. He and his 'Communitarian Movement' brought the term into popular political use, and this has meant that many positions which could be described in other terms were interpreted and presented in the 1990s as communitarian and as evidence of a new way of thinking. Thinkers as diverse as Giddens and Macmurray, and their ideas, are widely referred to as 'communitarian', which arguably would not have been the case if the term had not been brought to prominence by such a skilled publicist. This then is Etzioni's most significant and lasting contribution to 'New Labour's communitarianism': the fact that policy change is described and explained in those terms rather than others.

Etzioni's personal links with New Labour were significant in raising the profile of communitarianism and linking it with the party, but the bulk of the evidence subsequently adduced for their having adopted communitarian ideas was drawn from other sources: policy and rhetoric. Within these, especially in rhetoric, two key themes emerge as perceived indicators of communitarianism: community and duty. A focus on one or other of these two indicators often leads commentators to associate policies with different understandings of communitarianism, sometimes in turn associated respectively with different writers and traditions.

The concepts of 'duty' and 'community' used as indicators of communitarianism in policy and rhetoric

One conception, or aspect, of political communitarianism focuses upon the importance of community or communities, particularly their role as support mechanisms and in socialisation. These are frequently conceived of primarily as face to face, geographic or cultural communities, as traditionally understood. Links with this kind of communitarianism are inferred from politicians' talk *about* communities, the claim that people are not isolated individuals, and so on. One instance of this is Blair's speech to the Women's Institute in July 2000, in which he says 'At the heart of my beliefs is the idea of community ... our fulfilment as individuals lies in a decent society of others.'[7] This is sometimes associated with the work of John Macmurray (although often carelessly, as detailed in Chapter 4). This idea of a cultural community based on interdependence, mutual support and shared values, which can be, and in New Labour rhetoric frequently is, conceived of as encompassing an entire nation, is the conception most often to be found in that rhetoric, and is most likely to be noted by commentators. However, the idea of community as place – a geographic conception – is also to be found, in particular throughout New Labour's policy proposals on crime and anti-social behaviour, although this is not picked up so much by commentators. Both of these examples reflect the use, by commentators, of the concept of community as an indicator of communitarianism.

The inference of communitarianism from the use of the idea of duty, on the other hand, reflects a perceived emphasis in the work of Etzioni and his followers upon the importance of duties (as being owed in return for rights). In policy examples the idea of duty usually extends beyond face to face communities as far as the nation and 'fellow citizens' of it. This indicator is perceived in references to 'rights and duties', 'rights and responsibilities' and talk of 'moral regeneration'. Where this is present in New Labour discourse, an association tends to be made with Etzioni, although his views, as shown in Chapter 5, are not as stark as many commentators suggest.

These are by no means mutually exclusive, hard and fast defining categories: an overlap between the two arises from the way in which community is viewed as a locus of duties and responsibilities and as a training ground in these, and conversely, in the way in which the inculcation of a sense of duty and responsibility is seen as a prerequisite of building successful communities. However, the two 'indicators' do reflect views and perceptions of what communitarianism is, and therefore what its policy implications are, which are different in potentially important ways.

The two areas of policy, and associated rhetoric, which have been taken by commentators as most indicative of communitarianism are welfare and law and order. As in any case (as suggested earlier) it is often difficult to draw a clear line between them, policy and rhetoric will be considered in parallel for each of these areas. The instances cited here complement those in Chapter 1; while both evince the perception that New Labour are communitarian, commentators cited in Chapter 1 focus on the communitarian aspect and those in this chapter are primarily concerned with the examination of particular policy areas and frequently offer alternative interpretations – while never dismissing communitarianism entirely. Other areas, including education, citizenship, the voluntary sector, employment and industrial policy, are considered in succeeding chapters where they are examined in the light of specific communitarianisms. In this way a broad range of policy areas is covered.

Welfare policy

Broadly, welfare policy is about what the state does for people who lack resources. It is narrower than the broadest definition of the welfare state, which includes not only the National Health Service, but also education and even (where it exists) subsidised public transport. It is taken here to relate to provision via the state to individuals and families to alleviate, in the main, poverty and its effects. This at least is what it meant until the relatively recent (in Britain) introduction of the concept of 'welfare-to-work' which is now at the heart of welfare policy. Evidence of communitarianism in welfare policy might be inferred from a focus on the reciprocal relationship between rights and duties; it might also be discerned in a search for community solutions to problems of poverty and unemployment traditionally (since the 1940s at any rate) dealt with by government and state. Most commentators on 'communitarian welfare policy' have focused upon the former.

Emma Heron and Peter Dwyer argue that

> The communitarian identification of social decay (rectified by the restoration of moral order and achieved through the imposition of individual responsibility), family values and the 'correct' balance between rights and responsibilities with its emphasis on duty can be seen to typify New Labour's approach to welfare policy issues[8]

They note that 'many of the Communitarians' concerns are echoed in New Labour's literature',[9] suggesting a strong basis in rhetorical evidence, unsurprising given the time of writing. They identify four main strands in policy and literature: Macmurray, Etzioni, stakeholding of various kinds, and the 'remoralising' approach to welfare of former Labour spokesman on welfare, Frank Field.

In Heron and Dwyer's view, their policy on welfare indicates that 'Labour feels comfortable with notions of communitarianism and stakeholding.'[10] The adoption of these concepts, at least nominally, enables the government to mark a change of emphasis from previous, Conservative, policy, while remaining, as it promised prior to the 1997 election, within the previous government's spending limits. Aspects of the stakeholding agenda, in particular Will Hutton's[11] relatively radical vision of it, have not been developed. What remains has become conflated with the doctrine of individual responsibility. The apparently communitarian strand, however, seems to be going strong.

Both Heron and Dwyer, and Alan Deacon[12] take as their starting point the government's 1998 Green Paper on welfare reform[13] – the work of a new administration seeking to make its mark in a significant area of government. Both conclude that the policy outlined therein shows traces of communitarianism, but that there are also many other influences and outcomes at work. Heron and Dwyer make it clear that they are using a fairly narrow conception of communitarianism: 'the form of communitarianism, currently being popularised by Etzioni'.[14] This, as they present it, is characterised by a concern with 'what makes a "good society", and is centred around both the relationship between the individual and the wider community, and the expected roles they ought to play'.[15] Heron and Dwyer draw their claim about Labour's communitarianism from, among others, the Driver and Martell article examined earlier,[16] although the communitarianism the latter find is far, far broader than the concept that Heron and Dwyer claim to be working with. This is essentially a conception of communitarianism as a moral or moralising doctrine, which they find in Etzioni. In Etzioni's work, as presented here, there is a 'moral deficit' in society which arises from the overemphasis of rights at the expense of responsibilities. His proposed solutions include re-emphasising the role of responsibility, and developing community solutions.[17] 'A crucial element of the communitarian agenda,' Heron and Dwyer claim, 'is to regard community-level structures as the new currency for achieving desired goals.'[18] This, however, relates more to the government's communitarianism than to Etzioni's. For Heron and Dwyer, then, New Labour is communitarian because its welfare policy appears to reflect key tenets of Etzioni's doctrine as expressed in his *The Spirit of Community* and *The New Golden Rule*, in particular through its stress on rights in exchange for responsibilities, and the notion of autonomy being bounded by community norms to create a 'good society'. As they acknowledge, however, this is only one strand among many, of which they identify four, in Labour welfare policy. Although these other strands, particularly Macmurray, are frequently identified by other commentators with communitarianism, for Heron and Dwyer they are alternatives to it. This highlights the value of an approach which is explicit in identifying specific writers rather than a more generalised 'communitarianism'.

Similarly, Alan Deacon identifies strands in welfare policy which he (in contrast to other commentators) considers not to be communitarian. Deacon takes the Green Paper on welfare reform as an explicit starting point, asking how far it appeals to 'enlightened self-interest'. Such an appeal would not appear to be communitarian, but the reverse – an appeal to the classical liberal rational self-maximiser. This is in fact one of three strands which Deacon identifies: 'welfare as a channel for the pursuit of self-interest'; 'welfare as the exercise of authority', and 'welfare as a mechanism for moral regeneration', all three of which in their various ways lead 'people to act in ways which promote social well-being'.[19] The very aim of the promotion of social well-being is, on many accounts, sufficient evidence of communitarianism, but it is the latter two, and particularly the last of these, which would appear on the face of it to echo a specific communitarian agenda of the kind which has already been identified. What the three 'formulations' have in common, according to Deacon, is firstly, that they are more concerned in their general approach to welfare with *dependency* than *poverty*, (tied to which is the Green Paper's emphasis upon paid work) and, secondly, that each 'sees the prime task as the creation of a social order in which people behave differently, rather than one in which resources are distributed differently'.[20]

The importance of this Green Paper, as Deacon points out, lies in part in the fact that 'it attempts to provide an explicit statement of the scope and purpose of a "modernised" welfare state, and the values which should guide its design and implementation'.[21] He notes 'a striking similarity between the language of the Green Paper and that used by Tony Blair in speeches both before and after the election',[22] and concludes from this that Blair has had significant personal input on welfare reform issues.[23]

The key point raised by Deacon's work is this: like other commentators, he finds a great many references to rights and responsibilities, opportunities and duties, and reciprocity in the language both of the Green Paper and of Blair's speeches. But this does not lead him to characterise the proposals as communitarian, and he finds hardly any echoes of Etzioni – despite the language. What Deacon discerns in the policy is the influence of ideas about dependency and welfare-work incentives and disincentives, reflecting the work of writers like Charles Murray[24] and David Ellwood,[25] brought to prominence in the Labour Party by Frank Field, and also popularised in Britain by the Institute of Economic Affairs.[26] These themes, of independence versus dependency, work versus welfare (with its subtext of welfare's distortion of the labour market),[27] gained currency in the 1980s, and are generally considered to be defining positions of New Right thinking, rather than being associated with even the centre left. In this article Deacon provides signposts to an alternative interpretation of the language of Blairism – language which other commentators have taken as a decisive indicator of communitarianism.

Having examined a couple of the responses to it, this chapter now turns to the 1998 welfare Green Paper itself, and to the previous year's Labour Party policy document on unemployment and the 'New Deal',[28] to consider at first hand the evidence for communitarianism which they offer. In the process it flags up some issues which are given more detailed consideration in later chapters, and which, in the light of particular writers' communitarianisms, lead to different and surprising interpretations.

The first point to note is that in his introduction, Tony Blair credits Frank Field with starting the process of reform 'in this Green Paper'.[29] Field was appointed to the Department of Social Security when the government took office, with the brief of 'thinking the unthinkable' on welfare. He left in frustration when the government proved less keen to put his thoughts into effect. This is important because Field has a distinctive approach and attitude to welfare issues, and it is not a communitarian one, at least as conventionally understood.[30] He is, notably, a strong advocate of private provision, particularly for old age pensions, and an adherent of the view that poverty is by and large the product of a 'dependency culture' which the benefit system usually only serves to exacerbate. His position reflects that of Charles Murray who, in a booklet written for the IEA, puts forward his views as they relate to Britain. While other contributors to that volume take issue with Murray's conclusions (that there is an underclass emerging in Britain comparable to one which he had identified in the USA), Field offers qualified support.[31] Finally, as both Ruth Lister[32] and Fran Bennett[33] point out, the very use of the term 'welfare' rather than 'social security' reflects the term's pejorative use in the United States, suggesting both an American influence and a (linked) new moral judgementalism.

The second interesting aspect of the Green Paper is that it makes very little mention of community, and where it does, this is clearly community understood as more or less synonymous with nation (e.g. benefit fraud damages the whole community),[34] or the general public ('The new welfare state should provide public services of high quality to the whole community, as well as cash benefits').[35] If there is evidence of communitarianism to be found in this document it will be in the form indicated by references to duty rather than to community. However, such evidence and the assumptions drawn from it need to be examined in greater depth. There is indeed a great deal of use of the familiar terminology of rights and responsibilities in the Green Paper, but they themselves stand in need of closer scrutiny.

For example, rights and responsibilities are presented in the context of a contract, 'between citizen and state' and 'between us as citizens'.[36] The title of the document is *A New Contract for Welfare*. This new way of looking at welfare issues is presented as a 'third way' between 'dismantling welfare, leaving it simply as a low grade safety-net for the destitute' and 'keeping it unreformed and underperforming'.[37] But rights and duties created by a contract are legal ones, and it can be argued that the resort to legalised or quasi-legalised relationships represents the antithesis of the ideal of community. This may be intended only as a hypothetical or tacit contract (although it is probably more than that) but the very introduction of such terminology moves us away from the communitarian ideal in which the reciprocity between rights and duties arises from a moral sense, rather than either legislation or contract.

Furthermore, while the mere invoking of the concept of duty might suggest a communitarian agenda, it is certainly not sufficient in itself to identify one. Which duties are emphasised, and which are downplayed, is more important, and may suggest a different set (or sets) of underlying values. An emphasis on duty itself does not mean that a policy or position is communitarian. It is the content of the duty which provides the real pointer: what sort of agenda or values do *particular* duties suggest? For example, the duty to look after fellow members of your community might be seen as a communitarian one; the duty to take out a private pension policy might not be.

The duty most emphasised in the welfare Green Paper is the duty to work whenever possible; to be self-supporting and independent.[38] Other commentators have observed that the Labour government's conception of social inclusion[39] and citizenship[40] revolves to a very great degree around the idea of paid work. A focus on paid work as the best – indeed, for those capable of it, the only – route out of poverty is a key feature of this paper, although where it refers to social exclusion this is taken to be a more extreme, and narrowly defined condition.[41]

The ideas behind the proposals in the Green Paper begin to emerge on page one, where 'three key problems with the existing system' are set out.[42] These are, firstly, rising poverty and social exclusion, despite rising social security spending; secondly, 'barriers to paid work, including financial disincentives', and thirdly, fraud. The second of these reflects the pervasive emphasis on paid work as the primary solution to welfare problems and, inasmuch as inclusion is seen in terms of participation in the labour market and work as the best route out of poverty, solving this will also address the first; the third, a concern with benefit fraud, is well established, and is known to be of particular concern to Field, although some commentators have suggested that it is misplaced.[43] It is interesting, however, that these are described as problems of 'the existing system' (presumably meaning the welfare system). While fraud is clearly a problem within the system, and disincentives can be seen as resulting from its operation, to lay social exclusion – even when this is taken to mean lack of paid work – at the door of the benefits system is a new departure, indicative of New Labour's supply-side approach to dealing with unemployment.

The long-term aim (by 2020) of the policy outlined is to have

in place a **new welfare contract** between the citizens of the country and the government. This will deliver greater trust, transparency, responsibility and responsiveness
and people will be empowered to seize the opportunities to lead independent lives.[44]

Dependency is the key theme of the welfare Green Paper. Reform is justified by the claim that '[f]or many people the system is increasing their
dependence on benefit, rather than helping them to lead independent
and fulfilling lives'.[45] A key long-term aim is to 'restructure the institutions of welfare in order to promote people's opportunity and independence'.[46] Independence is seen as leading to 'empowerment',[47] another
theme which frequently arises in talk about community. Yet this pejorative use of the term 'dependency' and the extolling of independence seems
somehow at odds with the perceived communitarian themes of interdependence, mutual aid and reciprocity – until it is understood that New
Labour has given these concepts a 'spin' that turns them into useful rhetorical tools, as the issue of benefit fraud demonstrates.

In the Green Paper it is claimed that fraud costs an estimated £4 billion per year; enough to 'provide every family with an extra £10 a week'.[48]
In 1996 Frank Field was criticised for claiming that 'literally billions of
pounds' could be saved by cracking down on benefit fraud.[49] The claim,
however is still being made. The Green Paper acknowledges that a large
proportion of the money lost through fraud is accounted for by a relatively small number of individuals, mainly organised criminal gangs making multiple false claims, and of the remainder a further significant amount
is down to fraudulent housing benefit claims made by landlords rather
than by tenants.[50] However, this point is not stressed. The Green Paper
still appeals to the popular sentiment that it is individual, poor, benefit
claimants 'bending the rules' (e.g. claiming benefit while working) who
account for a significant amount of the fraud which penalises 'genuine
claimants', and the government continues to do little to dispel this misapprehension.

A long-running government advertising campaign played heavily on
these ideas, explicitly encouraging newspaper readers to feel that they
personally were suffering by the actions of people who worked while claiming benefit. Associated television advertisements showed a man being
dropped off at the pub from his job in the black economy, tucking away
a large wad of cash, and taking advantage of the misplaced sympathy of
his mates who stood him drinks in the belief that he was living on benefit.[51] In this campaign an attempt is made to transpose the ideals of
mutual support and reciprocity appropriate to a group of friends onto
the relationship between the individual claimant and the state, with the

aim of giving greater moral force to the crackdown on individual fraud.

Three aspects of New Labour's attitude to welfare policy are illustrated in one short passage from the Green Paper:

> Work is at the heart of our reform programme. For those able to undertake it, paid work is the surest route out of poverty. A pay packet also gives people independence and status in the community, and the chance to insure against risk and save for retirement.[52]

Firstly, there is the pragmatic strand – getting people into work is the most efficient and cost effective way of addressing poverty. Secondly, there is a moral agenda: independence is seen as a good in itself, and the idea that work confers status is endorsed and legitimated. Thirdly, it indicates the government's movement towards private provision for old age pensions and unemployment insurance, with the individual being handed back responsibility by the state in these areas which were at the heart of the traditional welfare state. Also, in focusing upon the costs of welfare provision, and in particular on benefit fraud (as opposed to tax evasion, which, it has been suggested, could yield far greater savings)[53] a clear populist streak is revealed.

Concerns about dependency, however, and, specifically, the shift of emphasis from claimants' rights to their obligations, is not a novel feature of New Labour policy, although their clever use of rhetoric has helped ensure that they will forever be associated with it in the public memory. In an article assessing Thatcherite welfare policy, published in 1991 and referring specifically to the Conservative Social Security Act of 1986, Alan Deacon notes that '[c]entral to this new aggressive stance were ideas about dependency, a "benefits culture", and the *obligations* rather than the *rights* of claimants'.[54] This was attributed to the influence of New Right thinking emerging from the US, particularly that of Murray, on the then Social Security minister John Moore.[55] The Conservative introduction of Jobseeker's Allowance in place of Unemployment Benefit and Income Support for the unemployed had already made the vital shift towards a work based welfare system, but it is only under New Labour that such policies have been identified as communitarian.

This section has shown that the area of welfare policy has been cited as providing prime examples of communitarian policy by some commentators, but as representing completely different sources of influence by others. Evidence of communitarianism is primarily furnished by frequent references to responsibility and obligation. Where there is explicit mention of reciprocity, however, in the Green Paper, this is contractual rather than communitarian. Far stronger, however, is the language of what might be termed 'dependency theory'. The focus in New Labour welfare policy is squarely upon work and independence, with a strong emphasis on tackling fraud, especially fraud by individual claimants. An alternative communitarian welfare policy, very different to New Labour's, might be characterised by reference to local support networks rather than direct state provision and direction, interdependence and responsibility for others rather than independence and responsibility for oneself, and a greater emphasis on organised social security fraud and tax evasion as factors which reduce resources for alleviating poverty.

Law and order policy

The other major policy area focused upon by writers who find New Labour to be communitarian is that of law and order, and it is to this that this chapter now turns, again, dealing with the perceived influence of Etzioni before going on to examine the evidence of policy and rhetoric.

Many commentators have found strong evidence of communitarianism, especially of the Etzioni variety, in Labour's law and order proposals before and after coming to power in 1997. The general 'feel' created by talk of 'zero tolerance', 'fast track sentencing' for persistent young offenders, and Home Secretary Jack Straw's famous comments about aggressive beggars and 'squeegee merchants' are taken as evidence of a hard, authoritarian communitarianism. From a slightly different perspective, the policy proposals are communitarian because they stress the responsibilities of individuals to their community, and of communities for their individual members, and, crucially, seek to utilise or empower communities to 'tackle' (a favourite word in these policy documents) criminal and antisocial behaviour by their members. This section considers claims about communitarian law and order policy, referring to policy documents and commentaries published both before and after May 1997, as well as more recent policy developments in this area and responses to them. As in the section on welfare policy, it examines what sort of evidence of communitarianism is drawn from these sources, and assesses how far commentators' conclusions are borne out by direct reference to the policies cited, raising issues which are addressed in succeeding chapters. Firstly, though, it considers the other major 'source' of evidence: New Labour's perceived links with Etzioni.

Some writers are in no doubt that Etzioni himself has been a significant, and direct, influence on Labour law and order policy. For example, Bill Bowring follows a critical commentary on the uses of 'community policing', which concludes that 'New Labour's rhetoric of community is inextricably coupled with the targeting of dangerous, even barbaric,

individuals and groups ... [which] is the inevitable consequence and coun-
terpart of the communitarianism which they have espoused'[56] with the
statement that: 'The source of this philosophy is well known: the 1994
[*sic*] book *The Spirit of Community: The Reinvention of American Society* by
Amitai Etzioni.'[57] Although Bowring goes on to describe Etzioni's position and criticisms of it in some detail, he does not demonstrate any
further quite how Labour policy relates to it. Indeed, the community
policing measures which he begins by criticising are well entrenched
Conservative measures.[58] Part of his evidence is formed by Etzioni's own
claims of influence. He cites both the preface of the British edition of *The
Spirit of Community* in which Etzioni claims that his ideas have been
taken up by 'visionary people', taking it that the politicians referred to
include Blair and Straw,[59] and says that Etzioni is 'probably right' to
claim to have influenced the wording of the new Clause IV.[60]

Another pre-1997 commentator, Gordon Hughes[61] argues that the
government has espoused Etzioni's morally authoritarian communitarianism in preference to other, radical, versions of communitarianism.
He refers to 'Etzioni's self-consciously populist and commonsensical
communitarian manifesto and its particular influence over Tony Blair's
"New" Labour Party'.[62] Alongside Etzioni, Hughes also notes the influence of Charles Murray, and writers at the IEA such as Norman Dennis
who have helped to promulgate Murray's ideas in Britain. As was found
with welfare policy, on law and order issues also some writers have found
a strong affinity not only between the government and Etzioni, but also
between both of these and the 'new right' as represented by Murray and
the IEA.

Hughes says that '[i]n Britain, Etzioni's message has been taken up
with particular gusto by ... Tony Blair and ... Jack Straw, in a series of
well publicized interventions on street incivilities and the "parenting deficit"'[63] but notes that it is not only the Labour Party (still in opposition at
the time Hughes wrote) who had fallen under Etzioni's influence:
'Communitarian ideas on law and order have in fact been taken up with
enthusiasm across the party political spectrum in Britain.'[64] But again,
after lengthy discussion of Etzioni's views and proposals, no more evidence is offered of the ways in which these might be reflected in British
policy. This is another example of the way in which the *assumption* that
Labour is broadly communitarian, and specifically influenced by Etzioni,
is largely self-perpetuating and circular.

Hughes does trace the apparent influence of – in particular – Dennis
and the IEA in some of the assumptions which sometimes explicitly, but
more often tacitly, underlie recent Labour positions and rhetoric. Primary

amongst these is the theory that family breakdown leads to criminality, in particular, in the view of Murray and Dennis, because of the absence of appropriate role models (i.e. fathers) for young men.[65] However, although Hughes pinpoints a similarity between these views and the government's, this could be seen as an alternative, non-communitarian, aspect to policy. Although it is, up to a point, compatible with types of communitarianism, it is not explicitly communitarian, and predates Etzioni's work and the popularisation of the doctrine. Sometimes, then, the assumption that New Labour is communitarian remains even after alternative accounts of policy have been set out. This tends to be self-reinforcing; Labour are taken to reflect communitarian ideas, and those ideas are frequently the subject of trenchant criticism, by commentators who do not really demonstrate that the party's policies and rhetoric actually do reflect such ideas.

Both Bowring and Hughes base their assessment on Labour Party policy documents published in 1995 and 1996.[66] The most immediately surprising thing, on examining these documents, is that where there is an apparent communitarian strand, this is far more likely to be found in references to community than to duty. The message that comes through most strongly in these papers is that crime needs to be reduced *for the sake of communities* and to enable communities to flourish. Many of the measures proposed are about *protecting* communities. This is the reverse of what might have been expected – that communities have a responsibility for crime and its reduction through inculcating or enforcing common values, socialisation of children, and by members discharging their duties to the community; there is very little emphasis on these aspects.

This is surprising because these proposals were drawn up at what was supposedly the height of Etzioni's influence on the Labour Party, and Straw was assumed to be one of Etzioni's biggest fans. In *Tackling the Causes of Crime* there is a section entitled 'rights and responsibilities',[67] but it is only seven sentences long, and even here it seems that reducing crime is seen as a prerequisite for rather than an outcome of establishing a 'stakeholder society'. Crime reduction is clearly seen as a government responsibility: 'Government has an obligation to tackle the conditions which foster crime, to ensure we all have a stake in society, do all in its power to reduce crime ...'[68] Although the document says that '[i]ndividuals must be held responsible for their own behaviour' and reiterates that 'as citizens we all have responsibilities as well as rights, duties as well as freedoms' and 'real freedoms and liberties can only be effectively exercised if we have a society in which government and people accept their civic duties and obligations',[69] these are the only such sentiments expressed in the whole paper, and their context suggests that they are there as a deliberate counterbalance to an otherwise pragmatic results-orientated approach centred upon proactive government measures to benefit communities *by* cutting crime.

Surprisingly, perhaps, there is no mention of morality or moral education (or its lack) as a factor in crime – the factor Etzioni stresses above all others. Conversely, *Tackling the Causes of Crime* recognises that poverty and lack of opportunity represent underlying causes of crime – factors which Etzioni is frequently criticised for downplaying or even ignoring. Where Etzioni (and influential commentators like Melanie Phillips) stress the role of family structure and the decline of the 'traditional' two-parent family[70] in rising crime and community breakdown, this Labour policy document cites almost every family related factor *but* family structure, and stresses research showing that 'it is the effect of relationships *within* the family that appears to have the greatest bearing upon whether an individual commits a criminal offence'.[71] Again the approach is the reverse of what might be expected, stressing the need to help families, both directly through education for parenthood, and indirectly by addressing the 'prevailing social circumstances', such as poverty, which adversely affect families.[72]

There are, certainly, even in this policy document, measures which have been criticised as potentially (and where they have been implemented, actually) authoritarian. These include Community Safety Orders (special injunctions which criminalise behaviour which is a nuisance to others) and Child Protection Orders – effectively curfew powers. These are frequently cited as examples of communitarian policy. But whatever their virtues or otherwise, it is very hard to see what makes them, in themselves, examples of or pointers to communitarian policy. They are legal, not moral approaches; they are about compulsion, not education. They are, if anything, a substitute for the morality which is presumed to have failed, not an expression or rebuilding of it. From a communitarian point of view they should surely be seen as an admission of failure – communities can no longer maintain order without new tools from the government.[73]

Other policy documents from this period provide similarly vague and ambiguous evidence of New Labour's communitarianism. *Protecting Our Communities* presents 'communities' as having a role in 'tackling' anti-social behaviour, but two things need to be noted about this. Firstly, the involvement of 'the community' is seen as a matter of effectiveness rather than of moral responsibility; and secondly, 'community' here is clearly meant to be understood as 'local authority' – a statutory body. 'Communities' are frequently defined in opposition to local government, but here

they are conflated with it. So while the proposals claim to be giving powers to communities to act (as if spontaneously) against disruptive elements
in their midst, the powers are actually vested in local councils, which have
their own agendas, and as Janet Foster has shown,[74] frequently hold different views from those on the ground in communities both as to what constitutes unacceptable behaviour and the best ways of addressing it.

The earlier paper, *Safer Communities, Safer Britain* notes that '[t]he
breakdown in law and order is intimately bound up with the break-up of
strong and cohesive local communities'.[75] This appears at first glance to
be a clear claim that the decline of communities is implicated in the rise
of crime. But the opening sentence of the paper sheds a different light on
this. It says: 'Crime is damaging the lives of individuals and communities
throughout England and Wales'.[76] So while rising crime and declining
communities might be 'intimately bound up' with each other, the clear
message is that this is a two-way process, and increased lawlessness is as
responsible for the breakdown of community as vice versa.

'Community', as a term, comes up quite frequently in law and order
policy. The stress, already mentioned, upon the importance for communities of cutting crime, continues in a Fabian Society pamphlet of 1999
in which Straw reiterates that: 'Tackling crime is at the heart of our plans
to build a better society. Crime damages individuals and disfigures communities ... strengthening communities through welfare to work, supporting families, better housing policies, improved education [and]
encouragement of volunteering'[77] is still seen as a means of reducing crime.
There is no mention here of individual responsibility, or even, save the
above, of community responsibility.

New Labour's law and order proposals, like their welfare policy, are
open to a range of interpretations. Taken by some commentators as evidence of communitarianism, they can also be taken to indicate other
outlooks, including the purely pragmatic. Law and order policy does not
indicate communitarianism in the same ways welfare policy does: where
the latter is strongly moralistic, the former is surprisingly less so; where
welfare policy has focused on ideas of duty and called upon norms of
reciprocity expressed as pertaining across the nation as a whole, law and
order proposals have focused on small scale local communities. These
limited examples, especially when combined with those in Chapter 2,
have shown that while there is an enormous range of approaches and
discourses which can be – and often are – taken as indicative of a
generalised, generic, communitarianism, these same approaches and discourses can frequently be taken just as easily as indicative of something
else entirely.

This confirms that such a generic conception of communitarianism is of little value in analysing and assessing policy, and a better approach to examining 'New Labour's communitarianism' is by comparison with specific communitarian positions articulated by a range of writers.[78] It is to that, its main purpose, that the book now turns: to examine apparently or supposedly communitarian policy in the light of a range of discrete examples of communitarian thought. Because many political observers attached significance to Etzioni and his work, he has already been the subject of some examination in this and the preceding chapters. However, his own work has not yet been examined in any detail, and an assessment of it, and its consonance or otherwise with New Labour's output is the subject of a later chapter in its own right, along with the work of John Macmurray, also frequently mentioned, including by Blair himself, and two other British communitarian writers, Jonathan Boswell and Henry Tam. Each of these is considered alongside the policy area or areas most relevant to their own position or approach. First, however, it is important to ask just what relevance academic communitarian philosophy has to the politics of New Labour, and that is the subject of the next chapter.

Part II

Communitarianism

3

Communitarian philosophy and New Labour

During Prime Minister's Questions in February 2002, Tony Blair was asked by a Labour backbencher about 'the political philosophy ... which underlies his policies'.[1] Blair did not mention the philosophy of Alasdair MacIntyre, or Michael Sandel; he did not even mention John Macmurray. In fact, his fumbled response referred to investment in the health service. This has not, however, prevented these and other philosophers from frequently being linked with New Labour, nor commentators from carving out a philosophy for New Labour and its Third Way. A reason is suggested by unrepentant Old-Labourite Roy Hattersley: that '[u]ntil Tony Blair came along, Labour had an implied philosophy', which was based upon egalitarianism, but that this has been destroyed by the party's modernisation and thus required replacement by 'a set of overt beliefs'.[2] It did not take much for these putative beliefs to become associated in the public mind with the work of established political philosophers whose positions have been labelled communitarian.

This chapter considers what has become known as communitarian philosophy, or communitarian political theory.[3] It very briefly outlines relevant aspects of the work of its four major proponents, and considers one attempt to derive political prescriptions from it. As the term 'communitarianism' seeped into coverage of politics and current affairs some commentators suggested that the ideas being popularised by Etzioni had roots in this highly theoretical academic work and even, in a few cases, that communitarian philosophy had been a direct influence on New Labour. These claims are illustrated with examples and assessed in the light of the communitarian philosophy itself.

Communitarian philosophy, political communitarianism and New Labour

Press commentators, and a few academics, have suggested that New Labour has been influenced by communitarian philosophy, either directly (in a few cases), or, more frequently, through the philosophy's having fed into political communitarianism which has in turn been picked up by New Labour. Some political communitarians themselves claim to consciously be building on the work of communitarian philosophers, but an examination of the ways in which these philosophers' work is used suggests that such claims are misleading.

Anthony Giddens, in a review of Etzioni's *New Golden Rule*, has suggested that Charles Taylor is Etzioni's 'illustrious predecessor', and that Etzioni takes the former's work to a greater level of detail.[4] Etzioni himself makes a similar suggestion, comparing his 'responsive communitarianism' with the work of 'old communitarians': Taylor, Michael Sandel and Michael Walzer, and sociologists Philip Selznick and Robert Bellah. The suggestion is that the 'old communitarians' had a somewhat one-sided view: they 'tended to stress the significance of social forces, of community, of social bonds,' whereas the 'new communitarians have been concerned ... with the balance between social forces and the person, between community and autonomy ...' and so on, suggesting in effect that his work is a considerable improvement on theirs.[5]

Philip Collins, writing in *Renewal*, calls communitarianism 'a loose set of ideas ... usually associated with' Etzioni, but goes on to say that '[t]he more substantive body of communitarian thought was named and given its most eloquent advocacy in Michael Sandel's *Liberalism and the Limits of Justice*. It includes in the canon Alasdair MacIntyre, Charles Taylor, Michael Walzer and Joseph Raz.'[6]

Driver and Martell include MacIntyre and Sandel (along with Macmurray, Tawney, Hobhouse and T.H. Green) as 'communitarian influences [which] are clearly apparent among Labour modernizers'[7] in addition to Etzioni, who, as usual, is mentioned first. To these examples can be added Geoff Mulgan's claim that New Labour's communitarianism has 'drawn upon' and been given 'intellectual backbone' by communitarian philosophy,[8] and Melanie Phillips' suggestion that Gordon Brown has explicitly proselytised for 'the MacIntyre position' within the Labour Party.[9]

These claims tend to give the impression, firstly, that there is a continuum, or a stronger link than actually exists, between communitarian philosophy and political communitarianism, particularly that of Etzioni; and secondly, that communitarian philosophy has been a direct source of ideas for New Labour. Although the proportion of commentators suggesting this link is not large – the profile of communitarian philosophy beyond the academy is not high, and within academic work it is generally dealt with at a philosophical level[10] – it is nonetheless significant and worthy of attention.

A number of political communitarians, including some of those considered in this book, have referred in their work to communitarian philosophy. Etzioni has certainly gone furthest in associating himself with it, presenting himself as having had a major role in turning a previously obscure, academic debate into 'a widely known public philosophy, a social force'.[11] Interestingly, he does not refer to communitarian philosophy in his definitive statement of 'responsive communitarianism', *The Spirit of Community*, but in his follow up to it, *The New Golden Rule*, in which he attempts to flesh out a theoretical underpinning for his doctrine.

Etzioni mentions MacIntyre (among many other writers) as someone who expounds a 'particularly moderate but powerful articulation of the importance of virtues', and referring to his reluctance to call himself a communitarian, suggests that MacIntyre is 'a moderate social conservative'[12] although the quotations he selects are among MacIntyre's more apocalyptic, as are the sentiments he paraphrases: 'the modern world, obsessed with liberty, has slain virtue, leaving us morally bereft, in a world of darkness'.[13] Etzioni claims that there is a need to 'go beyond' Sandel and Taylor's ontologically founded criticisms of the liberal conception of the individual (the unencumbered self and atomism respectively) 'to note that not only are human beings social by nature but that their sociability enhances their human and moral potential'.[14]

The suggestion that these writers fail to recognise this implication does not seem well founded; the idea that a certain kind of society is necessary to realise (even) the liberal conception of the self is central to Taylor's 'Atomism'.[15] Sandel is also drawn upon to provide a response to the potential dangers of 'a politics that tries to be neutral with regard to the common good'[16] – providing, incidentally, an example of the myth that seems prevalent among political communitarians: that the contemporary state is actually neutral with regard to values. Finally, Walzer is introduced as an example of an attempt to 'bridge the differences between individualist and communitarian views by allowing for different definitions of the good for different social areas' – but claims that what Walzer is advocating has long been recognised by sociologists to be the case, 'especially in open, democratic societies'.[17]

On the whole, Etzioni does not so much draw on the work of communitarian philosophers as use selected aspects of it to illustrate specific points, and it could be argued that in so doing much of the philosophical argument and intent is lost. In the primary statement of his communitarian position, communitarian philosophy is not drawn on at all; it is only in this later work, with its ambitions to theoretical credibility, that it makes an appearance, and then in a somewhat ad hoc fashion. Etzioni's claim to have provided a conduit by which communitarian philosophy is introduced to the world of policy and politics does not, in the end, convince.[18]

Similarly, Henry Tam utilises communitarian philosophy in two main ways: he employs, in general terms, philosophical arguments against liberalism as a defence of communitarianism in principle,[19] and he uses snippets to illustrate points, combat potential criticisms, and simply to illustrate that he is not alone in his views, but none of the communitarian philosophers' theses provides the framework of his thought, or the basis of what he advocates, despite his stated intent of formulating a 'unified theory' from communitarianism's various strands. Jonathan Boswell mentions only MacIntyre and Walzer, and each only briefly.[20] Macmurray's work, of course, predates that of the communitarian philosophers of the 1980s.

The three political communitarians who refer to communitarian philosophy all use it in similar fashion, using quotations because they neatly sum up a particular idea of the political communitarian writer, rather than because they are considered representative of the philosopher's position. Overall it seems clear from their work that political communitarians have not drawn significantly on communitarian philosophy (even in the case of Etzioni, who calls upon it for a degree of post hoc theoretical ballast for his own position), and therefore it would be a grave error to suggest that political communitarianism has provided a route for philosophical ideas to enter the political sphere. Indeed, as the remainder of this chapter shows, there is little if anything to suggest that such ideas can even be discerned in politics.

Communitarian philosophy

Notwithstanding the efforts of Daniel Bell (considered at the end of this chapter) to derive a set of practicable political principles directly from it, most of the many levels at which communitarian philosophy operates do not correspond directly to the formulation of policy and the everyday practice of politics. This means that any attempt to relate them, whether to derive policy or to assess whether existing policy is communitarian, needs to be approached with caution. It is nonetheless important not to ignore the abstract political philosophy which has been brought together under the communitarian label, not least because the names of these writers are still invoked by commentators on policy, and nailing this error is worthwhile and necessary to any understanding of the kinds of communitarianism we see in policy. Furthermore, although these philosophers do not engage in any immediately accessible way with policy as such, ideas about the nature of the human self, the place of justice, and what makes a good society, are certainly relevant, and can – albeit less directly – contribute to the context in which policy is examined and assessed. To exclude these theorists would be to rule out an important part of the background against which the degree of communitarianism in policy can be understood.

In its modern philosophical usage, the term 'communitarian' was applied, from the early 1980s, to a range of responses to modern – and in some cases explicitly Rawlsian – liberalism, before it was adopted by Amitai Etzioni for his political movement. In this respect at least, communitarian philosophy preceded communitarian politics, although it can be argued that the politics was around long before that particular name attached to it and Etzioni and others developed it into a more codified creed.[21]

The 'liberal-communitarian debate' in political philosophy took (almost exclusively) as its starting point the work of four writers, and four respective books, published during the 1980s: Alasdair MacIntyre's *After Virtue* (1981), Michael Sandel's *Liberalism and the Limits of Justice* (1982), Michael Walzer's *Spheres of Justice* (1983) and Charles Taylor's *Sources of the Self* (1989). These are obviously not the only works by these writers which are significantly communitarian: in particular, Taylor's article on 'Atomism'[22] does much to set out what is recognisably communitarian in his approach, but the publication of four books within a clearly defined decade usually proves too neat a boundary to resist. Mulhall and Swift note that it was with the publication of the second of these works, Sandel's *Liberalism and the Limits of Justice* that the debate began. Although *After Virtue* had been published the previous year, 'it was Sandel's book that first elicited the label "communitarian" and brought about the retrospective recruitment of other writers to that flag'.[23] Even as political philosophy has moved in recent years beyond this 'debate' its terminology has crept into political discourse.

Of the four writers, at least three have not been entirely happy with being classified as communitarian. MacIntyre claims to 'have strenuously disowned this label, but to little effect'.[24] Sandel says that '[t]he "liberal-communitarian" debate ... describes a range of issues, and I do not always find myself on the communitarian side' and that he 'wish[es] to register some unease with the "communitarian" label that has been applied to the view advanced in *Liberalism and the Limits of Justice*'.[25] Walzer endorses a liberalism in which 'the communitarian critique ... is ...

transient but certain to return', saying that '[i]t is a consistently inter-
mittent feature of liberal politics and social organisation' but will never
'be anything more than an inconstant feature of liberalism'.[26] He is critical of cruder, more oppositional communitarianisms.[27] Taylor suggests
that the 'liberal-communitarian debate' oversimplifies and contributes
to the confusion of the issues at stake.[28] In contrast to these writers, political communitarians like Etzioni are happy to be known as
communitarians; in many cases they have proudly claimed the term for
themselves despite its wide and varied use elsewhere.

There now follows a brief and by no means comprehensive outline[29] of
the most relevant aspects of the work of each of the four philosophers.
While there are some common strands in communitarian philosophy,
these four writers do have very different approaches and concerns, making it most appropriate to assess their work's relevance to New Labour
policy by dividing this section by author rather than thematically. I have
not tried to give a full account of each thinker's position, but to draw out
the most important aspects for policy, which can then be compared with
New Labour's position. This itself presents difficulties: firstly, this area of
philosophy does not on the whole concern itself with the quotidian business of politics, and secondly, although the same terms occur (for example, community, contract, person), they frequently carry different
meanings which can be a trap for the unwary, and have indeed led to
some of the misconceived impressions set out above.

Michael Sandel

While some commentators[30] tend to define communitarianism in relation to John Rawls's *A Theory of Justice*, Sandel, in *Liberalism and the Limits of Justice*, is one of only two (the other being Walzer) of the four who
specifically take it as their starting point. Sandel's approach has been
described as epitomising a communitarianism in which justice and community are in conflict.[31] He questions Rawls's assertion that 'justice is
the first virtue of social institutions,'[32] claiming instead that it is a 'reme-
dial' virtue, necessary only when other social virtues, such as benevolence
or solidarity, are lacking. Too great a reliance on Rawlsian justice is likely
to cause these communal virtues to atrophy still further – or at the very
least, 'reflect a lessening of the moral situation, rather than a moral improvement'.[33]

While Tony Blair has shown no sign of familiarity with communitarian
philosophers like Sandel, he has referred to Rawls – suggesting that *A
Theory of Justice* epitomises a highly individualistic model of human

behaviour which began to take root in the 1960s and by implication led
to the excesses of selfishness and greed widely perceived to characterise
the 1980s. According to Blair, 'the Left was captured by the elegance and
power' of Rawls's work. His comment on it is intriguing: '[Rawls's] manifesto for an egalitarian society is a brilliant exposition of the argument
that an equal society is in the interests of anyone who does not know
which position in that society they would occupy. *But it is derived from a
highly individualistic view of the world.*'[34] That derivation is apparently
sufficient to condemn the theory in Blair's eyes. However, this reflects a
confusion between the theory's 'philosophical anthropology' – 'its general account of the human person' and other background factors – and its
'prescriptive principles'.[35] Rawls's theory may be implicitly individualist
at the anthropological level, but the political and social arrangements
yielded by its explicit prescriptive principles are anything but.

In practice, however, it is not Rawls's individualism that Blair rejects,
but his egalitarianism. Blair's avowed support for meritocracy, illustrated
by his wish to 'build a new social order in Britain ... based on merit,
commitment and inclusion',[36] is at odds with Rawls's view that people
should not (except when to the benefit of the worst off) gain from 'arbitrary' attributes like talents which happen to be marketable. This egalitarian principle is one which many communitarians – including Sandel
himself – share with Rawls.

Sandel's key objection to Rawlsian liberalism is its idea of a self which
can abstract from its particular circumstances, as the choosers of the principles of justice are supposed to do in Rawls's 'original position'. Such an
'antecedently individuated' self would similarly choose its own ends – its
social goals, and the kind of person to be – from a position of detach-
ment. This, Sandel claims, is a dangerous illusion, which will lead us to
accord priority to the 'wrong' values in our search for justice:

> The vaunted independence of the deontological subject is a liberal illusion. It misun-
> derstands the fundamentally social nature of man, the fact that we are conditioned
> beings 'all the way down'. There is no point of exemption, no transcendental subject
> capable of standing outside society or outside experience. We are at every moment
> what we have become, a concatenation of desires and inclinations with nothing left
> over to inhabit a noumenol realm. The priority of the subject can only mean the
> priority of the individual, thus biasing the conception in favor of individualistic
> values[37]

This clearly has implications for political principles – for example, it
raises the questions of whether justice should have the primacy Rawls
accords it, and even if so, how justice is to be understood. For Sandel, our
social roles are not chosen, but discovered. As Kymlicka puts it, '[d]eciding

how to lead one's life ... is not a matter of choosing one's social roles, but rather of understanding the roles we already find ourselves in'.[38] Our selves are neither separable nor distinguishable from our ends, but constituted by them.[39] To insist otherwise both violates our own self-perceptions – we do not in practice consider ourselves, our identity, as entirely separate from what we seek to achieve or become – and 'ignores the way we are embedded in our social roles'.[40] Sandel is concerned that the liberal conception of the self as antecedently individuated, and separate from its ends, leads to an undervaluing of those ends and attachments, one of the most important of which is the community of which the person is a member.[41] A politics which recognises and values, rather than ignores or rejects, these communal attachments will be far healthier than one based on abstract principles of justice.[42]

All this however is generally taken as given at the everyday level of politics. This is an example of a term – individualism – having a very different meaning and different connotations in philosophy and politics. When we talk of individualism in an everyday sense we are not referring to whether we are constituted prior to our ends, or even whether we can consider ourselves independently of the communities which we inhabit. It is taken as read that we have ends which (at least in part) constitute our identity and that we are embedded in all kinds of communities. Individualism in this context refers to how we pursue those ends and behave *within* those communities and towards those others who help constitute them, and it relates to how we see ourselves in relation to the rest of society, rather than how we view society as a whole. When Blair refers to 'crude individualism'[43] and Labour's 1997 election manifesto hails the passing of the 'era of the rampant and narrow individualism of the Tories',[44] they are using the term 'individualism' wholly in this second sense.

In a more recent work, *Democracy's Discontent*, Sandel engages far more directly with 'real' politics – albeit those of the US. In this he continues to criticise the liberal ideals of what he calls the 'procedural republic' and the priority of the right over the good, but he defines his own position as republican, rather than communitarian, although in some forms the two are quite compatible; for example, in rejecting aspirations to state neutrality. A key feature of republican thought, in its traditional forms as well as in Sandel's version, is the ideal of the pursuit of the common good as distinct from the (liberal) aggregation of individual goods. Sandel's assertion that the republican tradition is characterised by an 'emphasis on community and self government'[45] would further suggest that such a tradition would be attractive to those same people as espouse some forms of political communitarianism, including New Labour. The fact that it is one political tradition that has not explicitly been mined in the construction of the 'Third Way' may be attributable simply to the associations that the term 'republicanism' has in the UK, with the IRA and with anti-monarchism, both (albeit to different degrees) unpopular causes.

However, although with its appeal to the common good the republican tradition might be superficially attractive to New Labour, there are aspects of it which are not compatible with their approach. The first is the ideal of informed, critical citizen participation. As Chapter 6 will show, the New Labour conception of citizenship is at least apolitical and in some manifestations profoundly anti-political. The second objection is more fundamental, however. The aim in republicanism is to arrive at a form of polity which enables, or even causes, citizens to live a good life. There is not necessarily any objection to achieving this (for example, in Machiavelli's vision) through threat and deception; what matters is the good of the republic which is identified with the common good.

New Labour, on the other hand, seeks to change the people while leaving the polity the same. An example of this is the government's reaction to the low turnout at the 2001 General Election, which focused upon individuals' failure to vote and sought ways of changing people's behaviour within the existing system – but still in the name of good citizenship. The 1998 White Paper on local government talked of giving people a 'bigger say' in local government, but this turned out to mean no more than more frequent elections and 'making it easier to vote through new ideas like electronic voting, mobile polling stations and voting on different days'.[46] The structures of government remain the same, and the idea that voting for representatives is the only conceivable expression of democracy is reinforced. New Labour's promotion of elected mayors in major towns and cities (one option being a mayor and executive council manager, greatly reducing the role of conventional elected councillors), while increasing opportunities to vote, actually decreases the already limited opportunities for participation in local politics. Although republicanism is by no means synonymous with communitarianism, this brief digression should serve to clarify New Labour's attitude to a key aspect of both: the idea of the common good.

Alasdair MacIntyre

MacIntyre describes *After Virtue*[47] as having arisen from his 'negative view of late twentieth century bureaucratised consumer capitalism and the liberal individualism which is its dominant ideology' and concludes that 'the moral philosophy which informs that ideology had been generated by the fragmentation of an older moral tradition concerning human goods, virtues and the social relationships in and through which goods can be pursued, of which the classical expression is the ethics of Aristotle'.[48]

MacIntyre's criticism of liberalism is thus far broader than Sandel's. His objections are to the entire post-enlightenment liberal tradition, rather than to any specific work, and he expresses concerns about liberalism's substantive moral implications, in addition to questioning its conceptual coherence. His thesis is that liberal societies are in a state of confusion, clinging to the vestiges of traditions destroyed by liberalism itself, which thus no longer make sense. Liberal societies are beset by effectively irresolvable moral arguments – irresolvable because there is no one set of basic premises, shared by the whole society, on which to base moral judgements. Instead, there is a plurality of incommensurable moral assertions,[49] which must ultimately be arbitrary, but are cloaked in the antiquated language of moral authority – vestiges of a lost tradition of which only the language remains.

True human morality, destroyed by the enlightenment project of seeking its rational justification, must, for MacIntyre, be teleological, directed toward the end of the good life, and this, for any individual, cannot be separated from the social roles which that individual holds, and which prescribe what is 'good' for a person who inhabits those roles. MacIntyre uses the analogy of a watch: we cannot judge whether a watch is a good watch or not unless we know what it is that a watch is meant to do – what its role is, in other words. Human potential cannot be realised, nor human ends fulfilled, in isolation from such communal, social and moral roles.

To illustrate how we are to understand these roles and the ends they offer, MacIntyre introduces the concepts of a 'tradition' and a 'practice'. Inherent in the idea of a practice is the concept of an 'internal good'; a good which can be realised only within that practice.[50] These then provide an internal standard against which to make moral judgements about human action, and which itself, unlike liberal moral assertions, is not arbitrary. It is because such practices and traditions are realisable only in society that the concept of community is vital to MacIntyre's thought, and this is one of the reasons why his criticism of liberalism is a communitarian one, although it is also neo-Aristotelian and, in subsequent work,[51] neo-Thomist.

A third aspect of MacIntyre's communitarianism is his insistence on the 'narrative unity' of a human life.[52] What this means, in part, is that people make choices not in the vacuum of the moment, but in the context of a whole life, and thus, again, in terms of their ultimate human ends.[53]

For MacIntyre, therefore, the possibility of attaining, or even identifying, any kind of good, but particularly the good life for human beings, and the possibility of moral behaviour, is dependent upon the standards given by the traditions and practices which are, in turn, social phenomena, requiring membership of a community.

The virtues whose loss MacIntyre laments are again those of Aristotle's political ideal.

> The notion of the political community as a common project is alien to the modern liberal individualist world. This is how we sometimes at least think of schools, hospitals or philanthropic organizations; but we have no conception of such a form of community concerned, as Aristotle says the *polis* is concerned, with the whole of life, not with this or that good, but with man's good as such.[54]

Although in appeals to the idea of 'one nation' and 'national community'[55] it might appear that New Labour is pursuing this ideal, they are not, on two counts. While New Labour does have a clear view of the good citizen – one who works for a living and brings their children up properly – this only reflects their narrow view of citizenship, which is defined in those very terms. It does not reflect a conception of what is good for 'man as such' or of the human *telos*. Rather, it reflects a view of what is good for the British nation or society – economic competitiveness and social order. People's *human* fulfilment, on the other hand, is to be sought on the basis of individual choice, sometimes in the public sphere but equally possibly in the private, and subject only to the liberal constraints of not impinging on others' ability likewise to seek fulfilment: 'We seek,' Blair says, 'a diverse but inclusive society, promoting tolerance within agreed norms.'[56]

Government and politics simply does not concern itself with what is good for man 'as such', i.e. as an entity with given ends. MacIntyre is right to say that we no longer think of people in this way. In the terms of MacIntyre's particular brand of communitarianism (although we must not forget that he himself has eschewed the label) New Labour, like every other major Western political party and polity, is irredeemably and inescapably liberal; they are among his 'barbarians'.[57]

In the same way as New Labour's invoking of the idea of citizenship superficially but misleadingly suggests congruence with MacIntyre's communitarianism, so too might Blair's frequent appeals to 'tradition', a key anchor for the modernisation of the party in the early years of his leadership. However, in a very significant sense New Labour understand this concept also in a different way from MacIntyre, because for Blair, tradition and its continuation is something which is consciously *chosen* – impossible on MacIntyre's conception of it. Furthermore, Blair suggests that we can chose rationally between different traditions, or between 'values' and 'attitudes':

> When I think of the values and attitudes of my parents' generation, I distinguish between the genuine values that underpinned the best of Britain and the attitudes we can safely and rightly leave behind. Old-fashioned values are good values. Old-fashioned attitudes or practices may simply be barriers that hold our values back.[58]

'Values' worth keeping here include good manners, respect for others, courtesy, rejection of crime, respect and support for teachers, and doing voluntary work, while 'other things from the past' which Blair 'chose[s] to leave behind' include opposition to women working and to wearing jeans in church, and failure to be 'fair-minded to gay people'.[39] Nowhere does Blair give any basis – other than personal preference or an intuition of the spirit of the age – for these distinctions; they are essentially arbitrary. In this, Blair is actually exhibiting what MacIntyre sees as one of the manifestations of the modern age which he condemns. In addition, in suggesting that it is possible rationally to choose to keep some traditions and reject others Blair is utilising a wholly different conception of a 'tradition' from MacIntyre.

Charles Taylor

In *Sources of the Self*, Taylor sets out to 'define the modern identity in describing its genesis'.[60] This modern identity, the ways in which we understand ourselves, is central to any understanding of 'modernity' in general – a theme which is also MacIntyre's. Taylor's approach is a historical one, because he believes that this question of identity can only be understood in the context of past conceptions.

A central issue is where we find apparently objective standards of right and wrong, those standards which go beyond mere preference and enable us to undertake what Taylor calls 'strong evaluation'.[61] Morality, or 'the good' is strongly intertwined with the idea of 'selfhood', but, Taylor claims, modern moral theory focuses on 'what it is right to do' rather than what it is 'good to be'.[62] Ideas about the good, and strongly evaluative standards must come from a social or communal context. This context provides 'frameworks' which enable us to judge by standards which are above and beyond our own immediate reactions and which can give us something to aspire to, and which we can recognise without necessarily being able to articulate why we subscribe to those particular standards. Indeed, these frameworks only logically need to be capable of being articulated theoretically if they appeal to reason; not all do, and it is perfectly possible – or at least it has been in the past – to live according to a framework without being able to define it philosophically.[63]

The kinds of community which give such meaning to our lives (and which in this work at least mark Taylor out as a communitarian) are far broader and deeper – encompassing history, culture, religion and, above all, language – than what is generally understood by the term, and the conception of community employed by New Labour. Taylor rejects individualism (in the form of the concept of a 'disengaged rational self')[64] on the grounds that 'my identity is defined by the commitments and identifications which provide the frame or horizon within which I can try to determine from case to case what is good, or valuable, or what ought to be done, or what I endorse or oppose'.[65]

A key feature of modernity, in Taylor's thesis, is the elevation of 'ordinary life'. In the past, ordinary life was not an end in itself, but a necessary prerequisite for the pursuit of 'the good life' which defines a life which is fully human (compared to that of animals, or, in the classical model, slaves). In Ancient Greece, or under the Italian republican revival, this was epitomised by a 'citizen ethic'; to be a good citizen was to be and to aspire to far more than the domestic necessities of ordinary life[66] – but in New Labour's conception, being a good citizen is identified very closely with the two most ordinary fundamentals of ordinary life: working for a living, and taking care of one's family. This identification is made explicit in Blair's promise to his party conference that once given the 'chance' to join the labour market, single parents, 'no longer the butt of Tory propaganda ... will be the citizens of New Britain who can earn a wage and look after the children they love'.[67]

The apparently absolute ideals, like human dignity, justice and democracy, to which in the modern age everyone – even their most extreme transgressors – pays lip service, are in fact historically contingent, the end result of the development of the idea of 'the free, self determining subject' which in turn arises from the 'erosion of all those pictures of cosmic order which could claim to define substantively our paradigm purposes as rational beings'.[68] Taylor claims that in modern societies 'the individual has been taken out of a rich community life and now enters instead into a series of mobile, changing, revocable associations, often designed merely for highly specific ends'.[69]

Taylor clearly considers this a matter for regret, but when those 'revocable associations' take the form of short-term employment contracts, say, this is a model of society endorsed by – or at least acceptable to – New Labour. For Blair, community is not primarily the framework which provides us with our bearings, but is itself a means to an end; for example, helping people in 'the struggle of balancing work and a family' and in the adjustment to a global economy: 'to become the masters of change, not its victims, we need an active community'.[70] Taylor notes that 'a society of self-fulfillers, whose affiliations are seen as more and more revocable, cannot sustain the strong identification with political community which public freedom needs'.[71] This means that two aspects of what New Labour wish to achieve – in a nutshell, meritocracy, mobility and flexible employment practices on the one hand, and a strong and cohesive national political community on the other – are, in terms at least of Taylor's communitarianism, incompatible.

Moreover, Taylor continues in a direct reference to policy,

> the atomist outlook which instrumentalism fosters makes people unaware of these conditions [i.e. the conditions 'for the public health of self-governing societies'], so that they happily support policies which undermine them – as in ... neo-conservative measures in Britain and the US, which cut welfare programmes and regressively redistribute income, thus eroding the bases of community identification.[72]

Taylor wrote this in 1989, but policies of this sort have been implemented to increasing degrees since then on both sides of the Atlantic; New Labour in its first term of government, for example, implemented cuts in lone parent benefit and increased (regressive) indirect taxation. Granted, it has more recently put into place a range of measures which arguably have redistributed resources to the least well off. Nonetheless, this was not the case in the party's first years in office, when claims about its communitarianism were at their height. Furthermore, help for the worst off has been in the form of the minimum wage, childcare provision, and tax credits, all of which are available only to those in work, thus underscoring the conception of citizenship and inclusion rejected by Taylor.

Neither Taylor's theory in general, nor his specific allusions to policy, offer any comfort to New Labour, and his communitarianism is not one with which the party could identify.

Michael Walzer

Like Sandel, and unlike MacIntyre and Taylor, Walzer writes in direct response to *A Theory of Justice*. According to Walzer, the way in which different social goods are distributed, and by whom, depends upon particular cultural understandings of those goods, and the 'idea that principles of justice must be culture-specific entails a hostility to any political theory that embodies claims to universality' such as Rawls's theory of justice, and many other liberal positions. The next stage of Walzer's argument is that different criteria for distribution are appropriate in different 'spheres'; injustice arises when, say, a criterion for the distribution of goods in one sphere intrudes into another:

> Every social good or set of goods constitutes, as it were, a distributive sphere within which only certain criteria or arrangements are appropriate. Money is inappropriate in the sphere of ecclesiastical office; it is an intrusion from another sphere. And piety should make for no advantage in the marketplace[73]

By keeping the spheres separate, Walzer seeks 'complex equality', by which although simple inequalities of wealth and all sorts of social goods will remain, they will lose their capacity to 'dominate'. (A dominant good is one which reinforces inequality by commanding goods from other spheres.)[74] What kinds of goods belong to which sphere, and what principles of distribution are then appropriate, can only be the product of shared cultural understandings, which will vary across cultures. He views the role of the philosopher as to interpret the cultural meanings shared within his own society, rather than to seek a distanced, detached view.[75] It is this 'radically particularist'[76] view, as well as the cultural particularity of his principles of justice and concomitant rejection of universalism, rather than any substantive objections to liberalism, that mark Walzer out as a communitarian.

Even a society as diverse as Britain's in the late twentieth century has a stock of shared understandings, in Walzer's terms. These are socially constructed meanings and ways of understanding things which depend as much upon history and tradition as on current agreement; they govern what 'feels' natural and right. These shared understandings can be and are called upon to decide which criteria are appropriate for the distribution of certain goods, and the criteria which those understandings yield are sometimes in conflict with the potential outcomes (intended or otherwise) of government policies. In a booklet published by Demos, John Gray explores some of the implications for policy of Walzer's position. For example, he notes that

> In Britain most people think it unfair that access to decent medical care should be restricted by income rather than need, or that the provision of such care should be distorted by market forces. This common understanding condemns the neoliberal commercialisation of the NHS, if – as available evidence strongly suggests – the introduction of market mechanisms within it has partly decoupled patient care from medical need and made access to care to a significant degree an accident of the policies of the NHS trust currently in force in one's locality. Moreover, it demands the reversal of these policies, insofar as they have effects which violate it.[77]

Written in 1996, this clearly refers to the policies of the Conservative administration, but while Labour in government have amended the internal market in the health service, market mechanisms play an increasing and more direct role, through the Private Finance Initiative and the increasing use of private health facilities for NHS patients.

Their extension of the Private Finance Initiative (PFI) and 'public/private partnerships' (PPP) in the NHS and other areas of public provision, under which profit making companies operate public services, is another policy in which New Labour themselves have arguably violated the shared understandings of the society they govern. This suggestion is borne out by the widespread public unease and opposition which the proposals have met.[78] It is seen as simply wrong – or inappropriate – that public services should be run for private profit, *even if* this would result in the cheaper delivery of those services.

This is illustrated by the case of prison policy. In opposition, Jack Straw opposed private prisons on the grounds that it is morally wrong for anyone to profit from people's incarceration. A 1995 policy document unequivocally stated that '[t]he Labour Party is opposed in principle to the privatisation of prisons ... It is not appropriate for people to profit out of incarceration'.[79] In government, however, this was outweighed by economic considerations, and existing prisons continued effectively to be privatised while considerable amounts of new prison building were undertaken by the private sector. As well as being cheaper, inspectors' reports suggest that in at least some cases the private prisons provide better facilities and conditions for inmates. None of this, however, assuages public unease at the *concept* of making profits from public services.

In everyday terms, this might be described as a case of the government 'moving too fast' in introducing policies for which the public are not yet ready. While there is often a case to be made for governments doing this, any government so doing is failing in that instance to legislate according to our shared understandings, and is thus not communitarian in Walzer's terms.

In short, on the relatively few occasions on which a communitarian philosopher has anything to say, either directly or by implication, about policy, their position is opposed to or critical of New Labour's. MacIntyre wholeheartedly rejects a model of politics and society which Blair and his colleagues accept without question and are happy to operate within. His understanding of the concepts of citizenship and tradition bear no resemblance to the government's. Sandel's rejection of Rawls's particular understanding of individualism has been widely misread as a criticism of Rawls's entire *Theory of Justice*, whereas in fact Sandel endorses Rawls's egalitarian position (but rejects his method of arguing for it). New Labour, on the other hand, prefer meritocracy, which is excoriated by both Rawls and Sandel. Taylor's understanding of the pivotal concept of community is completely different from the party's, as is his view of the nature and role of citizenship, leading to very different conclusions about what the aims and direction of policy should be. Finally, Walzer's philosophy effectively warns against the extension of the market into public services.

Overall, however, the reader who scours the work of MacIntyre, Sandel, Taylor and Walzer for clues to the ideas behind New Labour policy is likely to be disappointed by discovering a wide gulf, on many levels, between their (themselves very heterogeneous) positions and the communitarianism familiar from the press of the 1990s. This is in part an inevitable result of the fact that their work is, to varying degrees, far removed from the sphere of policy and politics. One writer, however, has sought to bridge that gap by developing a set of politically practicable principles from communitarian philosophy. The final section of this chapter explores this attempt, and asks whether similarities can be found between New Labour policy and rhetoric and this model of implementation for communitarian philosophy.

From philosophy to policy: Daniel A. Bell

In *Communitarianism and its Critics*,[80] Daniel A. Bell uses communitarian philosophy as the basis for a political communitarianism that is fairly conservative, nationalist and potentially authoritarian, and is certainly not the only possible interpretation of the work of (at least) Sandel, Walzer and Taylor (significantly, Bell additionally calls on Heidegger as a source for his ideas). On the other hand, Bell's book has been favourably reviewed by MacIntyre.[81]

Bell's theoretical starting point is the claim, most strongly made in Sandel's work, that it is impossible to conceive of any individual as completely separate from and independent of their community. However, rather than simply accepting this as an ontological claim, he develops it into normative claims about *how* individuals should relate to their communities. One of his more controversial claims is that an individual who attempts to leave their community will be 'damaged'; not merely ontologically (in the sense that it would no longer be coherent or even possible to think of them *as* a person), but in their experience of life as an individual living in the real world.

Such 'damaged human personhood'[82] as he calls it, could well take the form of mental illness, or at best, emotional disturbance; certainly unhappiness. However, he does not cite rising rates of mental and/or psychological illness as the symptoms of the social problems which he perceives, but more familiar worries like 'unshackled greed, rootlessness, alienation from the political process, rises in the rate of divorce and all the other phenomena related to a centring on the self and away from communities in contemporary Western societies ...'[83] He claims 'loneliness, divorce, deracination, political apathy, and everything else connected with the breakdown of community in contemporary Western societies' as particularly communitarian concerns, to which liberalism has no satisfactory response.[84]

Bell's argument seeks to extrapolate political prescriptions from communitarian philosophy. He begins by sketching a 'communitarian ontology', for which he draws heavily on Taylor and Sandel, but also, explicitly, Heidegger. This ontology, Bell claims, is fully compatible with, but does not entail, either communitarian 'methodology' or the concrete policy changes which he proposes. (His innovation, he claims, is in 'shifting the debate from ontology to advocacy'.)[85] The basis of Bell's communitarian ontology is the 'idea ... that "society" is ultimate in the order of explanation – whether we like it or not, whether we know it or not, we're deeply bound up in the social world in which we happen to find ourselves'.[86]

Certain communities are viewed as 'constitutive', and human well-being is closely tied to the ability to express commitment to, and live through, such communities. Bell defines three key kinds of constitutive community: 'communities of place', 'communities of memory' and 'psychological communities'.[87] Such communities are characterised by their basis in 'shared understandings', (the influence of MacIntyre and Walzer is apparent here) and, for Bell, 'the whole point of communitarian politics is to structure society in accordance with people's deepest shared understandings'. 'Constitutive attachments' (almost exclusively meaning membership of constitutive communities) are 'essential components of the self, stripped of which we would no longer be the same person in the relevant sense ... these essential components – one's family, one's nation, one's religion, and so on – constitute what it is that's valuable in our lives'.[88]

More strongly still, Bell claims, '[w]e identify so strongly with our constitutive communities that we deem the community's purposes to be our own'.[89] As a result, in a properly ordered and educated communitarian society, there would be little if any conflict between individual and community. Indeed, he argues that: 'If you ask yourself what matters most in your life ... the answer will involve a commitment to the good of the communities out of which your identity has been constituted [and] a need to experience your life as bound up with ... "constitutive communities".'[90]

This perceived need heavily informs the 'communitarian moral vision' and policy proposals which Bell outlines at the end of his book.

Bell's central aim is to 'try to provide a ... systematic statement of the communitarian position from which one can derive certain political measures meant to stem the erosion of communal life and nurture the fragile communities that still bind us together'.[91] The third part of *Communitarianism and its Critics* seeks to identify

> a palatable and feasible politics that allows people to experience their life as bound up with the good of the communities which constitute their identity, as opposed to a liberal politics concerned primarily with securing the conditions for individuals to lead autonomous lives.[92]

This will entail subjecting society 'to a very delicate operation that involves removing a certain idea propagated by liberal theorists, an idea which has "infected the body politic"'. This idea is the 'liberal myth that choice *per se* is good'.[93] Bell backs this up with examples of cases in which choice is not good, from the crude – it is not desirable that people should have the choice of buying bombs at their local shop – to the more sophisticated (taken from Singer) – there should not be the option of a market in blood.[94] He goes on to conclude from this that 'some choices currently available to individuals in society have undesirable consequences at the collective level, and that these ought to be curtailed if individuals are to realise what really matters to them'.[95]

Bell advocates the restriction of choice in two particular policy areas, which may be intended as guides to a broader position. The first of these is divorce, and Bell's reasoning goes thus:

> If the agreed-upon end is a society of secure, strongly constitutive families, political measures should be implemented that help realize that end ... It's not implausible to suggest that the easy availability of legal marriage dissolution reduces the probability of a successful long-term marriage.[96]

He stops short of seeking to outlaw divorce, however, instead rather mildly advocating that it 'can be made a more time-consuming procedure, thus allowing for a certain period of reflection before the knot is permanently untied'.[97]

This, interestingly, was one aspect of a new divorce law passed by the House of Commons in 1997, under the Conservative government but with the support of the Labour opposition. The law was initially intended to introduce 'no-fault' divorce and thus reduce conflict in the courts, but pressure from moralists within the Conservative Party and from the media led to the introduction of a 'cooling off period' during which the prospective divorcing parties would attend 'information meetings' in the hope that they might reconsider. Despite having supported the law in opposition, the new Labour Lord Chancellor, Derry Irvine, quietly dropped it when it became clear that other aspects of it (mainly the requirement that divorcing couples use the services of professional mediators) were proving unpopular, unworkable and expensive.[98]

New Labour – particularly Tony Blair, and especially prior to coming to power – did employ a certain kind of 'pro-family' rhetoric which made the same links between the break-up of families and the breakdown of community and society. For example, in 1994 – during his campaign for the party leadership – Blair said:

> The break-up of family and community bonds is intimately linked to the breakdown of law and order [...] The values of a decent society are in many ways the values of the family unit, which is why helping to re-establish good family life and community life should be a central objective of government policy[99]

Even here, though, Blair is concerned more with the effects of education and employment policies on the family, rather than with setting out a blueprint for the family as such, and this is a recurring theme in his pronouncements on the subject. He told the 1997 Labour conference:

> we cannot say we want a strong and secure society when we ignore its very foundation: family life. This is not about preaching to individuals about their private lives. It is addressing a huge social problem. Attitudes have changed. The world has changed [...] Every area of this Government's policy will be scrutinised to see how it affects family life.[100]

Perhaps mindful of how the Conservative government was made to look foolish and worse, hypocritical, by its 'back to basics' campaign, New Labour tended not to moralise about the family – as Polly Toynbee and David Walker point out, 'despite an extravagantly uxorious Prime Minister' the Labour front bench 'was a fair reflection of society at large' with its share of divorced, childless and gay ministers.[101]

While sharing Bell's view of the link between family and social breakdown, New Labour did not seek to address it directly through legislating on divorce. Indeed, against some moralising opposition, New Labour abolished the married couples' tax allowance – of little real but great symbolic value – and replaced it with a child tax credit available to all families with children. They also brought in legislation to ensure divorcees' – usually women's – entitlement to a share in their spouse's pension. Instead they talked about 'strengthening' the family through employment and welfare, and education policies.

The second area of policy for which Bell's communitarianism has direct implications concerns his advocacy of compulsory (civilian) national service. The purpose of this is to reinforce people's commitment to the nation, one of the most fundamental of constitutive communities, in Bell's view. The idea behind this is 'that by maximising contributions to the nation's purposes early on, more would come to acknowledge the nation's purposes as their own, and subsequently participate in the political life of the nation as virtuous citizens committed to the nation's well-being'.[102]

Again, this throws up the question as to whether such policies aim to enable the expression of pre-existing commitments, as Bell claims, or seek to establish commitments which, although desirable for whatever reason, do not already exist, as the perceived need for compulsion would suggest. In this instance, however, Bell addresses the question, and his answer is, in effect, that compulsion is necessary to make people act in their true interests, which they would not otherwise realise, being blinded by short-term desires.[103] As his imaginary liberal objects that the proposal 'comes down to implementing laws that limit choice so as to help citizens realise that their true interest lies in seeking the good of their nation', his defender of communitarianism replies that 'it's not so bad ... it's not too implausible to suppose that certain laws can be implemented on the grounds that they favour the structure that enables citizens to manifest their love of country'.[104]

New Labour are, on the whole, keen on the idea of service to others, usually understood in terms of voluntary work, and serving one's community. Where this is the fourth and final option under the New Deal, it is effectively compulsory. But this is very, very far short of Bell's proposals for service which is universal, compulsory and national. Firstly, the intention behind New Labour's plans and rhetoric is not the inculcation of identification with and loyalty to the nation as a whole, but, insofar as this is a primary intention at all, to the local community. The hope is that getting them to play a part in their local area will give people a 'stake' and reduce, for example, the likelihood of vandalism. Accordingly, schemes are organised on a local rather than a national level, and service is carried out through myriad existing, autonomous voluntary organisations[105] rather than being centrally organised and directed. Furthermore, the inculcation of even local loyalties is arguably not the primary aim of New Labour's promotion of voluntary and community activity: two other key aims are firstly, the effective and local provision of services, such as childcare (which in turn feeds into their economic objectives), and secondly, the development of *individual* responsibility.

Finally, Bell suggests, education policies have a part to play in ensuring that 'people's deepest needs of membership and participation in psychological communities are tapped at a young age'.[106] This would include encouraging a cooperative approach to joint working, but more than this, identification with the classroom community would be encouraged by 'implementing a reward scheme for the best classrooms ... and meting out collective forms of punishment to the members of classrooms that perform less well'.[107]

While Labour have continued to support 'whole class' teaching their approach to education is almost exclusively focused on improving results in the interests of employment and economic competitiveness. In schools, as in the community (and across all policy areas), they differ markedly from Bell in promoting individual rather than group responsibility. Proposals for specific citizenship education (discussed in Chapter 6) focus on the kind of voluntary work and community service outlined above, and on an understanding of the workings and importance of democracy and the British political system.

Bell's communitarianism, then, is unashamedly at odds with many aspects of liberalism in practice; he is far less reticent about its implications than Etzioni, but, as Kymlicka points out, still shrinks from pursuing his communitarian ideal to its logical conclusion.[108] The political communitarianism which Bell derives from communitarian philosophy is not the only possible interpretation. Walzer's work explicitly, and Sandel's and Taylor's too is quite compatible with many forms of liberalism; in the case of Walzer, of course, this would be so if a society's shared understandings were fundamentally liberal.[109]

Although many of its leading members are happy to promote a 'tough' image, and some are not afraid of being called authoritarian, New Labour is not – at least not explicitly – prepared to take communitarianism to the conclusions Bell advocates. Their aims are different. For Bell, community, society and nation are ends in themselves, inevitable and ultimate ends. Community in this sense is inescapable, and individuals must learn to fit in for the common good. For New Labour 'community means what we share'.[110] It is voluntary; a coming together of individuals, usually to cooperate to achieve a common purpose. When there is coercion in Labour policy – for example, in the New Deal – this is presented as being in the interests of personal responsibility and, in the broader picture, economic efficiency, rather than of preserving or promoting the sort of homogeneous community Bell envisages.[111] New Labour promotes community in terms of its advantages to individuals, both separately and in groups and communities of all kinds. In this, and in the comparable specific policy proposals, it is very largely opposed to Bell's communitarianism.

Likewise, New Labour's very understanding of the concept and significance of 'community' is largely on a different level from that of the philosophers considered in the first part of this chapter. The fact that they employ the term does not mean that New Labour share or reflect the views of those writers. Superficial similarities, such as those with MacIntyre's lament for lost moral standards or Sandel's rejection of individualism, prove, on closer examination, to be references to ideas which are conceptually quite different and do not entail one another. Indeed, where the philosophers do consider the implications of their thought for policy, as Taylor does, and as Gray does on behalf of Walzer, they tend to suggest the need for a more egalitarian, less competitive and less economically orientated policy than New Labour pursues.

4

'The wickedest idea of all is the idea of duty':[1] John Macmurray on community, society and service[2]

We now go on to consider in greater depth aspects of New Labour policy and rhetoric in the context of four further writers, who all, in different ways, have relevance to assessments of the party's 'communitarianism'. Three of these – Amitai Etzioni, Jonathan Boswell and Henry Tam – are contemporary writers who refer to themselves and/or their ideas as communitarian. The fourth, the subject of this chapter, is not. John Macmurray died in 1976, and his most important work was produced in the 1930s. He is nonetheless of considerable importance, because he has been widely claimed (not least by Blair himself) and perceived as a communitarian influence, via Blair, on New Labour. However, the actual content of Macmurray's work has largely been forgotten. It is well worth reconsidering, both as something which has been called a form of communitarianism, and in what it might mean as a standard for judging policy. While there is obviously a danger of anachronism in undertaking a comparison involving work written seventy-odd years ago and current policy, this will be avoided by focusing on Macmurray's work on the nature of humanity and society in general, rather than his comments on the specific politics, economics and religion of the period in which he was writing.

The second section of the chapter examines in detail the specific content of Macmurray's philosophy, and, in particular, his conception of community. Firstly, though, it looks in broader terms at New Labour's community-orientated policy and rhetoric, and the ideas and attitudes about what community is and what it is 'for' which underlie these. This will focus mainly on the policy area of the voluntary and community 'sector'. It will go on to outline the main relevant features of Macmurray's thought, primarily on the subject of community, in order to draw a detailed comparison between his position and that of New Labour and, especially, Tony Blair.

New Labour and Community

Community-orientated policies cannot be clearly identified with any one government department or approach but can be found, *inter alia*, in law and order, regeneration, employment and welfare policy. The importance of 'community' as a theme for New Labour is reflected in a range of areas. Although the first steps were taken by Conservative governments (through the City Challenge programmes of 1992–98)[3] to involve communities in economic regeneration (seen as an issue of efficacy), under New Labour it has become necessary to have community involvement to access government funding for almost any local project, including SureStart, Health Action Zones, Health Improvement Programmes, Lifelong Learning Partnerships, Early Years Development and Childcare Partnerships, and Local Cultural Strategies to name but a few.[4] Voluntary work and the involvement of individuals *in* their communities is being encouraged on a number of fronts – through the New Deal (both for Young People, where voluntary work is an option, and through the New Deal for Communities), through the Working Group on the Active Community (previously the 'Giving Age'); as part of the government's plans for citizenship education in schools; in the government's proposed relationship with the voluntary sector, and through the promotion of community and voluntary approaches to economic problems – e.g. to provide childcare to enable parents to undertake paid work. Community involvement in what is now known as local governance has increased in importance over New Labour's successive governments. Community is seen as both an end in itself, as a generally desirable thing to have, and, increasingly, as a tool or resource which can be tapped into to deliver other specified policy objectives – in areas which do not have any direct connection to community development.

Behind all these policies appears to lie the idea that by encouraging people to 'get involved', giving both their time and money to support and participate in voluntary activities, communities will be strengthened (a good in itself) and the people involved will gain in experience, esteem and, above all, will develop and express a sense of citizenship and duty. This in turn will 'empower' communities to take responsibility for themselves and their members (morally desirable) and in the process, if successful, lead them to take over some of the roles which are perceived as a burden upon the welfare state (fiscally and thus politically desirable).

As almost every writer on the topic has acknowledged, the word 'community' is problematic. Its uses range from a synonym for both local government and the entire nation (and beyond, as in 'international community'), to a meaningless word thrown in to any policy to create a 'warm glow'. This policy area is no exception, although in general the term's use is better thought out here than in other areas and avoids such extremes. Generally, the communities referred to are (usually implicitly) geographically based (as opposed to historic communities, communities of interest etc.). Here community is seen as a group of people who live in the same area – frequently meaning a housing estate, or perhaps a local school's catchment area.

Community activity is perceived as something which is done *with* other people; it is essentially a collective enterprise, rather than anything done by an individual acting alone but for the benefit of the community. In extreme cases (which are perhaps more prevalent than the government appears to presume) it will be the activity which engenders the community, rather than vice versa. It is generally assumed that the activities which bring communities together will be positive and constructive (despite the evidence that it is frequently protest which brings a community together, uniting in opposition to, for example, local or national government plans to build a road, or a rubbish tip, in their area). The Working Group on the Active Community in their report *Giving Time, Getting Involved*, note a number of ways in which people might do this, concluding that '[s]ometimes participation will take the form of advocacy, lobbying or *even* opposition to issues, but that is an important part of active community involvement in a democracy'.[5]

Volunteering, and all that it entails, was, in the early days of the Labour Government, 'badged' as 'Active Community Involvement' and the government set up an Active Communities Unit[6] to support and encourage voluntary activity. The Active Communities Unit was relaunched in 2002, and later came under the umbrella of the Civil Renewal Unit, established by the government in June 2003.[7] The kinds of voluntary activity envisaged have a significant place in the vision of society presented by New Labour, and although previous Conservative governments have also sought to encourage such activity, the emphasis is now subtly different. The rhetoric around this subject could, as much as any other, be taken as suggestive of some kind of communitarian agenda, but commentators have focused largely upon law and order and welfare policy. Whereas these look superficially communitarian as a result of their emphasis on duty, it is in the area of voluntary sector policy that the potentially communitarian themes of interdependence and mutual support are most clearly developed, and the ideal of a civil society of involved citizens can be seen.

The development of the 'active citizen' is seen as desirable in a number of ways, some easier than others to pin down. It will be good for society in a practical sense, providing better and more services and support than the state ever could. In an extension of this it will benefit the economy, for example, by providing childcare services, and also via the expansion of the voluntary sector[8] with its significant proportion of paid workers and managers. People, it is claimed, will be happier with the more localised, face to face and flexible services which the voluntary sector can provide. As a policy tool, tapping into community knowledge and expertise, and voluntary labour, is said to make for the more effective and responsive provision of services.[9]

The perceived benefits of what the government terms 'voluntary action' can roughly be characterised as 'practical' and 'moral'. Both approaches are evident in party and government literature. On the practical side are claims that voluntary action provides services which are more flexible and responsive, and generally better and better received than similar services provided directly by the state, as well as providing services which would not otherwise be provided owing to financial, political or practical constraints. Practical benefits for those participating in voluntary action are also pointed out, notably increased self esteem and the gaining of skills which will be useful in the employment market.

Because of its perceived independence from political and bureaucratic constraints the voluntary sector is seen as a locus for innovation, and for the development of good practice which can then be adopted by the statutory sector. These practical aspects are not ignored. The Working Group on the Active Community note that without volunteers there would be 'no voluntary reading schemes in schools, no victim support schemes, no mentors. This would have serious implications for those who receive this help ... [T]he economic value of volunteering has been estimated to amount to £40 billion so the public expenditure implications are considerable.'[10] This last would also have clear electoral implications. The ability to use volunteer time as matched funding in many of the government schemes mentioned above explicitly demonstrates that voluntary activity is viewed as a quantifiable economic resource. Community involvement is seen to offer added economic value through activities like 'credit unions, food co-operatives, LETS and the whole range of mutual interest groups' which 'create free services, increase mutual aid ... [and] reduce living costs'.[11] The economic benefits of people 'getting involved' in their communities are recognised by New Labour to be considerable, and this is a large part of their motivation for pursuing policies towards this end.

On the 'moral' side, the government stresses the importance of voluntary action in developing and promoting its particular vision of citizenship. For example, 'Volunteering and community activities are central to the concept of citizenship and are the key to restoring our communities'.[12] (Although the restoration of communities clearly has a practical dimension as well.) Linked to this is the perceived role of voluntary activity in creating and developing a 'sense of community' – viewed as a good in itself. Blair is quoted as saying that 'the government's overall aim would be "to rebuild a sense of community throughout the United Kingdom, by encouraging and supporting all forms of community involvement"'.[13] This ties in with normative arguments about individual responsibility and the character building nature of doing things for oneself (rather, implicitly, than relying on the state). This rationale, although important in the rhetoric of community involvement, is less explicit in actual policy initiatives, which generally have a more practical focus and emphasise benefits to, rather than duties of, participants.

It is also claimed that voluntary activity is important to the healthy functioning of a democracy; that it engenders citizenship and can contribute to improving democratic legitimacy, if – and it's a big if – it leads to greater engagement with the political process.[14] The Working Group on the Active Community's *Giving Time, Getting Involved* states that '[a] strong and vibrant democracy requires active citizens participating in their communities'.[15] This is an interesting development of the traditional conception of both democracy and citizenship, cutting it off from the political sphere and moving it into the social. Also on the moral side falls the issue of dependency. Voluntary activity is seen as a way for individuals, working together in their communities, to do things for themselves and thus avoid dependency on state agencies with all its perceived moral disbenefits.

Finally, there are a few themes which link practical and moral reasons for encouraging voluntary action. The face to face nature of voluntary, as opposed to state, aid not only makes it more efficient and responsive to need, but engenders a relationship in which the recipients can be made aware of their reciprocal duties, in contrast to the mere claiming of rights which is perceived as being attendant upon the receipt of aid, in the form of benefit, from the state. The personal nature of such voluntary aid lessens the risk of dependency, and because, unlike the state, it does not have to be neutral, gives (in theory at least) scope for what used to be called 'moral improvement'. This is of course frequently perceived as one of the less desirable aspects of Victorian charity, but similar sentiments underlay key features of Fabianism and are also clearly reflected in the work of David Green and Robert Whelan for the IEA.[16]

Secondly, the benefits which are seen to flow from the voluntary sector's 'independence' from 'politics' also reflect a moral assumption: that politics is not an appropriate medium for dealing with these issues, or, to put it more crudely, that the populace, while it has a democratic duty to vote in elections, should not further concern itself with the business of politics. This is considered in greater detail in chapter 7, where New Labour's conception of citizenship is examined. Finally in this section, there is an element of overlap between moral and practical reasons for encouraging voluntary activity insofar as the practical benefits of voluntary activity are harnessed by government to further policies which have a broader moral thrust. The Working Group perceives that 'community self-help is an integral part of what the Government wishes to achieve'[17] in terms of its broader policy objectives.

Voluntary action is implicitly defined by the government in fairly narrow terms. It tends to refer to the unpaid provision of services to others within the volunteer's locality. Carrying out voluntary service overseas, for example, is completely ignored, as is working in an unpaid capacity for national charities, except where these are operating at a local level. Voluntary action is clearly defined as unpaid: the *giving* of one's time. This has always been implicit in the understanding of voluntary work, and is not contentious, although a moment's thought shows that paid work can be, and usually is, voluntary too (and unpaid work can be involuntary, as in slave labour). Where there are subtle and (perhaps from employers who stand to gain kudos from their staff undertaking voluntary activity) less subtle pressures upon people to undertake these kinds of activities the distinctive nature of voluntary activity in which, in large part, its moral value resides, may become blurred. This might turn out to be the case both with requiring schoolchildren to undertake community[18] work as proposed by the Active Community Unit,[19] and, should it come to fruition, the proposal, mentioned above, that participation in community activity should be used as a criterion in allocation of university places.[20]

More explicitly, the voluntary sector 'option' under New Deal is sometimes effectively compulsory. There is, famously, 'no fifth option', but the other three options (work, training and various combinations of employment and training placements) may not be available to some participants (for reasons including lack of skills, criminal record, mental health problems and lack of local availability), leaving voluntary work, the fourth and final 'option' as compulsory by default. All of these point to the risk that if voluntary work becomes effectively compulsory, at least to a degree, while its practical benefits may increase, its distinctive moral value will diminish in proportion to the degree of compulsion or pressure.

Finally, the concept of voluntary activity as understood by the government in this context carries with it a strong bias towards service to other individuals or to groups. It excludes political and campaigning activities (although these may have a role in building a sense of community) and it excludes activities which, although voluntary, one would undertake in any case for one's own pleasure. Attempts are clearly to be made to promote voluntary activity as enjoyable and beneficial to those undertaking it, but it is at the same time expected to draw upon, inculcate and develop a sense of duty, which is to some degree undermined by the manner of its promotion. The Working Group on the Active Community propose a 'media campaign ... to raise awareness, demonstrating that community involvement is both a right and a responsibility of every citizen, and that everybody has the opportunity to be involved'.[21] 'Key promotional messages' would include: 'everybody gets something out of the experience' and 'it can be fun and interesting'.[22] So community activity is promoted on the basis of its benefits to those who undertake it, rather than appealing to a sense of duty or responsibility.

The rhetoric which accompanies these proposals for voluntary activity and the community sector provides insights into New Labour's understanding of the whole concept of community and its role. The concepts of community, rights and duties and citizenship can not, of course, be divorced from each other. They are very closely interrelated – perhaps especially so in New Labour rhetoric. Therefore although it is the conception of community which is under consideration here, this needs to be read in conjunction with the accounts of New Labour conceptions of the other concepts undertaken in following chapters.

New Labour's relating of community to state or government displays a range of attitudes. When embodied in voluntary activities and services, community is viewed as an alternative to government; community provision complements or displaces state provision, and this is seen as desirable for a number of reasons. On the other hand, community is sometimes identified with the nation as a whole. Indeed, in saying 'I don't think you can make the case for Government, for spending taxpayers' money on public services or social exclusion, *in other words for acting as a community*, without [a] covenant of duties and responsibilities together',[23] Blair seems to be suggesting that the government is at the very least acting on behalf of the (national) community if not actually embodying it.

Despite their constant stressing of the importance of community, New Labour does not consistently suggest that it is necessarily either logically or morally prior to, or more important than, the individual. They are not talking about community in the same sense that MacIntyre or Sandel are; something the absence of which is unthinkable. Indeed, a number of

policy positions make clear that the very absence of community is perceived as the root of the problem in question.

The most common position is that community is a necessary prerequisite for the advancement of individual interests, and that this is the
best basis on which to promote its desirability. Thus Gordon Brown talks
of his 'belief not only that individuals thrive best in a community and
that the potential of the individual is enhanced by membership of a community but also that a strong community is essential for the advancement of individual potential',[24] echoing Blair's frequent assertions to the
effect that (for example) 'the individual does best in a strong and decent
community of people … we are the party of the individual *because* we are
the party of community'.[25]

New Labour's starting point and priority is undeniably the individual,
with the community seen as the means to individuals' ends, and, in terms
of the fulfilment of potential, the (economic) ends of the nation as a
whole. It is in this way that the concept of community, and their particular use of it, enables New Labour to assimilate the individualism which
they claim is a product of Thatcherism – but which MacIntyre and others would trace back to the enlightenment – while marking their rejection of its Thatcherite associations. This, as the remainder of this chapter
shows, is in stark contrast to the views of the philosopher held to have
been a significant influence on Blair's thinking and through this, on New
Labour's development.

John Macmurray: community, society and service

The name of John Macmurray is creeping back into the public conscious-
ness, after having lain forgotten for forty-odd years. While it may not be
on everyone's tongue, it is common currency among journalists and academics analysing New Labour and offering explanations for the party's
perceived shifts of policy under Blair's influence. Macmurray in turn is
asserted to have been a significant influence on the party leader's thinking. According to Blair's biographer, John Rentoul, Macmurray is Blair's
'philosophical mentor',[26] and 'Blair's idea of community, which is perhaps his most distinctive theme as a politician, derives directly from
Macmurray.'[27] This claim is repeated and reinforced by Driver and Martell,
who note that 'Blair read and discussed the communitarian philosophy
of John Macmurray'[28] while at Oxford, and, elsewhere refer to Macmurray
as 'the Scottish philosopher who influenced Tony Blair'.[29] In another
biography of Blair, Jon Sopel notes that he 'became fascinated by his
[Macmurray's] work [which] introduced him to an idea that would later

become central to his political thinking, the notion of "community".[30] Sopel also refers to Macmurray as 'the Scottish philosopher ... whom Blair was so influenced by when he was an undergraduate at Oxford.'[31] Elizabeth Frazer, in her generally sceptical work on communitarian politics, says that 'Tony Blair's communitarianism was influenced by the philosophy of John MacMurray [sic]'.[32] Norman Fairclough, in his study of New Labour's use of language agrees with Driver and Martell that it is their use of communitarian discourse which differentiates New Labour both from Thatcherite conservatism and 'Old' Labour, but attributes this to Blair having 'been heavily influenced by the communitarian philosophy of John Macmurray',[33] similarly suggesting both that Blair's philosophy is Macmurray's, and that the latter is communitarian. The *Observer* has called Macmurray 'an important influence on the Prime Minister',[34] and the *Guardian* has described him as 'influential on Tony Blair'.[35]

These claims have two main bases: Blair's documented interest in and admiration of Macmurray; and the emphasis on community in Blairite rhetoric and, to a lesser extent, in New Labour policy, which is seen to reflect one of the primary themes of Macmurray's work. Political commentators have not been slow to note that Blair was at least aware of Macmurray long after others had forgotten him, while the former was a student at Oxford in the early 1970s. Blair's interest in Macmurray came about via Peter Thomson, an Australian theology student some years older than Blair and his contemporaries, around whom an informal Christian discussion group coalesced, to which Blair was an enthusiastic contributor. It is from this period, and this friendship, that Blair's own Christianity dates.

Thomson in turn was an enthusiast for Macmurray's particular brand of active Christian Socialism. Legend has it that that Blair and Thomson made a pilgrimage to Edinburgh to visit Macmurray in 1974, shortly before his death, although in the event only Thomson went into his home and met him. In some versions this was in deference to Macmurray's frailty, but others have the future Prime Minister simply losing his nerve at the last minute, and waiting on the pavement outside.[36]

Specific references by Blair to Macmurray are, however, thin on the ground, and most can be traced to a couple of primary sources: a frequently recycled comment made by Blair in an interview just days after his election to the party leadership, in July 1994, and a couple of interviews with Thomson (who was until the mid-1990s, when Blair recommended that he apply for the post of Vicar of St Lukes, Holloway,[37] a cattle rancher in Australia).[38] In the former, Blair is quoted as saying: 'If you really want to understand what I'm all about, you have to take a look at a guy called John Macmurray',[39] going on to say that 'he was influential – very influential. Not in the details, but in the general concept.'[40] This was still being quoted by journalists at the time of the 2005 General Election.[41]

Blair also mentions Macmurray as one of many writers to have influenced his 'interest in religion and philosophy', alongside Kierkegaard, Jung and Kant, saying: 'One of the best things I have read on the subject of Christian duty was an essay by the Scottish philosopher John Macmurray, a socialist thinker whose writings I was introduced to as a student at Oxford.' What Blair understood Macmurray to mean in this (unnamed) essay was that 'there is a human impulse within, which can be fulfilled only through duty'.[42] One Labour chronicler, Andy McSmith, offers an alternative account of Macmurray's influence on the student Blair, attributing the latter's inspiration to Thomson's 'blending his own mix of liberation theology based *partly* upon ... Macmurray'.[43]

Community and society

The 'general concept' that Blair refers to is generally taken by commentators to be the concept of community. To many eyes, the Blair trademark, the unique selling point with which he has provided his party, is the rediscovery (or possibly reinvention) of this ideal. Even (perhaps especially) within Blairite rhetoric, the concept of community covers a range of interpretations, some of which are evident in this single paragraph from a speech in 2000:

> At the heart of my beliefs is the idea of community. I don't just mean the villages, towns and cities in which we live. I mean that our fulfilment as individuals lies in a decent society of others. My argument to you today is that the renewal of community is the answer to the challenges of a changing world.[44]

Community is also one of Macmurray's key concerns. Therefore, the assumption has it, Blair's emphasis on community must reflect Macmurray's influence. From an academic perspective this might easily be dismissed as journalists' sloppy reasoning; however, such assumptions are not confined to journalists. Academic commentators also have repeated and lent credibility to these claims.[45] This chapter suggests, however, that Blair's 'philosophy', as reflected in both his words and his deeds (in the form of New Labour policy) is markedly different from Macmurray's and frequently in stark opposition to it, with very little common ground; and that only an extremely superficial reading of Macmurray could have led commentators – and Blair himself – to believe otherwise.

The problem lies in that 'the general concept' cited by Blair – which most commentators understand as referring to the concept of community

– is notorious for the broad range of interpretations which it invites, yet throughout discussions of Macmurray's perceived influence on Blair it is treated as if it is an uncontested, unambiguous term, which necessarily means the same for Blair as for Macmurray, which, as we shall see, is far from the truth. This in turn leads to the superficial posthumous characterisation of Macmurray as a communitarian in the mould of Amitai Etzioni – the most blatant example of this is provided by Sopel, who says that Macmurray's ideas

> find voice nowadays through the American Communitarian Movement, Amitai Etzioni [*sic*]. The central proposition is that individual rights and responsibilities must be properly balanced, and that this new settlement must take place in the context of the community.[46]

and that Etzioni's work has a message 'not so very different from that of … Macmurray'.[47] This misunderstanding[48] of Macmurray's views is fairly common currency, with only a couple of writers questioning it.[49] Therefore, although significant differences can be identified between the positions of Macmurray and Blair on almost every issue on which the former pronounced (including the themes of tradition, Christianity and the role of the church, socialism, capitalism, equality and democracy) this chapter focuses in the main on the key theme of community.[50]

John Macmurray, already unfashionable by the time of Tony Blair's interest in him, was until recently all but completely forgotten, at least as a philosopher.[51] The vast 1998 *Routledge Encyclopaedia of Philosophy* does not have an entry for him. Yet from the 1930s to the 1950s he was widely known; a populariser of moral philosophy through radio appearances and lecture series, collections of which were being published into the 1960s,[52] and pamphlets/short volumes on a number of topics.[53] As well as this relatively popular work, he wrote more academic volumes[54] and held chairs at London and Edinburgh, and in South Africa and Canada. The publishers of the 1968 edition on *Freedom in the Modern World* (first published in 1932) claim that the work 'has probably had a deeper and more lasting effect than any other book of a philosophical character published this century'.[55] Even allowing for publishers' established tendency to hyperbole, this demonstrates that Macmurray was considered a very important figure in mid-twentieth-century Britain.

The main thrust of Macmurray's work is his assertion that people's humanity and human potential is only realised through their relations with others – but only through certain kinds of relationship. Relations, according to Macmurray, may be either social or communal. Where people come together to cooperate for common ends, a social relationship is formed. In this, we associate with others in order to achieve some purpose that we all share. Out of this there springs a life of social co-operation through which we can provide for our common needs, and achieve common ends. We may define this social life in terms of purposes. That is its great characteristic.[56]

Social relationships are, in other words, instrumental. The definition of society is that it is founded upon, and composed of, instrumental relationships. This is highly necessary to human survival, but it is not the form of relationship which expresses and realises humanity itself.

> The satisfactory working of social life depends upon entering into relationships with other people, not with the whole of ourselves, but only with part of ourselves. It depends upon suppressing ... the fullness and wholeness of our natures.[57]

Personal relationships – 'the personal life' – in contrast

> demands a relationship with one another in which we can be our whole selves and have complete freedom to express everything that makes us what we are. It demands a relationship with one another in which suppression and inhibition are unnecessary.[58]

The personal life is in contrast to both the social life and the individual life.[59] Whatever we call this kind of relationship (and Macmurray points out that all the possible terms, such as '[f]riendship, fellowship, communion, love' have all taken on a partial meaning too specific for this purpose) at the heart of it

> is the idea of a relationship between us which has no purpose beyond itself; in which we associate because it is natural to human beings to share their experience, to understand one another, to find joy and satisfaction in living together; in expressing and revealing themselves to one another.[60]

It is this type of relationship which characterises Macmurray's highly specific and very *pure* conception of community, providing for a very narrow definition of the term. Certainly, in Macmurray's view, society and community are two very different things, defined in opposition to each other. Society arises through external pressures and needs; community from internal human impulses.

> the difference between a community and a mere society is ... clear cut. When we consider the forces which give rise to human relationships and which create and maintain human groups, we see that they are of two opposed types. Some are external and compulsive. Others spontaneous and intrinsic. We are forced into relationship with other people, in many cases, by conditions over which we have no control. We are compelled by our necessities to co-operate with people who do not attract us, and whom we should not choose as our friends or associates if we could help it. In other cases we are drawn into relationships by the need to share our experience, by the need for mutual companionship.[61]

The former kind of relationship characterises Macmurray's conception of society; the latter, of community. The entire point of his advocacy of community is as a contrast and necessary complement to social relations.

Society is built upon interdependence, but dependency is, for Macmurray, corrosively destructive of *community*. If we are dependent upon other people – however much it may be mutual – we cannot be in true fellowship with them, but only in an instrumental relationship which diminishes our humanity.[62] For Blair, on the other hand, '"[c]ommunity" implies a recognition of interdependence',[63] and 'The idea of community resolves the paradox of the modern world: it acknowledges out interdependence; it recognises our individual worth',[64] while Gordon Brown 'think[s] of Britain ... as a community of citizens with common needs, mutual interests, shared objectives, related goals ...'[65]

Macmurray has been claimed as a communitarian because of his stress upon the importance of community for humankind. Although he is much else besides, there can be little objection to this provided that it is borne in mind that his conception of community is of a very narrowly defined form of relationship, of a particularly rare and precious nature. Macmurray's work cannot be used to confer the value that he ascribes to this conception of community upon what he calls 'mere society'.[66]

However, New Labour tend to conflate the two concepts and use the terms 'community' and 'society' interchangeably, as in 'At the heart of my beliefs is the idea of community ... that our fulfilment as individuals lies in a decent society of others.'[67] In doing this they reject the distinction at the very heart of Macmurray's work, and thus negate everything he has to say about the desirability of community.[68] The fact that New Labour have ideas of what community and society respectively mean and entail which are so different from those of Macmurray mean that they can conflate the terms without internal inconsistency – but this only serves to demonstrate the distance of their conception from his ideal.

Notwithstanding this, it is Blair's claims about the relationship of the individual to society which have done most to draw comparisons with Macmurray. A typical example is his claim, quoted earlier, that: 'our fulfilment as individuals lies in a decent society of others'.[69] However, such claims (i.e. claims that these sentiments are a reflection of Macmurray's views) would appear to be based upon a very superficial reading of Macmurray. A closer reading suggests that Blair's position is almost diametrically opposed to Macmurray's. This confusion arises because Macmurray's vital distinction between society and community, discussed above, is ignored. Blair's (and the government's) constant conflation[79] of the terms is sufficient in itself to demonstrate that this aspect at least of their thinking owes nothing to Macmurray.

In fact, many of the themes and ideas attributed to Macmurray, most explicitly by Rentoul, and by Driver and Martell[71] are far closer to those of the contemporary communitarian philosophers discussed in Chapter 4, than to Macmurray's own work. For example, Rentoul claims that

> Macmurray saw his purpose as being to challenge the starting point of modern philosophy, the idea that people are individuals first who then choose how to relate to others. He insisted that people exist *only* in relation to others ... he argued that the liberal self was incomplete, because people's personalities are created by their relationships to their families and communities.[72]

The use of the term 'modern philosophy', and its description by Rentoul, suggest something like Rawlsian liberalism; something far more recent than Macmurray could have been responding to.[73] Driver and Martell also present Macmurray's position as 'a direct attack on liberalism',[74] although nowhere does Macmurray explicitly, nor, arguably, implicitly, attack liberalism. Indeed, In *The Self as Agent*, he defends liberalism against communism.[75] Macmurray's attacks are primarily directed toward capitalism and tradition, and generally toward those forces which *suppress* the individual human impulse.

Individualism

Communitarian politics is often presented as an antidote to the individualism perceived to have been engendered under Thatcherism. It is fashionable to stress that there '*is* such a thing as society'[76] in implied contrast to Thatcher's claim to the contrary.[77] For Macmurray, however, individualism – which he perceived in his own time – was not the cause of social ills, but a symptom of them, in particular of insecurity, in a world dominated by fear rather than love.

> Fear accomplishes [the] destruction of life by turning us in upon ourselves and so isolating us from the world around us. That sense of individual isolation which is so common in the modern world, which is often called 'individualism' is one of the inevitable expressions of fear.[78]

Duty, responsibility and rights

Blair is frequently labelled communitarian because of his constant emphasis on rights and duties or rights and responsibilities. Examples include Blair's assertion that '[i]f we invest so as to give the unemployed person the chance of a job, they have a responsibility to take it or lose benefit'[79] and '[f]or every new opportunity we offer, we demand responsibility in return'.[80] These reflect Blair's view that 'a decent society is not based on rights. It is based on duty.'[81] However, this finds few echoes in Macmurray.

Although, according to Macmurray, an ethos of service to others is inimical to the ideal of true community, he is adamant that this does not mean that there is no place for concerted efforts to help the worse off – in effect, for the welfare state:

> ... getting rid of unemployment, providing hospitals and recreation grounds and better schools for the poor and so on ... is very necessary but it is no substitute for personal morality. It is a matter of bare justice, and it has got to be done. But to erect it as a moral ideal is another matter ... What the unemployed need is not pity from a distance, but their bare rights as members of an astonishingly wealthy community. We have to see that they get their rights, and not pat ourselves on the back for our benevolence when we are merely being honest and decent.[82]

In other words, people should be able to depend, for subsistence and more, on rights, not charity. Macmurray talks about rights far more than he talks about duties, and when he refers to responsibilities, this is with a very different understanding from Blair's. Peter Thomson is quoted by Rentoul as saying that Macmurray

> was onto a concept of community. He used to say that the noblest form of human existence is friendship and that instead of being on a debit and credit ledger idea of 'If you do this for me, then I'll do that for you,' we ought to develop a sense of community where people were committed to the welfare of one another.[83]

This seems a far more accurate reflection of Macmurray's thought. But it is a long way away from current government policies in which the language of rights in exchange for duties; opportunity in exchange for responsibility, and 'contracts', 'compacts' and 'covenants'[84] strongly reflects the 'debit and credit ledger idea' rejected by Macmurray in his advocacy of the spontaneous generosity of truly human relations.

In fact, duty is a term that crops up extremely rarely in Macmurray's work. Responsibility for oneself plays a part in Macmurray's thought, but not in the way it is used in government rhetoric. For Macmurray, the ability to take responsibility for oneself is a privilege; even perhaps, in an ideal world, a right, but certainly not a burden. For example, in a discussion of democracy, Macmurray says that '[democracy] opposes privilege and social distinction, because these mean that some people or some classes of people are cornering freedom and responsibility for themselves at the expense of others'.[85] Responsibility is a precondition of freedom[86] which people will grasp if only given the opportunity, not something which has to be imposed upon them by New Deal type conditions. This might be said to reflect an unrealistically optimistic view of human nature.

Nonetheless, it highlights very clearly the difference between Macmurray's conception of responsibility and New Labour's, and shows that if New Labour are to be considered communitarian on account of their emphasis on responsibility, such a communitarianism is no reflection of Macmurray's work.

'Active community'

One aspect of the government's brand of communitarianism is to attempt to foster community by encouraging people to serve others. This ethos underlies the concept of 'active community', which encompasses voluntary work and charitable giving and is a key plank of proposals for the teaching of citizenship in schools. It is also widely promoted and practised in traditional Christianity. For Blair and his government, '[v]olunteering and community activities are central to the concept of citizenship and are the key to restoring our communities'.[87]

Such sentiments reflect, almost word for word, pre-election Labour Party policy documents.[88] The idea that '[c]learer expectations need to be set about the importance of people participating in their communities ... Children should grow up with these expectations' and the proposal that 'by 2010 all first degree courses should provide for a small element of credit towards the degree for approved community activity; and all universities and colleges should use community involvement as part of the criteria for entrance'[89] appears to bring us a little nearer to compulsory community service (although still a long way short of that advocated by contemporary communitarians like Etzioni[90] and Daniel Bell).[91] Macmurray scathingly condemns such an ethos of service to others, and in doing so unambiguously rejects the accepted communitarian conception of the individual's relationship to the rest of society. To understand why, it is necessary to look at Macmurray's philosophy in a little more detail.

Macmurray describes three kinds of morality: mechanical, social (or organic) and human.[92] The second of these, social morality, is very close to the communitarian morality endorsed by Etzioni and promoted by New Labour. Macmurray sets out what social morality says. For example,

> it will talk a great deal about purpose. Each of us ought to have a purpose in life and to work for its achievement, it will say. Then whatever draws us aside from our purpose will be bad and whatever advances it will be good ... If human life is to be good, it must not forget that the purpose which it serves is not its own purpose but the purpose of life as a whole.[93]

Macmurray outlines the justifications offered for this morality, which again, look like those of modern communitarianism:

> Each of us is born into a society and our lives are bound up with the community to which we belong ... We owe all we have and all we are to the community to which we belong. The community is our real environment and we live only in it and through it. Therefore the purpose which ought to control our lives is not our own selfish purpose, but the social purpose. We are part of a community of social life, and the goodness of our individual lives depends upon our devoting them to the common good ... The good man is the man who serves his country, serves his generation, identifies himself with the good of the community and devotes his life to the accomplishment of the social purpose.[94]

This passage is quoted at length because it is so exactly the sort of thing which Blair says. He could express such sentiments and truthfully claim to be quoting Macmurray. But it would be quoting out of context. This morality is being set out in detail by Macmurray only to be condemned. Such a 'morality of service ... is a false morality. It is false because it thinks of human life in biological terms, as if we were animals, not persons.'[95] Furthermore, it is 'a denial of human reality. It treats everybody as a means to an end.'[96] Finally, such a view of morality 'subordinates human beings to organization'.[97] In sum,

> The working morality of the modern world is a morality of social service ... The first thing we have to stop is the false idea that it is a good thing to serve society and its institutions. It isn't. *It is an evil thing.*[98]

Modern communitarian thinking is clearly not that new. Macmurray was already taking issue with it in 1932, on two fronts: firstly the view that the individual owes his existence, and therefore a duty, to the community, and secondly the idea that serving one's community is morally good. This makes very clear the danger in claiming Macmurray as a modern communitarian or even a progenitor of modern communitarianism. It also must cast serious doubts on any claim that Blair's substantive views owe anything to the philosopher. Macmurray sets out in detail the kind of morality currently espoused by Blair, only to condemn it as false and evil.

Far from contributing to the development of New Labour's conception of and attitude to community, then, Macmurray's philosophy actually provides strong and explicit criticisms of their position. We have already seen quite clearly that New Labour does not have one single conception of what 'community' means. All their understandings, though, are broader than Macmurray's. Usually, they use the terms 'community' and 'society' interchangeably, whereas for Macmurray the terms represent two completely separate concepts. New Labour's use of the term 'community' varies between policy areas. In law and order policy, it tends to refer to the places where people live and the people they live amongst;

a very practical, concrete meaning. In terms of the voluntary sector policy which has been considered in detail in this chapter, community is perceived as an expression of people's interdependence, which manifests itself in the giving of services to others. Such interdependence is of course completely antithetical to Macmurray's ideal of community, but much closer to his conception of society, while service to others, or to society, is seen by him as a denial of humanity and therefore evil.

We have seen, therefore, that contrary to New Labour's position, Macmurray rejects any role in community for duty or interdependence, and thinks voluntary service is a bad rather than a good thing. He defends both (welfare) liberalism and socialism, and sees individualism as a symptom, not a cause, of the erosion of community.

Blair might well have been influenced as a student by Macmurray's thought; indeed, parts of his maiden speech to the House of Commons in 1983 – for example:

> at its best, socialism corresponds most closely to an existence that is both rational and moral. It stands for co-operation, not confrontation; for fellowship, not fear. It stands for equality ... because only through equality in our economic circumstances can our individuality develop properly.[99]

has more than a ring of Macmurray. However, this predates New Labour by a decade or more. Tony Blair's early socialism might have owed something to John Macmurray; New Labour's 'communitarianism' very clearly does not.

5

Rights, responsibilities and morality:
Amitai Etzioni versus New Labour

In discussions of 'New Labour's communitarianism', the name which comes up most frequently is that of Israeli-American sociologist Amitai Etzioni. Some academics and journalists have boldly suggested that New Labour (and often other British parties, as well as European and American politicians) have been directly influenced by Etzioni's work, while many others note affinities and parallels between New Labour's rhetoric and Etzioni's creed. Some examples have already been given in Chapter 1, where they served to demonstrate the widespread perception that New Labour had become communitarian in more general terms. Many further examples can be found.

These examples may again be subdivided into 'academic' and 'press', with the academic examples being both fewer in number and generally more cautious and considered. These will be considered first. To the claims of Anthony Giddens, David Gilbert, Gordon Hughes, Gillian Peele, John Dearlove and Peter Saunders, Emma Heron and Peter Dwyer, and Bill Bowring, which are all detailed in Chapter 1, may be added these further examples of perceptions on the part of academic writers that Etzioni's work is at least compatible with New Labour's positions, and in some cases that it has directly influenced them.

The first of these claims is an explicit one, and comes directly from Etzioni himself – or at least, from his publishers. The British edition of *The Spirit of Community* reflects in its preface the view, which I have already described in detail, that the book, in its American edition (published two years previously), had already been influential in Britain, noting that communitarian ideas 'have been endorsed by a wide spectrum and growing number of political leaders, although they rarely utter the six syllable word'.[1] These politicians are said to include Tony Blair, David Willetts and Paddy Ashdown in Britain, as well as others from across the political spectrum in Germany, France and the US. This claim appears to be a clear reflection of views expressed in the British press around 1994, although Etzioni bases it on his observation that all these politicians 'often speak communitarian'.[2] This in itself could encompass a broad range of positions, and indeed, elsewhere Ashdown at least has been reported as being uneasy with Etzioni's ideas. (For example, only a year later Polly Toynbee claimed that 'Ashdown points with alarm to Labour's infatuation with American communitarianism and the work of Amitai Etzioni, the high priest of the new left moralism. He fears this tyranny of the majority crushes any dissenting voice, ruling by collective shame through the law of the lace curtain.')[3]

Etzioni suggests, with a sort of double-edged modesty, that '[c]ommunitarians like myself have not implanted these ideas in their heads; they are visionary people who have seen the power of a compelling set of ideas whose time has come'.[4] The publishers of Etzioni's follow-up to *The Spirit of Community, The New Golden Rule: Community and Morality in a Democratic Society* are not so modest, stating on the back cover that 'Etzioni has been very influential on New Labour'.[5] In contrast, the back cover 'blurb' of Etzioni's 2000 pamphlet for Demos, *The Third Way to a Good Society*, suggests that the 'Third Way', as pursued by New Labour among others, would benefit from paying more attention to Etzioni and his nostrums.

Ruth Levitas,[6] as has already been noted, observes that New Labour's rhetoric owes more to Etzioni than to Macmurray, and although she does not posit a crude relationship of influence between Etzioni and Blair's party, her careful examination of New Labour's use of 'inclusion discourses' shows how Etzioni-type language has helped the party make its significant political shift away from social democracy and enabled it to occupy territory mapped out by the New Right, while claiming to remain true to its roots.

Levitas identifies three types of 'inclusion discourse'. The one most closely identified with traditional social democracy is the 'redistributive egalitarian discourse' – RED for short. The other two, 'moral underclass discourse' (MUD) and 'social integrationist discourse' (SID) are more apparent in the rhetoric of New Labour. The former is most strongly associated with American writers like Charles Murray, and is characterised by the suggestion that the 'excluded' are largely to blame for their position (exclusion largely being identified in practice if not in principle with poverty), because they lack certain moral attributes, such as the capacity or willingness to work, or to maintain a stable two-parent family. SID, meanwhile, is a discourse which identifies inclusion very strongly with paid employment, and thus sees exclusion largely as arising from the lack of a job. This carries shades of the conceptions of inclusion employed in continental Europe, especially France, but the British incarnation tends invariably to see exclusion in terms of the excluded individual's responsibility to make themselves employable, rather than being looked at in the context of structural economic factors upon which the state can and should act. Each discourse can be summed up by what it perceives the excluded as lacking: money in RED; morals in MUD, and a job in SID.[7]

It is important to stress that these discourses should not be seen as 'versions' of communitarianism: they are descriptive accounts of more or less ideological approaches to exclusion. However, there are many overlaps between them and some identified kinds of political communitarianism, and it is possible to use Levitas' accounts to describe some aspects of different forms of communitarianism. For example, John Macmurray's communitarianism might be described as a form of RED, while Etzioni's has most in common with MUD, especially insofar as he explicitly calls for a 'shoring up of our moral foundations'.[8] It is through couching the discourses of SID and MUD, and the shift from collective to individual responsibility which their adoption signals, in the language of community, that New Labour has disguised the move, and Etzioni's identification of individual responsibility and duty with the concept of community certainly parallels this even if Etzioni himself has not provided the vocabulary.

In particular, Levitas views Etzioni as representative of one aspect of what she calls the 'new Durkheimian hegemony', to which New Labour also subscribes, 'with its appeal to social integration, solidarity and social cohesion',[9] although Etzioni's reading of Durkheim is a particularly right-wing one.[10] Simon Prideaux has suggested that Etzioni's entire communitarian ouevre is no more than functionalist organisational theory writ large.[11] Although Levitas does not claim that Etzioni has been an influence on New Labour's inclusion discourses, she does note a number of parallels, and, importantly, her work shows how communitarian language may be used to 'smuggle in' shifts in ideological approach without unduly alarming core supporters, simply by attaching new ideas to terms, like community, with positive but flexible connotations.

Joan Smith explicitly suggests that this is the case, claiming that rather than confront the New Right head on, New Labour, like the 'New Democrats' in America, have sought a 'New Settlement' which is 'acceptable to Conservatives, industrialists and bankers'[12] and which avoids the issues of how governments might regenerate the economy and society without reflationary measures. This is achieved, in Smith's opinion, by redefining the problems as a new kind of social crisis, drawn from communitarian theories like Etzioni's. According to Smith, '[t]he role played by Charles Murray in promoting the underclass thesis in both the US and the UK has now been taken over by Amitai Etzioni on behalf of the communitarian position',[13] and in *The Spirit of Community* 'Etzioni displayed an almost complete acceptance of the New Right agenda on social order'.[14] Like Levitas, Smith charts the changing language of New Labour (in particular its gradual acceptance of the very concept of an underclass), and suggests that it 'was in this context that communitarian arguments became important inside the Labour Party, offering a theoretical legitimation for the New Right perspectives on social welfare but dressing them in the language of family and community responsibility, and increasingly of "law and order"'.[15]

However, these similarities between the language of Etzioni and the New Right point to the possibility of misconstruing the latter for the former. Where such language is employed by New Labour, it is arguably more likely to be the legacy of a general shift in attitudes under previous administrations both in Britain and the US, than the ground-breaking ideas of a writer who to all intents and purposes is new on the scene. Blair's language might, as Smith perceives, look like Etzioni's on issues like the linking of law and order to family values. But these are equally the ideas of the New Right, developed and pursued by the Thatcher and, to a lesser extent, the Major governments. Etzioni's contribution, if such it be, is to provide a context and a language within which these ideas might be rendered acceptable to those traditionally on the left.[16]

Although she concedes that there are some policies where 'Blair's speeches and writing differ considerably from the more right-wing communitarian statements of Etzioni',[17] (albeit that these include areas like 'stakeholding' where Labour policy post-1997 did move appreciably away from an economic model of stakeholding to the idea of stakeholding as a synonym for employment based inclusion), Smith concludes that '[t]he Responsive Communitarian Platform has had more impact on both Democrat and Labour policies than the many radical community initiatives … led by local activists seeking to counter the devastating effects of the social policies of the past two decades'.[18] In other words, Etzionian communitarianism *has* influenced significant areas of New Labour policy, and furthermore, has done so at the expense of more radical, 'bottom-up' (in Frazer's terms, vernacular) forms of communitarianism.

While both Levitas and Smith see Etzioni's communitarianism as a mechanism by which New Labour has covertly assimilated New Right ideas, Adam Crawford, in a review of the British edition of *The Spirit of Community*, notes that '[a]s *an explicit rejection of New Right politics*, Etzioni, and communitarians more generally, have met with a favourable reception within the Labour Party, as it seeks to redefine itself under the leadership of Tony Blair'.[19] In this Crawford unconsciously provides an example of the broad range of interpretations to which Etzioni's communitarianism is open, which he later remarks upon. Noting the range of politicians who are claimed to have been inspired by the book, Crawford suggests that '[t]his should immediately alert the wary or cynical reader as to how an agenda can appeal simultaneously to such diverse interests'.[20] According to Crawford, New Labour 'has seized upon *The Spirit of Community* as offering something which lies between the untamed "market" and the out-of-favour ideals of "socialist social solidarity"'.[21] He goes on to note that '"community" has become the policy "buzz" word of the 1990s', and that '[o]n the British Left, the Demos political think tank has done much to promote communitarianism and the work of Etzioni in particular', while on the right, 'conservative commentators ... draw heavily upon the concept of "community" and, implicitly if not explicitly, upon the insights of American communitarians'.[22] Crawford goes on to criticise Etzioni, and *The Spirit of Community* in particular, for the succour they give to 'conservative and reactionary forces'.[23] Overall, his review again reflects the strength of the belief that Etzioni, and in particular this book, have provided some of the ideas behind New Labour policy.

Finally, in their collection of profiles of the politicians behind the transformation of the Labour Party, Paul Anderson and Nyta Mann claim that 'Blair's thinking about the dynamics of crime, family and community drew heavily on the ideas of the American communitarian movement, especially as expressed by the sociologist-turned-polemicist Amitai Etzioni.'[24]

Perhaps drawing on these academic accounts, but more likely as the result, in large measure, of Etzioni's successful publicisation of himself and his book, the idea that Etzioni was a significant influence on New Labour was reflected widely in the quality press at the time of his most publicised visit, and this continued through to the next General Election and beyond. Again, many examples have already been detailed in Chapter 1. However, here it will be possible to examine more closely the extent and effect of these perceptions in relation to Etzioni himself rather than as an indicator of communitarianism more generally.

An interesting perspective is provided by Peter Wilby, at the time of the publication of Etzioni's Third Way pamphlet by Demos.[25] Wilby describes Etzioni as 'one of Mr. Blair's favoured gurus', saying that he (Blair) 'was very taken with Professor Etzioni's "communitarianism" until some people explained that it was an unreasonably long word with faintly fascist overtones' but that in the Demos pamphlet Etzioni 'sets some of

those fears to rest ... and now, it seems, the community is back'.[26] This is
a particularly strong linkage of Blair with Etzioni, in that it suggests that
Blair's espousal of the idea of community has waxed and waned alongside
Etzioni's perceived British acceptability; i.e. it is very strongly identified
with Etzioni. In their retrospective assessment of Labour's first term, Polly
Toynbee and David Walker claim that '[t]he sociologist Amitai Etzioni
became a guru figure as the author of the new "communitarianism"'.[27]

There are many more examples of the casual assumption of Etzioni's
significance. In 1994, Seumas Milne wrote that Etzioni's name was being 'dropped at every moderniser's Islington dinner party'.[28] *The Sunday
Times* noted that he had exercised considerable influence on the American government, and that his influence was spreading to Europe, with
Gordon Brown being one of the leading politicians to have consulted
him.[29] In 1995 *The Times* claimed that 'In this country, Dr. Etzioni's
beliefs are also finding favour among Labour modernisers.'[30] The *Independent* called Etzioni 'an influential figure' in the trend towards a political language of 'community, family, rights and duties – not government,
councils or individuals', whose '"communitarianism" is said to have influenced the Labour leader'.[31] The *Economist* confidently asserted that
Blair 'has read Mr. Etzioni's books',[32] having earlier noted that '[a]dvisers
to ... Tony Blair can quote Mr. Etzioni at the drop of a hat'.[33] Psycholo-
gist Oliver James wrote that '[i]f Baroness Thatcher's guru was Milton
Friedman, Tony Blair's is also American, Amitai Etzioni. The whole of
New Labour, not just its leader, repeatedly use his buzz-words ("rights"
and "obligations") and they have implemented some of his policy
proposals.'[34]

This last serves to demonstrate a trend which needs to be noted in
order to avoid the risk of over-estimating Etzioni's influence: many commentators have taken the mere presence of the words 'rights' and 'duties'
(or 'responsibilities') in any kind of conjunction to indicate the explicit
influence of Etzioni, and this is potentially misleading on two fronts:
firstly, these concepts are such common currency within the government
that, even if they were first drawn from Etzioni (and it is not really a
sufficiently striking phrase to be uniquely identified with one writer),
they are now used far more broadly and widely, and secondly, they are
now often used in ways, and in the course of justifying policies, different
from Etzioni's own. A perhaps more realistic assessment comes in a leader
in the *Independent* which notices the adoption of 'key words' such as
'community, family, rights and duties – not government, councils or individuals' and the 'new buzz terms [of] community, responsibilities, civil
society and cohesion', and calls Etzioni 'an influential figure in this

trend',[35] recognising that it is wider than either Etzioni himself or the
Labour Party.

Nonetheless, many press commentators suggest that there is more to
it than this. John Lloyd, in the *New Statesman*, sees Etzioni's influence in
the 'invocation of community' of the new Clause IV.[36] When Etzioni
visited Britain in March 1995, Martin Walker, writing in the *Guardian*,
felt that '[h]is speech could signpost a future Labour government's social
policy'. The speech would, Walker suggests, 'be scoured for clues' to such
policy, because 'the broad themes of [Etzioni's] thought find so many
echoes in the political philosophy of Tony Blair'.[37] This assessment illustrates an important aspect of these perceptions: when Labour were in
opposition, and not in a position to implement policies, all their policy
documents and proposals really had the status of rhetoric, widely and no
doubt rightly seen as a key weapon in an extended election campaign,
and the party was still being seen more in terms of what it was not – i.e.
not Conservative, but not 'old' Labour either. As a result of this, commentators were keen to find any clue as to the ideas that might inform
policy if – or rather, when, as victory was widely predicted – New Labour
formed its first government. Etzioni's visit potentially offered them a ready
made answer, and this could in part account for the large amount of
attention that he received.

Many of the earlier pieces claim that it is not only the Labour Party
who were receptive to Etzioni's ideas in the mid-1990s – while the Conservatives, under John Major, were still in government. Just prior to the
British publication of *The Spirit of Community*, Paul Anderson and Kevin
Davey wrote in the *New Statesman* that Etzioni's 'ideas have already at-
tracted the attention of the political class and the media'.[38]

Others went further. A *Sunday Times* feature claims that 'politicians
worldwide' have 'seized upon his thinking as a way out of the fixed battle
between left and right'.[39] According to this source, 'much of Bill Clinton's
[1992] election campaign was based on the "communitarian" principles
developed by Etzioni' and 'Vice-President Al Gore keeps in constant contact.' It is also reported that Etzioni had a five-hour meeting with the
German Chancellor, Helmut Kohl, who along with his main opponent
was 'intrigued at the electoral possibilities' of communitarianism. Finally,
it is claimed that both Gordon Brown and David Willetts have 'consulted' Etzioni.[40]

For the Conservative philosopher, Roger Scruton, in late 1995, '[c]om-
munitarianism is now an orthodoxy, not only in America, but also on
this side of the Atlantic, influencing both Labour and Tory rhetoric'.
Scruton's point here, though, is that communitarianism is suitable *only*

as rhetoric: 'Tony Blair may be able to win an election by spouting this stuff; but no society can be redeemed by believing it.'[41] Scruton's review shows that it is possible to criticise Etzioni's position from the Conservative right as well as the liberal left.

Anna Coote – who criticises Etzioni very strongly from the left – sees that Etzioni's communitarianism has appeal across the political board, but is especially attractive to New Labour, referring to 'the extraordinary cross-party infatuation of British politicians with the American communitarian Amitai Etzioni'. Coote says that while 'Blair is said to be intrigued with some of it', so are Paddy Ashdown and 'quite a handful of Tories. But its special appeal to New Labour is that it offers an intellectual security blanket, a philosophical agenda which appears to justify a shift towards civil authoritarianism.'[42]

Other press commentators have expressed greater or lesser scepticism about the idea that Etzioni's ideas have *influenced* New Labour, although very few, if any, question the idea that New Labour's positions *parallel* the writer's. Andrew Marr notes that 'From America has come "communitarianism", something like an intellectuals' political movement dedicated to spreading attitudes and policies for community feeling and social cohesion' whose 'guru' is Etzioni who 'rightly notes that British politicians, including Tony Blair, have shown an interest in these ideas'.[43]

Bernard Crick, in a review of Etzioni's *The New Golden Rule*, suggests that if Blair owes anything at all to Etzioni it is the idea of 'standing between the individualism of market liberalism and the community-based ideas of order common to both socialists and old Conservatives'. Blair's conception of community, he claims, is nothing like Etzioni's, being 'coupled with "nation" or "society as a whole", not with what most sociologists and political theorists think meaningful to call community'.[44]

However, there are many reasons to avoid leaping to the conclusion that Etzioni was a significant source of New Labour ideas, or even of vocabulary. For a start, there is nothing particularly distinctive about the coupling of 'rights and responsibilities' or 'rights and duties', nor of the invocation of the ideal of community by politicians. Furthermore, there is plenty of evidence that Blair was using such ideas and language certainly before *The Spirit of Community* was available in Britain, and even prior to its first publication, in the US, two years before (in 1993). For example, in a speech in February 1993, Blair said:

> We cannot exist in a moral vacuum. If we do not learn and then teach the value of what is right and what is wrong, then the result is simply moral chaos which engulfs us all. The importance of the notion of community is that it defines the relationship not only between us as individuals but between people and the society in which

they live, one that is based upon responsibilities as well as rights, on obligations as well as entitlements.[45]

Although the language used here is similar to Etzioni's, with its references to morality, community and rights and duties/responsibilities, the final phrase also echoes almost word for word Margaret Thatcher's claim in 1987 that '[t]here is no such thing as an entitlement unless someone first has an obligation'.[46]

However, this chronology does not necessarily rule out the possibility that New Labour's language came, albeit less directly, from Etzioni. Rentoul himself is certain that there was a noticeable change in language following the visit by Blair and Gordon Brown to Clinton's campaign advisors in early 1993, two months after Clinton's victory in the Presidential election, and before Blair became party leader. One of the main lessons passed on by the Democratic Leadership Council – the source of many of Clinton's political ideas – was the need to appear tough, and to shake off an image of the party as 'soft' and ineffectual. One of the policy areas with most possibilities for this was that of law and order. It was only three days after returning from America that Blair used the term (actually coined by Brown) 'tough on crime, tough on the causes of crime', and this, Rentoul says, is highly significant and indicative of the American influence.[47] Blair in particular was affected by the potential of this 'new social moralism', which chimed with his own views, and according to Rentoul, it was as a result of this that he requested the post of Shadow Home Secretary from John Smith.

Blair used other Etzioni-like language at this time, when it is still unlikely that he (or his advisors) would have read *The Spirit of Community*. In another speech, he said 'it is easier to do the difficult job of bringing up a child where there are two parents living happily together'.[48] Again, this sounds like Etzioni's view that two parents are better than one and three would be better still.[49] These are sentiments expressed in *The Parenting Deficit*, extracts from *The Spirit of Community* which were published by Demos in Britain in 1993, but might well have been brought to Blair's attention earlier by the founder of Demos, Geoff Mulgan. On the other hand, Blair's claim is carefully worded to reflect a widespread and fairly uncontroversial (because couched in practical rather than moral terms) common-sense position, particularly as he makes no reference (at this stage) to the desirability of those two parents being married to each other.

The above examples show that, particularly in the mid-1990s while Labour were still in opposition, but continuing at least until 2001, many commentators, academics as well as journalists, believed that the Labour

Party, as part of its transformation into New Labour, reflected the influence of Etzioni's ideas and work. A relatively small number of commentators questioned this assumption.[50] Very few if any questioned the assumption that there were significant similarities between Etzioni's ideas and the policies being developed by New Labour. Similarities there no doubt are, at the very least because of the flexibility of Etzioni's ideas, remarked upon by a number of commentators. For the same reason, glaring dissimilarities should not be hard to find either – but remarkably few writers have sought these out. Part of the purpose of this chapter is to do just that, but more than that, to show how Etzioni's thought (particularly in relation to British politics) developed through the course of the 1990s, and to ask why some aspects rather than others were the focus of attention, both from the press and academe, and also, if there was any, from New Labour itself.

Firstly, though, we need to look at Etzioni himself, and his communitarian writing of the 1990s. One journalist, commentating on Etzioni's somewhat panglossian view of communities, remarked that 'to argue with Etzioni is like arguing with a very slippery Santa Claus. How can anyone be against motherhood, truth and community?'[51] This has more than a ring of truth to it, and any careful reader of Etzioni will find many contradictions and inconsistencies (particularly in *The New Golden Rule*), and arguments which are circular rather than well founded. Most of the examples cited above are critical of Etzioni, although more for the perceived authoritarian implications of his position than for failures in his arguments.

Amitai Etzioni was born Werner Falk in Germany in 1929, to Zionist parents. Shortly afterwards, the family emigrated to Palestine, where Etzioni grew up an equally committed Zionist, helping to smuggle in refugees and fighting the British. He studied in Jerusalem under Martin Buber before moving, in 1957, to the USA to undertake further study. Etzioni settled in America, where he established a reputation as a sociologist, particularly of organisations.[52] He is constantly at pains to stress his academic credentials, being quoted as saying at one point: 'I can play the academic game as well as most. My last book had forty pages of footnotes. I can out-jargon and out-footnote them all.'[53] Despite his protestations, there is little doubt that Etzioni's communitarian output lacks the academic rigour of his earlier work. John Lloyd seeks to defend Etzioni from critics' charges of 'intellectual slenderness' by pointing out that the work in question is 'aimed at an audience of activists and policy-thinkers rather than one of intellectuals'.[54]

For our purposes this later work is the focus. Although criticisms of the status quo emerge in some of Etzioni's earlier work,[55] it is only his explicitly communitarian writing which is relevant here. The main publications are *The Spirit of Community: Rights, Responsibilities and the Communitarian Agenda*, published in Britain in 1995, and in the US in 1993 as *The Spirit of Community: The Reinvention of American Society, The New Golden Rule: Community and Morality in a Democratic Society* (1996), and *The Third Way to a Good Society* published first in Britain by Demos in 2000, and subsequently published in a revised version in the US under the title *Next: On the Way to the Good Society*.[56]

As we have already seen, it is the first of these which has done most to draw comparisons with New Labour, unsurprisingly, because it was its UK launch which did most to raise Etzioni's profile in Britain. *The New Golden Rule* represents an ambitious follow-up to *The Spirit of Community* and attempts to provide theoretical foundations for Etzionian communitarianism. According to the cover notes, Etzioni 'breaks away from the traditional mentality' in which 'one side laments the moral decay of their societies' while the other side sees 'individual liberty threatened by government, religious fanatics and increasing social control', to put forward 'the idea of a golden rule where order and autonomy are in equilibrium'.[57]

The formulation of the 'New Golden Rule' is: 'Respect and uphold society's moral order as you would have society respect and uphold your autonomy.'[58] This wording is clearly intended to reflect the 'golden rule' as traditionally understood: to 'do unto others as you would have them do unto you', but lacks the original's logical reciprocity and thus its philosophical and moral power. *The New Golden Rule* is about the need to balance personal autonomy with social order, and in particular, the importance of a 'thick' social order based upon shared values which people are taught to hold and defend, rather than a 'thin' (liberal) social order which enables individuals to pursue their own values.[59] Such a 'thick' social order, Etzioni claims, reduces the need for coercion in the interests of the common good; coercion which is likely to be both resented and ineffectual. For Etzioni, an increase in the numbers of police, or of tax inspectors, is a sign of 'a deficient moral order'.[60]

Communitarian social order, he stresses, is a very different thing from the general understanding of 'law and order'. Rather, the 'New Golden Rule requires that the tension between one's preferences and one's social commitments be reduced by increasing the realm of duties one affirms as moral responsibilities'[61] – i.e. compliance with society's requirements (however determined) is to be achieved by changing people's beliefs in preference to the use of overt coercion. The key questions which this throws up are these: firstly, how are the requirements of 'society' (as an entity distinct from the individuals who comprise it) to be determined; and secondly, how is the necessary moral consensus to be achieved? How can a society establish an order which respects personal autonomy, which in turn respects the social order? Under the 'old' golden rule, we know how to treat others because we all know how we would wish to be treated ourselves, but Etzioni's New Golden Rule does not contain its own answer. It is vitiated by its asymmetry.

The only reason such a rule is necessary is because individual autonomy and social order often conflict. Telling us to respect that order as we would have it respect our autonomy does not protect our autonomy, because the rule as formulated applies only to individuals, and not to 'society'. While aping one aspect of Kant's Categorical Imperative, it rejects an equally vital part: it is not universalisable. If everyone followed the New Golden Rule, only order would be protected; there would be no guarantee at all for autonomy.

The other main theory Etzioni expounds in *The New Golden Rule* is his idea of 'inverting symbiosis', which he also develops in an address to the American Sociological Association. The basic premiss of Etzioni's theory of society is that within it there are fundamental forces which need to be kept in balance if society is to remain healthy. These are the centrifugal force of individualism or autonomy, and the centripetal force of authoritarianism or collectivism. Sometimes these are characterised as impersonal, even natural or physical, forces, as here: '*All social entities are subject to both centrifugal and centripetal forces. Communities have social formations that protect the community from being pulled off balance by either of these forces.*'[62] These forces enjoy what Etzioni calls 'the inverting symbiotic relationship'.[63] In contrast with 'relationships we are familiar with',[64] the forces in an inverting symbiosis are symbiotic up to a point, but 'antagonistic if either force gains too much strength'.[65] Etzioni concludes that

> [a] common mistake is to view order and autonomy either as antagonistic (a zero-sum relationship, so that the more we have of one the less we have of the other) or as mutually enhancing. They are complimentary [*sic*] up to a point, after which they grow antagonistic. It is the role of those who care to fashion authentic communities to pull their communities into the highly responsive zone, into one in which mutuality between the basic elements of order and autonomy is high and antagonism low.[66]

The New Golden Rule is not, overall, very significant in terms of understanding New Labour's communitarianism and the extent to which that is similar to Etzioni's, being far more concerned with diagnosing the ills of American society in justification of Etzionian communitarianism.

However, one aspect is relevant. In a number of places in the book, Etzioni suggests that his diagnosis of excessive autonomy applies to the US in particular, and not the UK or other European countries. In the UK, he claims, in many ways people have less autonomy than in the US. He cites such things as the Official Secrets Act, the Prevention of Terrorism Act (with its provision for detaining suspects without bringing them before a court), closed circuit television in public places (in the US, according to Etzioni, CCTV is generally confined to privately owned, commercial, spaces), the recent restriction of the right to silence when being questioned by police, and 'mandatory prayers' in schools. While a Briton might well take issue with the suggestion that these necessarily mean that they have less autonomy than their American counterparts, this is significant for what it tells us about Etzioni's view of Britain: that it is 'a rather free and orderly society, a far from perfect – yet a relatively communitarian – society'.[67] Elsewhere he refers to Britain as 'a rather communitarian society'.[68]

Another way in which the Britain of the mid-1990s approaches more closely than his adopted country Etzioni's communitarian ideal is in the realm of electoral politics. Bemoaning the fact that in the US, elected officials are more accountable to campaign donors than to their electors and the communities they are supposed to represent, Etzioni explicitly suggests that a solution would be to adopt the British model of short election campaigns and strict limits on election expenditure (he notes with approval that agents who overspend in Britain can be sent to prison). In Etzioni's eyes, then, Britain was a relatively communitarian society before New Labour came to power. The question is whether it has moved nearer to or further away from that ideal under the New Labour government, and what direction Labour's pre-election policy statements and rhetoric suggested.

Those commentators who perceive Etzioni as having been an influence upon the party, or at least have perceived that the party has moved in line with Etzioni's position, often do so on the basis that New Labour's policies and rhetoric suggest a more authoritarian approach. Yet Etzioni's view, in 1996, was that Britain was already a fairly communitarian country, and did not suffer from the excess of autonomy which he perceived in America. John Lloyd, in the *New Statesman*, notes that Etzioni believes that Britain '"is about in balance"; and since it approaches closely to his golden mean, he is suspicious of proposals, advanced by the government, to reform it'.[69] This was written in June 1997, and the government referred to is the new New Labour government. Etzioni's central claim in

The New Golden Rule is that communitarianism is principally concerned with attaining the right balance between order and autonomy, and if Britain pre-New Labour had more or less achieved that, than any move towards greater order, as perceptions of authoritarianism indicate, could only be a move away from communitarian balance.

There are, however, a couple of caveats here. Firstly, many of Etzioni's critics have suggested that although he pays lip service to balance and autonomy, Etzioni's prescriptions are inevitably more authoritarian than otherwise, and these critics are largely the same people who have perceived authoritarianism in apparently Etzioni-friendly New Labour policies and proposals. Nonetheless, those who support such policies cannot claim that they would necessarily find Etzioni's approval, and as we shall see later, Etzioni has specifically criticised some of the policies which might be most closely associated with his ideas – or at least the way those ideas have been perceived and presented in this debate.

Secondly, Etzioni himself is not consistent on this point. In other pieces which appeared at around the same time he suggests that rather than being a paradigm of communitarian values, Britain is going downhill fast. True, he says, 'the United Kingdom has not yet reached the levels of moral anarchy that we witness in the United States, but the trends are clear. Increases in rates of violent crime, illegitimacy, drug abuse, children who kill and show no remorse, and political corruption are all significant symptoms', and asks whether anyone 'truly believe[s]' that the 'moral and social foundations of institutions' in the UK 'have not yet cracked'.[70] Although this was published in February 1995, before the appearance of *The New Golden Rule*, the latter was probably written much earlier, allowing for the time it takes to get a book published, compared to a newspaper article. Nonetheless, both refer to the Britain of the mid-1990s, and the difference might be accounted for by the intended audiences of the pieces, the US for the book and the UK for the article/lecture.

In an article published in the *New Statesman* in 1994, Etzioni claims to 'see British society slipping in an American direction in terms of its moral infrastructure', but also says (earlier) 'I leave it to readers to determine what the UK most needs next – rights enshrined in a written British constitution perhaps, or a greater sense of personal and social responsibility.'[71]

In terms of the more general social and legal climate, New Labour have enacted laws that are more 'authoritarian' than before and thus presumably take Britain from a position of Etzionian communitarian balance towards an undesirable level of authoritarianism. These include the recent Regulation of Investigatory Powers Act, which authorises broad

email surveillance and limits the use of encryption; the proposed reduction in the right to select trial by jury; the 2001 Terrorism Act, which
increases the number of organisations which it is a crime to be a member
of or even to give support to; and measures, taken following anti-
globalisation protests, which curtail the right to assembly and peaceful
protest. This does not include much stronger measures subsequently enacted in the name of security (including detention without trial), but
focuses only on those which were proposed or enacted while Etzioni's
supposed influence was at its zenith.

However, it is mostly from *The Spirit of Community* that commentators
have drawn parallels with New Labour, so it is to that book I will now
turn. The first noticeable thing is how surprisingly little of what is in *The
Spirit of Community* is taken up by those commentators who have claimed
to see in it the seeds of New Labour thinking. Whole chapters go completely unremarked, including those dealing with topics as significant as
political campaign funding,[72] public safety and public health,[73] and 'hate
speech'.[74]

The last two of these are examples of issues which loom larger in the
US than they do in Britain, largely because (in Etzioni's eyes at least) of
radical individualist civil rights campaigners who object to metal detec-
tors at airports and effectively random breath-testing of drivers for alcohol, and a range of measures in between which tend not to raise such
hackles in the UK. This in turn is linked to the reliance in the US upon
the positive rights granted by the constitution, particularly in the case of
the last, 'hate speech', under the first amendment, which guarantees the
right to free speech and effectively rules out measures comparable to
Britain's laws against incitement to racial hatred. However, Etzioni is not
in favour of curbing such speech, and indeed is scathing about various
attempts on university campuses to outlaw offensive speech, advocating
instead a cooperative approach of education and apology. This view is at
odds with the proposed extension of the laws against incitement to racial
hatred to cover religious as well as racial groups.[75]

Furthermore, in dealing with issues which involve infringing rights in
some way, Etzioni is very concerned to limit any measures taken with a
series of provisos which will cut 'notches' in the otherwise 'slippery slope'
towards authoritarianism. These include three criteria which he says should
always be applied before any measure (including breath-testing or air-
port searches) is undertaken: there should be 'clear and present danger';
'no alternative way to proceed', and 'adjustments should be as limited as
possible'. Etzioni's commitment to upholding and preserving individual
rights seems to be stronger than that of most Britons and certainly than

that of New Labour.

The issue of political funding is one which Etzioni returns to again and again, in *The Spirit of Community*, in *The New Golden Rule*, and in a volume in its own right, *Capitol Corruption: the Attack on American Democracy* (1984). In *The Spirit of Community* Etzioni again holds the British system up as an example of how politicians could be relieved of the need for large amounts of money, and so not be beholden to funders once in office, by limiting the length of campaigns and capping electoral spending: '[I]f Britain can conduct elections in less than a month and with a pittance, we should be able to cap both the period and the expenditures, even if at higher levels.'[76] These three issues comprise the part of the book entitled 'Too Many Rights, Too Few Responsibilities' and 'The Public Interest'. The way these issues are dealt with suggests that the problem of too many rights – and by extension, of the strident insistence on exercising them – is essentially an American one.

If we are to find direct relevance in *The Spirit of Community* to British politics and policy, then it will be necessary to look in the book's first section (the part which hard pressed journalists were perhaps most likely to have read); the one which deals with 'Shoring Up Morality', and addresses issues of the family, education and community, and what Etzioni calls 'the moral voice'. This last refers to the ways in which communities ideally keep their members in line by gentle 'suasion', examples of which include telling a neighbour that his lawn needs mowing, and that failure to do so will reduce property values for the whole area, by recommending the services of a gardener (this apparently happened to Etzioni himself).[77] Another example he proffers involves the way drivers on his university campus waited in turn at a busy intersection and thus kept the traffic flowing relatively smoothly. People who failed to wait frequently came from outside the community. Etzioni attributes this to the fact that community members who pushed in would be subject to 'mild ribbing at the faculty club, supermarket or movie theater'.[78] In general, he says, we should not be afraid to make moral claims on others and to make them feel guilty if they fail to meet those claims. This, and the other moral issues which Etzioni raises in this section cannot effectively be the subject of legislation, and are to a large degree outside the scope of politics, which limits their relevance to questions of New Labour policy. However, some of the rhetoric employed – again, by Blair in particular – does reflect a similar attitude.[79]

It might be argued that measures such as anti-social behaviour orders (ASBOs) are an extension of or a substitute for such 'suasion', but that would be to miss Etzioni's point: that the whole reason for shoring up 'moral voices' is to obviate the need for coercive legislation. In this way, much of what commentators have identified as communitarian in New Labour policy is actually its antithesis. Etzionian communitarianism seeks to avoid legislating to control people's behaviour: 'Communities gently chastise those who violate shared moral norms and express approbation for those who abide by them. They turn to the state (courts, police) only when all else fails.'[80] Blair's words in this area suggest superficial similarities, but also highlight fundamental differences: 'Strong communities depend on shared values and a recognition of the rights and duties of citizenship ... [W]here they are neglected we should not hesitate to encourage and even enforce them ...'[81] While such steps may be politically and socially necessary, Etzioni's position is clear: they represent the failure of communitarianism, not its realisation.

Indeed, in some areas there are clear conflicts between Etzioni's position in *The Spirit of Community* and New Labour policy. One of these is the area of children and the family in relation to employment policy. Again, Etzioni holds Britain up as an example of a more communitarian approach than is available in the US (for example, in terms of maternity rights and parental leave); again, New Labour is moving policy away from, rather than towards, what Etzioni advocates. Etzioni stresses the need for both parents to spend time with their children, in order to discharge their duties both to their children and to the wider community.[82] While conditions may be better in Britain than in the US, the UK still has the longest working hours in Europe, and New Labour has responded positively to calls from industry and commerce to apply the minimum regulation and limits on working times possible under European Union law.[83]

Etzioni is certain that most childcare, largely because it is poorly paid and undervalued and hence tends to have a high staff turnover, is usually inferior to parental care, at least in the early years, and damaging to the subsequent attainment and behaviour of children. New Labour, in contrast, is keen to expand the role of childcare, in some cases through voluntary (i.e. not just poorly paid, but unpaid) provision, as part of its commitment to a work-based inclusion strategy and welfare policy. This is evidenced by the introduction of, among other things, childcare credits, the encouragement of childcare initiatives in employment based regeneration programmes (such as the Single Regeneration Budget), the proliferation of 'after school clubs' for children of school age, and most clearly of all by efforts to get lone parents into paid employment once their youngest child has started school, with compulsory Employment Service interviews. Etzioni quotes research showing that children who had after school care outside the home tended to have more problems, get lower grades and to be less liked by their peers than those who were cared for by parents. He concludes from this that maximising parental contact with children, even at the expense of parents' employment, does not cease to be vital once children have started school.[84] This is clearly at odds with New Labour policy, in particular the New Deal for lone parents, which aims to get single parents into work as soon as their children have started school.

Finally, Etzioni is dubious about the apparent 'need' for income which he claims is driven by consumerism in a society in which 'parents are under pressure to earn more, whatever their income. They feel it is important to work overtime and to dedicate themselves to enhancing their incomes and advancing their careers.'[85] It is certainly true that contemporary British society (even if to a lesser extent than the US) embraces both a work and a consumerist ethic, fuelled by television (for example, fashion, and house and garden 'makeovers') that although not initiated by the government is certainly not condemned by New Labour (as it is, for example, by the Green Party) and is often lauded. Etzioni's recommendation that '[c]orporations should provide six months of paid leave and another year and a half ... of unpaid leave', the costs of which should be shared by the employers of *both* parents, with a further six months of the unpaid eighteen being 'covered from public funds' seems unlikely to be realised in New Labour's business-friendly policies. Etzioni takes up a similar point when considering the decline of traditional community; it has, he says, been 'cannibalized' as 'more and more people have been gobbled up by the economy'.[86] One might perhaps imagine such sentiments being expressed by Prince Charles, but not by Tony Blair.

In short, then, the central messages of *The Spirit of Community*, which is the work of Etzioni most closely associated by commentators with New Labour, actually offer the party very little comfort.

Finally, this chapter examines Etzioni's 2000 pamphlet, published by Demos, entitled *The Third Way to a Good Society*, in which the author explicitly engages with British politics. The idea of his brand of communitarianism as a 'third way' is not new to Etzioni; he has himself referred to it as such in, for example, *The New Golden Rule*.[87] What is new in this pamphlet is the explicit attempt to fit it into the British Third Way debate initiated by New Labour and led by Anthony Giddens.[88]

This is one of many ways in which Etzioni's *The Third Way to a Good Society* differs from the books by him already considered in this chapter. Firstly, and most obviously, it is written explicitly as a contribution to a British debate, for a British audience, about British politics and society.

The Spirit of Community and *The New Golden Rule* offered only passing nods to the British situation (for example, in the brief preface which was fairly obviously tacked on to the British edition of the former), and as noted above, Etzioni's attitude to Britain in these works was sometimes contradictory and often superficial. However, having said that, there is actually very little in *The Third Way to a Good Society* which does relate exclusively to Britain. Examples are primarily drawn from US experiences,[89] the language used is American, and references to Britain are frequently parenthetical[90] and often seem poorly understood.[91] Nonetheless, this is a British publication and as such at least nominally addresses British questions in a way not attempted by the earlier books.

Secondly, there are signs in *The Third Way to a Good Society* that Etzioni has (although he does not specifically acknowledge this) taken on board some of the criticisms of the authoritarian implications or potential of his earlier communitarian work. (One such critic, interestingly, was Giddens, who in a letter to the *Independent* said that while '[n]ot all forms of communitarianism are authoritarian ... the authoritarian tinge of the more primitive versions advanced by Amitai Etzioni and others is plain to see').[92]

In part this is the result of a shift in emphasis: no longer focusing on the balance between order and autonomy (as in *The New Golden Rule*) but rather on that between state, market and community. As such it concentrates more on the role of community in the development of relationships, such as mutual aid, rather than the maintenance of order.[93] This is a different emphasis rather than a necessarily conflicting perspective, although Etzioni does come out strongly against legislating for 'good behaviour' and notes that 'attempts to suppress divorce, abortion and consumption of alcohol by law ... tend to backfire and should be avoided, whether or not one opposes those behaviours'.[94] Gone too are proposals for compulsory citizen service: in *The Third Way to a Good Society* social cohesion is to be furthered by reducing inequality[95] and ensuring a 'rich basic minimum for all',[96] which while requiring less than equality of outcome entails considerably more than mere equality of opportunity.

Etzioni appears also to have noted those critics who point out that communities can themselves be oppressive, saying that communities should not be able to 'violate the right to free speech, assembly and so on of anyone' – although these are defined vaguely and there is no indication of where and how a line would be drawn between the community's powers and individuals' rights, Etzioni does recognise that 'unfettered communities are no better than unfettered markets or states'.[97]

Similarly, in *The Third Way to a Good Society*, Etzioni articulates the relationship between rights and duties in a more measured fashion than previously (at least, certainly more measured than his position has been generally understood, and far more nuanced than New Labour's understanding of the relationship), saying that in many areas, where the relationship between them is 'complex and tense', 'it is a grave mistake to presume that either rights or responsibilities are dominant ... [they] should be treated as two cardinal moral claims'. Where they cannot both be maximised, 'no *a priori* assumption should be made that priority will be given to one rather than the other'.[98] This might reflect a shift in position in the light of criticism (insofar as it is different from his previously articulated position), but it might also reflect Etzioni's more generous attitude to Britain and its needs compared to those of the US (insofar as *The Third Way to a Good Society* is a British publication).

Finally, whereas *The Spirit of Community* and *The New Golden Rule* are books, *The Third Way to a Good Society* is a pamphlet, presumably intended as a contribution to a contemporary and more ephemeral debate, rather than as a statement of timeless truths – for although those books are no less rooted in, and indeed derive their relevance and force from, perceptions of prevailing social and political circumstances, they nonetheless aspire to a wider and more theoretical relevance. Because of its specific circumstances and intent, *The Third Way to a Good Society* is of particular interest in comparing New Labour's perceived communitarianism with that of Amitai Etzioni.

The Third Way to a Good Society is in large part a criticism of New Labour's Third Way, in particular its perceived neglect of community, in its understanding of the Third Way as being concerned only with the relationship of state and market. For Etzioni, community is the 'third leg' of a three-legged stool, and needs to be 'lengthened' to bring it into balance with the other two (state and market). Community provides what the other two cannot: an environment in which people are viewed 'holistically', and treated as ends in themselves rather than as means to others' ends. This, for Etzioni, characterises the 'good society' of his title, and the values most conducive to it include 'love, loyalty, caring and community'[99] – values which are largely to be found in the family and the community. In the other spheres, people are treated not holistically as ends, but 'only as employees, traders, consumers and even fellow citizens'.[100] This reference to 'citizens' suggests that Etzioni sees citizenship as part of the political, rather than the communal sphere, in contrast to New Labour's attempts to depoliticise the concept. This failure to allow community 'its proper share of the social division of labour',[101] Etzioni claims, is not just a feature of New Labour's Third Way, but of all conceptions of the Third Way to date. In other aspects, he says, the Third Way closely mirrors communitarian concerns,[102] and his Demos pamphlet is intended to provide the Third Way 'with a positive and normative characterisation as a public policy'.[103]

This entails many criticisms of New Labour policy. In the main, these are not explicitly directed at the Blair government, but the policies, approaches and attitudes which Etzioni criticises are clearly recognisable as theirs. Whether or not this avoidance is deliberate on Etzioni's part (most likely from a desire to give the pamphlet wider appeal and avoid significant rewriting for the US market) is not really relevant. What is relevant is that far from being an implicit supporter of, or even influence upon, New Labour policies, Etzioni emerges, in this work to a greater extent even than before, as a cogent critic of many of those policies, and, furthermore, a critic from a communitarian perspective, suggesting that New Labour's position is too authoritarian to be considered communitarian – and this from an author whose own position, at least in the past, has itself been considered worryingly authoritarian.

Firstly, Etzioni's general criticism of the Third Way as neglecting community is clearly directed at New Labour as leading proponents of, and closely identified with, Third Way thinking. Although Blair in particular talks a lot about community, the concept does not feature in New Labour's understanding of the Third Way itself – at least, not in the way Etzioni understands it. For New Labour, the community is a locus of responsibility, rather than of ends-based relationships; their approach is more society- rather than person-centred. Furthermore, as previously noted, in New Labour thinking, 'community' is often used as a synonym for the nation as a whole, and 'community activity' for voluntary work.

In his own pamphlet on the Third Way[104] Blair lists 'community' as one of four key Third Way values (the others are equal worth, opportunity for all, and responsibility),[105] but it is accorded a bare paragraph in the twenty-page pamphlet, in which it is equated with 'civil society'. The pamphlet goes on to consider civil society at slightly greater length, in a section entitled 'Strong Civil Society: Rights and Responsibilities' which covers policy on youth justice and the family, but here it is largely just another vehicle for familiar New Labour rhetoric about rights and responsibilities.[106] The 'core value' of community barely gets another mention, and even the single paragraph dedicated to it concludes that '[t]he truth is that freedom for the many requires strong government. A key challenge of progressive politics is to use the state as an enabling force, protecting effective communities [whatever that means] and voluntary organisations and encouraging their growth to tackle new needs, in partnership as appropriate.'[107] In New Labour's Third Way the community is subordinate and instrumental, where it is considered at all. Although lip service is paid to the concept, Etzioni's criticism that the Third Way neglects community – and indeed lacks any meaningful conception of it – is well-founded. A Third Way which accorded community the same importance as Etzioni's does, and in the same way, would be very different from New Labour's.

Secondly, Etzioni is very critical of 'the rush to legislate good behaviour', and again, this looks like a fairly explicit criticism of New Labour measures such as Anti-Social Behaviour Orders (ASBOs) which serve to bring aspects of behaviour, which are not in themselves illegal, within the scope of the criminal law. 'Third Way governments do best', Etzioni says, when they resist this rush,[108] as 'legislation often numbs the moral conscience', and can undermine the 'moral voices of the community'. Etzioni advocates 'relying on informal community-based processes' in preference to the law 'when there is a valid need to modify behaviour'.[109] While the potential effectiveness of this, and the concept of community which it invokes, is certainly open to question, there is again no doubt that this represents a very different approach from New Labour's. Tony Blair, for example, explicitly states that where the 'duties of citizenship' imposed by 'an inclusive society' 'are neglected, we should not hesitate to encourage *and even enforce them*'.[110] It is ironic that some critics of New Labour's communitarianism cite measures like these, which Etzioni actually opposes, as evidence of his influence.[111] In fact the opposite is the case: a government consistent with Etzioni's later work would eschew legislation like ASBOs.

Thirdly, New Labour's conception of community as expressed through 'voluntary activity' is somewhat at odds with Etzioni's understanding. We have already seen how the idea of voluntary service is seen by Macmurray as inimical to true community; perhaps surprisingly, Etzioni's view here is closer to Macmurray's than to New Labour's.[112] Etzioni draws a clear distinction between 'mutuality' and 'voluntarism', with the former being characteristic of community relations, and providing a more important foundation for the 'good society'. Mutuality, he says, 'is a form of community relationship in which people help each other rather than merely helping those in need'.[113] As examples of these, Etzioni cites community patrols in Balsall Heath, which he claims reduced crime in the area (these patrols were in fact directed against prostitutes and there was some controversy as to their methods, effectiveness and desirability),[114] credit unions and 'Local Food Buying Groups'.[115]

Although these are not very clearly defined, Etzioni is clear that '[i]n mutual relationships, people do not keep books on each other but have a generalised expectation that the other will do his or her turn if and when a need arises'.[116] On the basis that '[m]utuality is undermined when treated like an economic exchange of services', Etzioni explicitly criticises policies such as 'time banks' which by 'attempt[ing] to organise mutuality as an exchange will tend to undermine this moral foundation'.[117] Such a scheme was launched by Blair himself in March 2000 and it, and similar schemes, have frequently been invoked in the context of New Labour's community policy.

On the next page, though, Etzioni does recognise a place for such voluntary action, which he believes should be further encouraged, through measures like those announced by Gordon Brown in February 2000[118] – but as complementary to mutuality, rather than as expressions of it. In more general policy terms, although New Labour pay lip service to the ideals of 'commitment, trust and altruism [which] hold the fragile web of community together'[119] they do tend to see responsibility as being exercised in an explicitly contractual fashion: 'opportunity or rights ... need to be matched by responsibility and duty. *That is the bargain or covenant at the heart of civil society*'[120] – which is certainly at odds with Etzioni's professed community ideal.

It is the language of balancing rights and duties, of matching opportunities to responsibilities, which has done most to draw comparisons between Etzioni and New Labour. It is true that one important point made in *The Spirit of Community* and *The New Golden Rule* was that people have become too demanding of rights, too keen to expand the powerful language of rights, and insufficiently willing to perform the duties necessary to maintain an extensive network of rights. However, it is important to be aware that this reflects the situation in the US rather than the UK, and Etzioni says as much himself.[121] Because positive rights are enshrined in the American constitution, demands are more likely to be articulated in terms of rights, in an attempt to fit them into that pre-existing framework. Furthermore, the constitutional rights to privacy and freedom of speech lead – at least according to Etzioni – to strong objections to measures which in the UK are generally considered unexceptionable; for example, checking whether a potential childcare worker has been convicted of child abuse, or whether a school bus driver is working under the influence of drugs.[122]

Etzioni's approach in *The Third Way to a Good Society* is different, and places far less stress on the potentially destructive aspects of rights. However, this more measured approach is not entirely new. In 1995, Etzioni wrote:

Rights and responsibilities are two sides of the same coin. First, a right is a moral and often legal claim on another person and hence becomes their responsibility. If the other side will not assume that responsibility, the right is meaningless. Thus, my right to free speech is dependent upon your accepting that you have a duty to allow me to say things that you find quite offensive. Second, rights are best anchored when people are members of well-integrated communities, and most endangered when there is only a crowd of isolated individuals.[123]

This demonstrates a more analytical interpretation of the relationship between rights and responsibilities/duties than that understood by New Labour, who present the relationship as conflictual rather than reciprocal, a conception demonstrated in the claim that 'a decent society is not based on rights. It is based on duty.'[124] In *The Third Way to a Good Society*, Etzioni is more explicit about how this understanding of the relationship manifests in policy, and in the process is firmly critical of New Labour's position.

When New Labour talk about rights and responsibilities, although this is often couched in the language of community and/or civil society, the rights they refer to are usually *welfare rights*, i.e. money, goods or services provided via the state, and the duties or responsibilities (the terms tend in this context to be used interchangeably) are those of individuals, frequently and most specifically individual beneficiaries of state action. Furthermore, 'community' is often used to mean the nation as a whole (for example, Blair asserts that a 'covenant of opportunities and responsibilities' is a prerequisite of government 'acting as a community' – here explicitly understood as a synonym for 'spending taxpayers' money on public services or social exclusion',[125] and he has spoken of 'renewing our commitment as a nation, as a community of people ...'),[126] or even government itself acting on behalf of that nation (David Blunkett, being interviewed about proposed increases in fines for the parents of truants was referring to the government when he said 'as the community, a strong community, we have put support measures in place').[127] Thus duties to the community become duties to the state or government, as representative of the nation, while rights are seen not as absolute and inhering in the individual, but as being in the gift of the state; for example, 'A young country gives rights, but demands responsibilities.'[128]

For New Labour, then, the language of rights and responsibilities has become ever more explicitly contractual and conditional: 'For every new opportunity we offer, we demand responsibility in return. Responsibility means we no longer hand out social security benefits without conditions.'[129] Although this kind of language is still generally perceived as a prime example of Etzioni's influence, as has already been noted, this is not an accurate representation. In *The Third Way to a Good* Society he asks:

> What exactly is meant by 'rights *and* responsibilities'? Basic individual rights are inalienable, just as one's social obligations cannot be denied. However, it is a grave moral error to argue that there are 'no rights without responsibilities' or vice versa.[130] Thus a person who evades taxes, neglects their children or fails to live up to their social responsibilities in some other way is still entitled to a fair trial, free speech and other basic rights. The number of basic rights we should have may be debated, but those that are legitimate are not conditional … [N]obody should be denied the basic necessities of life even if they have not lived up to their responsibilities, such as to find work.[131]

It is interesting to compare this to the speech, explicitly entitled 'Values and the Power of Community' in which Blair states unequivocally: 'If we invest so as to give the unemployed person the chance of a job, they have a responsibility to take it or lose benefit.'[132] Etzioni has also explicitly criticised another manifestation of this kind of contractualism in New Labour policy, the proposal to remove or reduce the benefits of people who breach community service orders imposed by the courts, as justified by Social Security minister Alistair Darling in a letter to the *Guardian* (in response to an editorial criticising the proposal), saying,

> Surely it is not unreasonable to say to someone that if they enter into an agreement they should stick to it? … We are all responsible for our actions. Society is built on a contract. There are rights, yes, but there are responsibilities too.[133]

When asked by the author about this particular proposal, Etzioni condemned it as uncommunitarian, and was adamant that rights must be unconditional.[134]

Many more examples of New Labour's contractual view of the relationship of rights and duties could be provided, but this should be sufficient to demonstrate that on this point, on which comparisons are most frequently drawn, New Labour have much less in common with Etzioni than has been popularly supposed, and Etzioni has in fact been explicitly critical of their attitude, over a considerable period of time (certainly since 1995) and on a number of different occasions. While New Labour stress the dangers of people abusing an over-generous or insufficiently conditional welfare system,[135] and Blair says 'You only take out if you put in. That's the bargain',[136] Etzioni suggests that 'if there are some who abuse the system,' – and he considers that there are not likely to be many such people, if work is available – 'a good society will consider this a small price to pay in order not to deny anyone's basic humanity'.[137]

In his consideration of responsibilities, Etzioni makes a particular point of mentioning the responsibilities *of* the state: 'responsibility *from all* entails that people will do whatever they can for themselves and their communities,[138] while 'responsibility *for all* means, firstly respecting everybody equally and treating people without discrimination; secondly, and more importantly in this context, it means 'ensuring that everyone has access to the basic necessities of life'. While voluntary and mutual organisations, extended families, charities and churches can meet some of these needs, they 'cannot take on the final responsibility that all will be attended to. It is the responsibility of the state to ensure that such provisions are available to all.' Basic provision, including 'food, shelter, clothing and healthcare' is essential in a society that treats people as ends: a good society requires this.[139]

While this in itself is not in conflict with New Labour policy, the difference in emphasis, as with the issue of benefit fraud, is telling. In opposition, Blair could agree that the 'covenant between society and each of its citizens' 'involves duties from society to citizen as well as the other way about', but even then, this is quickly elided into the idea that '[a] society geared to extending opportunity [the extent of society's duty] is one then able to demand responsibility ... to be much tougher and hard headed in the rules we apply and how we apply them'.[140] Etzioni understands the state's, and society's, reciprocal responsibility to its citizens a good deal more broadly.

This theme, of the state's responsibility to individuals, is linked to two further areas in which Etzioni does not (to put it mildly) wholeheartedly endorse New Labour policy: the concept of equality and the ideal of meritocracy, and the role of the market. Blair has nailed his meritocratic colours to the mast, in a deliberate and explicit attempt to wrest back the language of 'Freedom. Choices. Opportunity. Aspiration and ambition' from the Conservative Party,[141] claiming that '[a] meritocratic society is the only one that can exploit its economic chances to the full; and that means exploiting the talent of all its people'.[142] In his vision of the Third Way, Blair expresses a desire to 'highlight opportunity as a key value in the new politics'. The left, he says, at its worst, 'has stifled opportunity in the name of abstract equality'.[143]

For Etzioni, recognising all citizens' fundamental equality means that the state must ensure the provision of a 'rich basic minimum for all'. While 'less than equality of outcomes' this signifies 'more than equality of opportunity', and is a prerequisite of treating people as ends.[144] Blair also says that what matters is 'equal worth, not equality of income or outcome, or, simply, equality of opportunity', but for Blair this means affirming 'our equal right to dignity, liberty, freedom from discrimination as well as economic *opportunity*.[145] For Blair this is a social question, resolvable by community, whereas for Etzioni it is primarily an economic issue. Where Etzioni advocates a 'rich basic minimum for all', New Labour's measures focus on minimum standards for the working poor. Elsewhere Etzioni makes a plea for greater economic equality: 'The gap between rich and poor is too great. It is destructive of community. You can't get equality and you don't want it. But you should make things less unequal.' More surprisingly still, this is said in the context of an endorsement of codified socio-economic rights for both the US and the UK.[146]

Etzioni asserts that the 'good society is one that balances three often partially incompatible elements: the state, the market and the community' keeping each 'properly contained'.[147] Not only has the community element been neglected; often, in Third Way discourse, the market has been allowed too much sway. A good society 'should view the market as akin to nuclear energy' as something which has great potential benefits, but 'must be watched over carefully'. A market which is not 'properly contained ... may dehumanise people and wreak havoc on local communities, families and social relations'.[148] Etzioni notes that the US and the UK have gone furthest down the 'Thatcherised' road toward allowing markets a free rein, but that 'all Third Way Societies should be much clearer about the areas into which market forces must be prevented from intruding. This is essential if the proper balance between the instrumental realm and that of ends is to be achieved and sustained.'[149]

New Labour in government has in fact expanded the role of the market into areas that even Margaret Thatcher baulked at: the Royal Mail, air traffic control and prisons, to name just a few examples. However, it is not only a question of privatisation, of the private sector taking over functions previously carried out directly by the state. Of greater influence on the lives of most people is the type and extent of government regulation of the private sector's activities, in particular in their role as employers. According to Etzioni, 'Third Way societies are currently making numerous incremental changes that favour market forces.'[150] This actually applied more strongly to mainland Europe than to Britain, but only because the latter had already gone a considerable way down that road under the Conservatives. New Labour has adopted the European Social Chapter and introduced a minimum wage, but both policies have been implemented in such a way as to cause as little distress as possible to the business sector,[151] and secured an opt-out clause, used only in Britain, which effectively emasculates the Working Time Directive.

The New Deal, and more broadly, Labour's approach to welfare is avowedly work-centred; furthermore, rather than attempt to create jobs directly (seen as a discredited Keynesian approach) it rests largely on supply-side measures to fit and encourage people to participate in the competitive labour *market*, in a country which has the longest working hours in Europe.[152] Participation in the labour market, especially when hours are long, is often at the expense of participation in family or community activities. For this reason, Etzioni was critical of the New Labour government's implementation of cuts, planned by the outgoing Conservative administration, to lone parent benefit, which he said were 'not very communitarian' – particularly as there was no evidence that work was even available.[153]

Although Etzioni recognises that there is a 'close association between work and a sense of self worth, which is a vital foundation of ends-based relationships',[154] he does not see longer hours and greater flexibility as the solution; rather, a fairer distribution of work opportunities and pay: 'Surely it is better for all who seek and are able to work to be employed than for some to have high salaries and benefits well protected, only to be highly taxed in order to pay unemployment benefits to those who are kept out of the labour market.'[155] In contrast, according to Polly Toynbee and David Walker, New Labour 'mocked the French version of New Deal which created thousands of jobs and introduced the thirty-five hour working week to try to spread work to the workless by easing overwork for the employed'[156] – the very solution suggested by Etzioni. It is also interesting to note here that Etzioni has a more optimistic view of the unemployed – perhaps of human nature in general – than that displayed by New Labour. While the latter focus on benefit fraud and ever stricter measures to 'make' people work, reflecting an assumption that the unemployed lack incentives to work, Etzioni's proposals are based on the presumption that most people desire a job, but are prevented from having one by others having an unfair share of the available opportunities.

As noted at the beginning of this chapter, it has been suggested that communitarian language has been used by New Labour as a cover for a shift away from egalitarian ideals, towards market neo-liberalism. Whether or not this is the case, Etzioni's communitarianism actually has little to offer such an endeavour, and finds much to criticise in moves in that direction. Perceived similarities between Etzioni's brand of communitarianism and New Labour policies and rhetoric prove to be more apparent than real. There are, it is true, some overlaps, especially in the language used, but these have been considerably overstated, looking only at the actual words used but not at the respective understandings they represent. Etzioni's 'influence' has been vastly overstated, and his position is implicitly and often explicitly critical of many significant aspects of New Labour policy – including those identified in the popular mind most closely with him.

6

The mysterious absence of British communitarians from the discussion of British communitarianism

It would appear, on the face of it, that communitarianism is not primarily a British phenomenon. The perceived influence of Etzioni has been criticised as an unwelcome and inappropriate intrusion of 'foreign' ideas. Macmurray of course was British, but is safely dead, and arguably cannot be counted a communitarian anyway.[1] So it might come as a surprise to discover that there have been, since the early 1980s at least, British writers who have (unlike most other 'communitarian' writers) labelled themselves communitarian, and who have developed explicitly communitarian ideas tailored specifically to criticise, and in some cases influence, British government policy. Why, then, have Jonathan Boswell and Henry Tam slipped under the radar of both politicians and commentators, while Alasdair MacIntyre, high theorist and scourge of all things modern, is proposed as a credible source for Tony Blair's modernisation of his party?[2]

It cannot be because they lack academic credibility: both are established academics, one with a background in British industry, the other with extensive experience of local government and community activism. This chapter will argue that it is precisely because of this that they have been ignored by commentators: because their work is so explicitly about particular aspects of British policy and politics and so detailed in its recommendations it is not possible to stretch and squeeze it to fit what New Labour have said and done as it was, apparently, for the American Etzioni, the historical figure of Macmurray, and the abstract philosophers. The reasons for their neglect by politicians are different, but linked; the writers' demands are clear and explicit – but far too radical for, arguably, any government to put into practice. This does not mean, however, that they are irrelevant. On the contrary, any study of 'New Labour's communitarianism' cannot afford to ignore these writers. They point to what a considered, British, communitarian policy might look like, and when we compare this with Labour Party and Labour government policy since 1994 the differences are thrown into sharp relief.

Boswell and Tam are both British; both self-styled communitarians;

both writing in the 1980s and 1990s. Nonetheless, their approaches and areas of interest are very different. What they have in common is the uncompromising nature of the demands made by their communitarian standards. Because of their lack of coverage elsewhere, this chapter will set out their respective positions in some detail.

Jonathan Boswell

Jonathan Boswell's *Community and the Economy: The Theory of Public Co-operation* was published in 1990, and thus predates Etzioni's communitarian work.[3] Boswell's primary focus is on economic life and economic systems, which he sees not as something separate from the social or communal sphere, but as important forces shaping both these and individual behaviour. The fact that the economic sphere has tended to be seen as separate from community means that it is in particular need of an injection of community values. This means more, however, than simply transferring a conventional view of community from the social realm to that of economic relations; Boswell begins by setting out a particular conception of community and its place in social, political and economic life which he calls *democratic communitarianism*.

Boswell's view that it is in economic life that the values of community are in greatest need of elevation and promotion, and furthermore, that the 'recovery'[4] or institution of such values in the economic sphere is possible, sets him apart from other communitarian writers. Etzioni, for example, has been criticised for ignoring the influence of economic factors, and although he does give them some consideration in *The Third Way to a Good Society* he is generally quite clear that his concern is with the social sphere. For Boswell, the two cannot be separated. Economic factors and economic policy play such an important part in people's lives that individuals, community and society are inevitably shaped by them.

While New Labour thinking may go some way towards this position it diverges sharply from Boswell's in its acceptance of economic factors – particularly in the context of 'globalisation' – as forces of nature beyond the control of government or society. Secondly, but linked to this, Boswell's views of what community consists in, as well as the role it can and should play, particularly in the economy, are considerably more radical than that of Etzioni (the only explicitly *political* communitarian to have been linked with New Labour) and, this chapter will show, both more radical and far more clearly defined than New Labour's.

The first tenet of democratic communitarianism is that community is a value in its own right, and furthermore, it should be considered as the supreme value, elevated above the more conventional foundational political values of liberty and equality, and the economic goals of growth and prosperity. This rules out any consideration of community as an instrumental value; as a means – as it has often been presented – toward attaining these more familiar goals. This is clearly an area in which Boswell's position is at odds with policy; not only that of New Labour, but as he himself points out, every British government in history (and those of most other nations too).[5] For Blair, 'the renewal of community is the answer to the challenges of a changing world';[6] community is something to be used 'to break down the barriers holding back opportunity for all … The idea of community resolves the paradox of the modern world: it acknowledges our interdependence; it recognises our individual worth.' Blair presents 'community' as a bridge, uniting and resolving conflict between old and new, traditional and modern.[7]

In all these varied examples community is not only instrumental to some other purpose, but is presented as a valuable entity rather than a value as such. Far from being a value in its own right (as it is for Macmurray as well as Boswell), for Blair it is based on or derived from other – more primary – values: 'the values of responsibility to, and respect for, others', and furthermore, these values, like those of socialism or 'social-ism', can change over time in response to changing circumstances.[8] In another speech, Blair identifies the value at the heart of his 'modern idea of community' as 'the belief in equal worth' which 'affirms our equal right to dignity, liberty, freedom from discrimination as well as economic opportunity'.[9] Even in expressing its values, Blair is looking at community instrumentally, and as a means to realising some other primary value; not always the same one.

The values which Boswell's 'democratic communitarianism' 'actively seeks to promote' are those of fraternity, 'associativeness in liberty'[10] and '(civic or democratic) participation'.[11] While the more conventional notions of freedom, equality and prosperity have been endlessly debated and made the basis of ideologies, Boswell claims, these values which, for him, characterise community, have been ignored in terms of serious discussion.[12] Ideas about community, he says, 'are all around us, but in immature, secondary or emasculated forms' producing 'a widespread illusion that they are alive and well and do not need intellectual effort'.[13] This description is clearly applicable to New Labour's concept of community, which encompasses many different and frequently confused ideas, but is almost invariably taken for granted as understood and uncontroversial.

Boswell draws on the work of Durkheim to assert that in order to realise its full value – indeed, to have any intrinsic value at all – community or solidarity must reflect relationships which are both free and *spontaneous*: "'What gives unity to organised societies ... is the *spontaneous* consensus of parts.'"[14] This aspect is often ignored or discounted in communitarian thinking[15] and is very difficult for government policy to take account of (for the obvious reason that there is little government action can do, other than remove obstacles, to engender spontaneous activity).

This is one of the distinct echoes of Macmurray's views which can be heard in some of Boswell's propositions, although he does not draw upon Macmurray as a source, even in his next section on 'personalist Christian democracy', where he draws primarily on the work of Jacques Maritain, a Christian philosopher of roughly the same period.[16] This is evident in his claim that it is the *quality* of interpersonal relationships which must be at the heart of any conception of community, and more significantly, in his attitude to interdependence and contracts.

On Boswell's interpretation of Durkheim (and in the view of most communitarians) the idea of a (social) contract can only reflect the 'classical liberal concept' of 'initially separate, isolated and "free" individuals'.[17] While a contract could conceivably reflect a spontaneous relationship, it is certainly true that the concept usually implies something more onerous, binding and long-term – its antithesis, in effect. Durkheim's words vividly convey another aspect: 'A contract is only a truce, and very precarious; it suspends hostility only for a time.'[18] A contract is, on this view,[19] and in everyday terms, a substitute for trust. It is interesting therefore that contract plays a large part – which will be explored in the next chapter – in New Labour's communitarian policy and rhetoric.

Interdependence is the second concept which in the eyes of Boswell (again drawing on Durkheim and reflecting the view of Macmurray) is destructive of community, but which for New Labour comprises a (defining) feature of it – for example, Blair claims that '"[c]ommunity" implies a recognition of interdependence'.[20] Interdependence is seen by Boswell, following Durkheim, as a largely economic phenomenon, arising from the specialisation and division of labour.[21] Boswell rejects (with the benefit of hindsight) Durkheim's somewhat optimistic view of where such developments would lead, but retains the concept of interdependence as a feature of advanced industrial societies; a feature which is more likely to lead to conflict and exploitation than to the development of community spirit.[22]

A final point which Boswell draws from his interpretation of Durkheim is the view that although excessive government intervention would be both tyrannical and inefficient, and should be guarded against by the buttressing of institutions between the individual and the state,[23]

government action, in particular a radical redistribution of wealth and
income, would be necessary in order to give 'solidarity' a chance to develop.[24] For New Labour, in contrast, the development of social solidarity
is seen as completely separable from – and sometimes as compensating
for – economic inequality.

The second of Boswell's 'roots of democratic communitarianism' is
'personalist Christian democracy'.[25] This is a doctrine based on the belief
in each individual's 'infinite worth' as a person, involving both the right
and the duty to develop one's full human potential, to which end social
arrangements should be geared.[26] This view sees the formation of communities as an intrinsic part and expression of human nature, and elevates love and fraternity above any economic goal.[27] While a religiously
based, teleological position like this may not have immediate application
in today's polity, Boswell believes that its conception of human nature
does have political implications.

Again, once we get beneath the surface similarities, these are often at
odds with the words and deeds of New Labour. In particular, in common
with the previous ideals of free associativeness and solidarity, the greater
(let alone full) development of human potential, for every individual,
would call for radical redistribution of resources and genuine opportunities, and, according to Boswell, the rejection of capitalist industrial
organisation as we know it and its replacement by a system which recognises
'the primacy of labour over capital'.[28] Finally, the ownership of property
would imply social duties: 'restraint in both acquisition and consumption' and the 'subordination to communal needs, particularly those of
the poorest'.[29]

The personalist Christian democratic doctrine implies social responsibility, but the creation of conditions in which this can be exercised would
require a degree of economic decentralisation unthinkable to the British
New Labour, or any other western, government. People need power and
resources in order to be able to exercise such responsibility meaningfully.
If the conditions do not exist, it makes no sense to expect, let alone demand, the other side of the equation, yet for New Labour, duty explicitly
comes first, before – even as a part of – creating the conditions in which
it can reasonably be expected to be exercised: 'Duty is the cornerstone of
a decent society ... It defines the context in which rights are given ... It
is at the heart of *creating* a strong community or society.'[30] For Boswell
the opposite is true: a decent, in particular, more equal, society, is a precondition of the exercise of duty.

Boswell's third 'root' is 'civic humanism', which provides a theory of
citizenship and the state. In this context, 'politics is first and foremost

about the pursuit of personal virtue in community'.[31] Hence the importance accorded to participation; people developing their 'full capacities'
through interacting with each other. However, participation 'cannot be
commandeered',[32] a further contrast to the New Labour's comparatively
heavy handed approach.[33] While government has a major role on this
view it is in the (now familiar) field of securing the conditions which will
enable this development, including 'safeguards against chronic poverty,
unemployment and ill health ... government was to promote personal
virtue only in these sorts of barrier-removing ways. The scope for personal moral choice was to be enhanced.' Freedoms would be extended,
allowing people to make up their own minds about how these choices
might be used.[34]

Boswell finds a 'guiding thread' running through all three of his 'roots
of democratic communitarianism' – 'the search for associativeness in liberty'.[35] This is the first of his three values of democratic communitarianism,
and is characterised by three beliefs: firstly, that there are 'distinct and
unique components' – individuals above all, but also 'person-enhancing
groups' – whose 'diversity and freedom are crucial';[36] secondly, that these
units should 'be brought together' in a community which is 'mutually
fulfilling' and *not* just 'convenient or necessary'[37] and thirdly, these ideals
will never be attained, but must constantly be striven for.[38] This leads on
to Boswell's main normative claim: that 'the starting point of enquiry,
the overarching model and the ultimate evaluative yardstick in social affairs is the standard of relationships between persons'[39] and his call for a
'deliberate moral effort to improve the quality of recognition, communication and mutual regard between persons'.[40] This both requires and
develops diversity, and the ultimate aim is 'unity in diversity'.[41]

Fraternity, the second of Boswell's communitarian values, also features
three components: conviviality, mutual aid and shared commitment.[42]
Obstacles to the development of fraternity include large distances between living spaces, shortage of time (a relevant point in view of the long
working hours in Britain and the time demands imposed by the economy
on many), lack of public spaces, geographical mobility reinforced by career structures and personal ambition (to which can be added the expectation that people should be prepared to travel in order to obtain work),
class divisions, the isolation and institutionalisation of elderly and dis-
abled people, and 'ghetto communities' including middle-class suburbia
and 'lifestyle enclaves' as well as the ghettos of the poor.[43] Some of these
are more telling than others in their effects on fraternity, and some have
increased while others have decreased since Boswell wrote, but they are
all to a greater or lesser extent features that can be found in present day

Britain. Boswell's position is unequivocal: these impediments to the expression of fraternity should be removed by government action. 'Fraternity,' he says, 'cannot be socially engineered; but the effort to destroy impediments is fundamental.'[44]

It is difficult to point to New Labour policy or proposals to address any of these, or indeed to any recognition on their part that these are particular problems. Some, particularly those relating to isolation and ghettoisation, would seem to fall within the remit of the Social Exclusion Unit, established by Blair in 1997 in an attempt to coordinate departmental activity on a range of issues. But the group of issues which New Labour perceives as central to social exclusion is not the same as those perceived by Boswell to be undermining the formation of meaningful community. New Labour defines social exclusion as 'a shorthand term for what can happen when people or areas suffer from a combination of linked problems such as unemployment, poor skills, low incomes, poor housing, high crime environments, bad health and family breakdown'.[45] On this definition, entire communities can be seen as excluded – from mainstream society – even though there may be strong relationships within them. Most of these indicators of exclusion are, as Levitas has pointed out, employment-related, as are the solutions offered – education and training, the New Deal, and childcare initiatives, for example. The idea of social exclusion has also served to swallow up another of Boswell's perceived obstacles to community – class division, which has been rejected by New Labour as any kind of basis for politics.[46]

For New Labour, the main solution to exclusion from society is a job ('work is the best form of welfare, the best way of funding people's needs, and the best way of giving them a stake in society');[47] for Boswell, many kinds of exclusion, destructive to community, are *caused by* employment, and New Labour's focus on broadening employment, while regulating it as little as possible can only exacerbate these. Blair has boasted that the UK is the most lightly regulated labour market in the advanced world,[48] and despite the hopes raised by New Labour's commitment to sign up to the Social Chapter of the Maastricht Treaty (which the previous Conservative government had opted out of), the British labour market is still the most 'flexible' in Europe. Flexibility is presented as a virtue, allowing Britain to compete in the global economy, but it also means less protection, fewer workplace rights and less consultation and involvement for employees.

New Labour in government rejected the French version of New Deal, which directly created jobs and redistributed employment opportunities by cutting the working week to 35 hours. Although it implemented the

Working Time Directive, which theoretically limits the working week to a maximum of 48 hours, the New Labour government negotiated a clause, only used in Britain, under which workers could 'voluntarily' give up their rights under the Directive. Four million workers have signed away those rights at the request of their employer,[49] meaning that the opt-out clause seriously undermines the effectiveness of the legislation.[50] Even 48 hours is a long week by EU standards, and time spent at work, especially as most employment is outside the community where people live, must qualify as a significant contributor to the lack of time which Boswell points to as a serious obstacle to the development of community. On top of this, Boswell cites the dislocation caused by labour mobility, which is a key feature of the flexible labour market. It is not just geographical mobility that militates against community. Flexibility means changing jobs and employers far more during the working lifetime, such high workforce turnover significantly reducing the potential for developing meaningful relationships *within* the workplace.

Boswell's third communitarian value of participation would certainly seem to find echoes in New Labour's promotion of 'active citizenship', but there are important differences. For Boswell, '[p]articipation means to share freely in activities which shape and express democratic community. It has to be voluntary. Coerced or conscripted involvements do not qualify'.[51] Participation is a duty insofar as it represents the fulfilment of human nature; it is essentially a duty we have to ourselves, rather than to others or society: 'if social groupings and civic life are fundamental for self development, involvement in them becomes a moral imperative'.[52] It could be argued that something as fundamental to human nature as this will happen in any case if only (again) impediments are removed; and impediments to participation, like those to fraternity, are far more within the power of governments and industry than they are of individuals and small social groups, suggesting that any duty imposed by the human need for participation falls upon those bodies rather than on people in general. For one thing, as Boswell notes later, the hegemonic party system characteristic of western democracies militates against the meaningful political participation which should provide a vital arena for free association.[53]

Although Boswell's overall conception of duty is in fact a little vague, certain key aspects come through clearly. Above all, he is adamant that the true meaning of duty must be 'recovered', rejecting the notions of 'enforced duty ... [or] duty towards a social abstraction or collective', and the idea that duty is 'necessarily uncomfortable or one-sidedly altruistic' in favour of 'duty related to one's own development through free associativeness ... which is as often relaxed, convivial or even festive as it is sober and determined'.[54] Participation, for Boswell, includes meeting your mates in the pub, and maybe not even discussing politics there. 'Participation involves not only acting together, but being together ... [it] involves play and dialogue as well as work.'[55]

This is a conception of duty which New Labour would find decidedly unhelpful. For them, duty is primarily, if not exclusively, duty to others, frequently mediated through the state. Any duty to oneself lies in developing one's talents and skills for employment and for deployment for the general good. Indeed, the idea of duty to oneself is associated by Blair with the very values New Labour rejects: while the left, he claims, focused too heavily upon people's rights, 'the Right started to define personal responsibility as responsibility not just for yourself but to yourself'.[56] This excludes any element of duty to oneself, even alongside duty to others, from the New Labour conception. Duty is the price paid for opportunity,[57] and 'defines the context in which rights are given'.[58]

Another key point, which reflects Boswell's overall view of community, is that participation is an intrinsic good; an end in itself. It is not valuable only or even primarily for the other benefits which might flow from it, in comparison to New Labour's conception of citizenship as a duty to others which will improve services and reduce government/taxpayer costs. In a speech to the National Council for Voluntary Service, in which the phrase 'civic patriotism' was coined, Gordon Brown recognises that 'volunteering provides something the state could never provide',[59] in terms of quantity of participants, breadth of service provided, and innovation. The Active Community Unit point out the practical and economic implications of declining voluntary activity: 'with no volunteers there would in 10 years time be no voluntary reading schemes in schools, no victim support schemes, no mentors ... the economic value of volunteering has been estimated to amount to £40 billion, so the public expenditure implications are considerable'.[60]

This represents the 'conventional wisdom' which Boswell's conception of participation 'turns upside down'. According to Boswell, the conventional view is that 'we participate in joint activities in order to get X, Y or Z done',[61] whereas in fact many goals are valuable not (primarily) for themselves but 'are worth doing precisely because we participate associatively in them and so develop ourselves as human beings'.[62] This is in stark contrast to Blair's defence of society on the basis that 'self interest demands that we work together to achieve what we cannot do on our own'. Also, Boswell's position explicitly challenges '"output", consumerist notions' of politics – he suggests that 'democracy's highest value' comes not from its delivery of security or prosperity, but from 'its communally participative attributes',[64] whereas the focus of New Labour's approach to participation is almost exclusively on its measurable outputs; it is advocated in those terms, and not in terms of intrinsic value.

So far this chapter has considered the values central to Boswell's 'democratic communitarianism' – fraternity, associativeness and participation – in terms of what they mean to him and where they differ from New Labour's understanding of community and communitarianism. But Boswell's conception of communitarian values is not, by a long way, what is most radical or original about his approach. The most radical aspect of his position is his view that 'all elements of the democratic communitarian heritage insisted that an advanced economic system could not be exempted from the search for free solidarity'.[65] The ideal is *economic community*; the cultivation of these communitarian values in the economic sphere. Not only is it not 'possible to separate "society" and "the economy" so that democratic community would be increased in society while the economy remained untouched'[66] but 'the economic system stands in *particular* need of change'.[67]

While it is clear that there is not much hope of democratic communitarianism taking root in any modern capitalist economy, Boswell claims that there are practical steps that can be taken to encourage its development. Mostly, however, such steps have been taken by governments in mainland Europe in contrast to the attitudes of governments in Britain and the US. In his chapters on public cooperation, Boswell moves away from the normative realm of democratic communitarian values and sets out to identify empirically where the phenomenon of public cooperation – the potential precursor of those values – is to be found in existing or recent economic systems. If democratic communitarianism is to be realised at all, then public cooperation must be nurtured, institutions and ways of working conducive to it encouraged, and obstacles removed. Only the state is in a position to attempt this task. The question is whether New Labour shares Boswell's view that such changes are either possible or desirable.

The first indicator of public cooperation in the economy is a degree of corporatism; a quasi-contractual role in the decision making processes of industry and government for both business and trade unions. This European model, successful in Germany, was considered (under the concept of 'stakeholding') but ultimately rejected by New Labour in favour of the continuation of an Anglo-American, free market, approach.[68] A second indicator is 'industrial peace' born of voluntary restraint and cooperation on both sides, rather than imposed by anti-union legislation or the legal repression of strikes[69] (a consistently key point is the necessity for arrangements to be largely voluntary and spontaneous in order to qualify).

New Labour, on the other hand, have retained and defended the vast bulk of the Thatcher government's union-control laws. Although people's right to join a union, and the union's right to recognition (in certain circumstances) in the workplace, have been established by New Labour,[70] the scope for action of the union itself remains as circumscribed by legislation as under the Conservatives. The very establishment of these new relationships between employers and unions – 'no more bosses versus workers, but partnership at work'[71] (this model of participation meaning the effective co-option of the unions into the alliance of government and employer rather than a European model of consultation and cooperation) – tends to rule out the spontaneous development of relationships and participation. The very competitive economic environment promoted by New Labour militates against the development of those traits which Boswell describes as the essential precursors of democratic community in the economy.[72]

Other structural factors necessary for the development of community in the economy include long-term stability and a long-term view (which might not bode well for the Private Finance Initiative), smaller rather than large business units (requiring greater restrictions on takeovers and mergers), and social transparency of economic actors.

More important than structural and institutional obstacles to cooperative behaviour, however, are what Boswell calls 'ideological barriers and supports'.[73] Ideological barriers include insecurity, exploitation, unemployment and disenfranchisement. While reducing unemployment has been a New Labour priority, and it could be argued that the introduction of the minimum wage is a move toward reducing exploitation,[74] insecurity of employment, of housing and even of education is widely viewed as part of the *zeitgeist*, and even leaving aside the issue of falling election turnout, it may be argued that the 'first past the post' system does more to disenfranchise people, particularly those with minority political views. De facto disenfranchisement through disillusion is a feature of today's politics which causes concern not only to the current government but to all governments, because it threatens their legitimacy; hence New Labour's initiatives on citizenship and participation.[75] Without a fundamental alteration of the system, however, these can only be window-dressing in Boswell's terms.

Boswell goes on to make some points about what he sees as the failure of democratic socialism to realise its potential democratic communitarian values which are interesting in the light of the claims staked by Blair and

New Labour to the democratic socialist heritage. Some of Boswell's criticisms of democratic socialism are equally applicable to New Labour attitudes. Democratic socialism, he asserts, elevates fraternity as an ideal; abstract and beyond the reach of rational analysis or debate,[76] but never takes the necessary steps to realise it. This happens because the extent of its abstraction as an ideal leads to fraternity being perceived as a 'total substitute' – something which is necessarily an alternative to the existing situation, and thus obscures the 'imperfect approximations' of fraternity which already exist. This in turn leads to the belief that not only is the change from capitalism to socialism necessary for the realisation of fraternity, but that that it will inevitably and automatically yield it. This reflects a particularly abstract, ahistorical and anti-empirical approach[77] i.e. in Boswell's view it ignores reality. In the third stage of this process the realisation of fraternity becomes identified with a particular economic policy, reflecting the aforementioned belief in quasi-mechanical solutions. This then tends to become an end in itself, and as it does not automatically issue in increased levels of fraternity, 'fraternity seeking is postponed'[78] leaving a vacuum which is filled by 'elements from the dominant paradigm'[79] – selfish liberal capitalism.

Clearly there are elements in this analysis – notably the commitment to traditional socialist economics – which do not chime with the actions of the current administration. But certain of Boswell's perceptions do apply. Firstly, fraternity – or community, to use New Labour's nearest term ('fraternity' itself perhaps, ironically, has too much of a ring of socialism about it) is still perceived as an ideal, and a universal solution,[80] while policies aimed at promoting community (but doing nothing in Boswell's terms to achieve it) operate at an entirely different level. While New Labour display less apparent dogmatic adherence to mechanistic economic solutions, social and welfare policy, with its direct and intentional effects on community values and potentially fraternal behaviour, has become increasingly rigid, based as it is around the paradigms of social inclusion through paid employment and the explicit criminalisation of behaviour which is judged 'anti-social' by politicians.[81] This last represents a far more direct attempt to influence behaviour than any economic policy, but still will not do anything to engender fraternal values[82] (not least because the essence of such values is freedom and spontaneity).

This brings us to the final point on which Boswell's criticism of democratic socialism is pertinent to New Labour: it cannot shake off the 'dominant paradigm'. A liberal, or a pragmatist, and no doubt the party itself, would say that such a sloughing off is neither necessary nor desirable. But without it there is no possibility of fraternity as Boswell understands it, and, we must not forget, fraternity is one of the foundational values of democratic communitarianism. At least the democratic socialists paid lip service to the idea of changing the economic system to let fraternity flourish. Even though they ultimately failed to achieve it, they realised that fraternity (except perhaps on a very small scale) is not possible under capitalism. In this sense, Boswell's criticisms are even more applicable to New Labour, who openly seek community values in the context of global capitalism; the reconciliation of an economic sphere based on competition with a social sphere based on cooperation. The spheres cannot be reconciled, and neither can they be separated. And it is the value of competition which wins out over that of cooperation. When people do cooperate, it is because they as a group are in competition with other groups, not because cooperation is the highest value. Britain's workers are exhorted to cooperate nationally in order that Britain may be competitive in the global economy. People are urged to 'shop' unemployed 'benefit cheats' in order to protect the interests of taxpayers, by definition a separate group, in the competition for resources. This inter-group competition represents the same competitive self-interest as individualism on a broader canvas, and has no greater moral value.

Furthermore, Boswell suggests, the political economy debate in the UK is exceptionally polarised and perceived in the extreme terms of 'free enterprise *versus* the state', 'public *versus* private'. Whereas some of Labour's 'Third Way' language has rejected this apparent dichotomy, for example, through 'public/private partnerships', these initiatives still perpetuate the image of public and private as discrete spheres, albeit ones which may work together for mutual benefit. It is still true to say, as Boswell does, that there is 'little emphasis on the economic system as a focus for socio-ethical ideals, civic co-operation or the growth of persons in community'.[83] The private sector may, under partnership arrangements, work with 'the community (sector)', but this generally involves the latter adapting to work within the paradigm of the former – for example, by producing business plans and costing the value of voluntary labour[84] – rather than the private sector taking on board any of the attributes of community, especially as understood by Boswell.

Boswell ends *Community and the Economy* by asking: 'What would a normative approach based on economic communitarianism entail? What sort of reforms does it advocate?'[85] On looking at Boswell's answers to his own questions, we can go on to ask: how far is this reflected in what New Labour are saying and doing, especially where this differs from the way in which Britain has been governed in the past?

What comes clearly out of Boswell's work is that genuine community

will not and cannot develop and flourish without radical economic reforms, which themselves must be preceded by significant – perhaps un-
imaginable – shifts in attitude. These are not going to happen – whether
because of lack of will, lack of belief or the simple fact that such reforms
on a national level are impossible in the context of a global economy (and
if this is so, then what are the implications for the attempt to create
community on a local level within a national economic structure which is
both competitive and capitalist?) The reason really does not matter. If
Boswell is right that communitarian ideals cannot be applied to the social sphere without equally applying them to the economy, then all Western communitarian politics is a lost cause.

Boswell's radical economic communitarianism can help to shed light
on claims that New Labour is communitarian. This is despite the fact
that Boswell has never been cited or claimed as an influence on or by
them. Firstly it helps demonstrate that communitarianism – even just
political communitarianism – is a vast and diverse body of work encompassing many approaches and areas of interest, and coincidence with one
of these is not sufficient reason to label something 'communitarian'.

Secondly, Boswell's key point, that the economic sphere cannot be
insulated from the search for community ideals, is a valid one, and certainly gives pause for thought, particularly as New Labour is actively
encouraging people (through welfare to work and the inclusion paradigm it represents) to identify themselves more with the sphere of economic activity. People participate in the economic sphere primarily as
workers and earners (this is certainly how New Labour sees it) but also as
consumers: consumption is an economic activity, and in many ways one
which characterises our age. In short, people today are more active in and
affected by 'the economy' than ever before, meaning that the (probably
inevitable) lack of community values in that sphere will be more telling
than ever before, and no amount of effort in promoting those values in
the 'social' sphere will have any impact on it.

Thirdly, Boswell's view, which he shares with Macmurray, that community, if it is to have any value, must be perceived and treated as intrin-
sically and not just instrumentally valuable, calls into question many of
the party's policies and statements on community. The promotion of
community is almost invariably justified in instrumental terms – the
taxpayers' money which will be saved, the additional and better services
which will be provided. Even when the benefits to the participant
(fulfilment, self-development)[86] are mentioned, they are followed up with
a note on their value in the job market – the economic sphere. Community is still subordinate to the economy. The only role that New Labour

appears to see for community in the economy is the participation of community groups in the economic sphere – for example, as service providers. This again subordinates community values to economic ones (you have to play by the rules of the economy in order to participate in it), and so represents the opposite of what Boswell has in mind.

In Boswell's terms, which are illuminating here, no initiative or policy, let alone an entire party programme, can rightly be called communitarian if it does not elevate community above all other values, in all spheres. While this is an extreme view, and not one which is amenable to practical application, it certainly puts other claims about communitarianism into perspective.

Henry Tam

The fourth and final political communitarian to be considered is Henry Tam, an English writer and community activist whose *Communitarianism: a New Agenda for Politics and Citizenship* was published in 1998. As well as working as an academic, Tam has held a number of posts in local and central government, and in 2004 was appointed head of the Home Office's Civil Renewal Unit. However, at the time his book was published, and New Labour was in the process of formation, Tam was Chief Executive of St Edmundsbury District Council in Cambridgeshire. Here he was instrumental in establishing the 'Communitarian Forum', based at Anglia Polytechnic University, a British response to Etzioni's Communitarian Platform, to which people were invited to sign up and offer endorsement.

While there are some similarities between the communitarianisms of Tam and Boswell – in particular, their recognition of structural factors – Tam focuses his interest and his policy prescription at a more personal and less organisational level, and is more concerned with social than economic policies. *Communitarianism: a New Agenda for Politics and Citizenship* has a number of chapters devoted to specific policy areas: education, employment and 'protection' (essentially law and order and welfare); and a chapter each for the three 'sectors': the public or state sector, the private sector, and the 'Third Sector', a term which is now widely used to refer to organised voluntary and community activity.

The focus here will be on the policy areas of citizenship and education, which are both an important part of New Labour's approach, and are key to Tam's understanding of communitarianism. However, comparisons between Tam's communitarianism and New Labour's position can and must be taken further than specific policy proposals. Tam's proposals are founded upon clearly defined and carefully chosen principles.

Similarly, New Labour claims to be guided by firm, unwavering principles and values. However, these concepts are often understood and used in different ways and at different levels, and this chapter will examine and contrast these. Tam's communitarianism is based upon three 'fundamental principles': cooperative enquiry, mutual responsibility, and citizen participation, and where these coincide with or approximate to ideas used by New Labour, these will be compared. More broadly, the respective conceptions and uses of the concepts of 'citizenship' and of 'values' will be compared and contrasted.

Like Etzioni, Tam takes 'individualism' to be a key problem in contemporary politics and society, but again, the similarity is only superficial. While for Etzioni individualism is identified with ever growing demands for social and civil rights, for Tam the villain is squarely identified as *market* individualism. This, he asserts, has 'cancerous effects on community life' and its 'hegemony ... must now be brought to an end'.[87] Market individualism is not destructive simply because it elevates the values of greed and selfishness, as suggested by popular criticisms of Thatcherism, and echoed by Blair, for example, in his endorsement of the view that 'economic and social inequality was in part attributable to a governing ideology of unfettered individualism'[88] and his claim that 'the 1980s were the time of "who cares?"'[89]

According to Tam, the real mechanism is both more complicated and more direct: selfishness arises from market individualism not via moral endorsement, but through the fear and insecurity which are an inevitable fact of life for the majority in a free market system.[90] Tam paints a bleak picture of a society in which, under the free market, those 'who are in control of more economic resources than others are able to set the agenda for everyone from a privileged bargaining position' – for example, by making financial contributions to political parties, controlling the media or by threatening to withhold their investment or purchasing power.[91] Thus a vicious spiral is formed whereby those with the most resources have the most power, and thus gain more of society's resources, and so on, leaving the majority of people insecure, afraid and under stress, working ever longer hours and with no thought, time or energy to spare for others, even their own children. This is of course compounded by the other side of the market, consumption and the pressure to consume in order to achieve what is perceived to be an acceptable lifestyle, which fuels both the need, and thus the insecurity, of those in work, and the exclusion of those without a job.

For Tam, there is a trade-off between economic prosperity and community; he does not perceive them as mutually reinforcing. Furthermore, this trade-off has become untenable, in part because it is failing even to deliver the economic benefits that are its *raison d'être*, but primarily 'because even with the growth that has been achieved, the harm to community life through the marginalisation of those with job insecurity, low pay – or no job at all – has reached a point where it can no longer be tolerated'.[92] In Tam's view this has dire social consequences: people turn to drink and drugs as an escape from the helplessness of their situation, and crime rises as people's hopelessness translates into a sense of having no responsibility for the future and a 'withdrawal from collective obligations'.[93] 'Civic discourse' is dismissed, and 'all attempts to articulate the public good' are 'denigrated' as 'authoritarian intervention'.[94]

This last sounds remarkably like Etzioni – but there is a very significant difference. For Etzioni this perceived breakdown of social life is the result of individual selfishness and the decline of community morality. Similarly, for New Labour, it reflects the 'who cares' attitude attributed to the 1980s exacerbating the 'anything goes' ethic of the 1960s[95] and individuals' unwillingness to meet their responsibilities to society. In stark contrast, for Tam the denigration of the public good is a *deliberate act* by 'individualist defenders of the dominant socioeconomic system' to defend their interest in the free market status quo.[96] It is essentially the act of an interest group, not of atomised individuals.

According to Tam, the dominance of the free market means that an economic paradigm is being inappropriately applied to social (or what should be social) life, 'removing discussion from civic forums and reducing them to private bargains between individuals, and … evaluating the trade-off solely in terms of what can be quantified economically'.[97] Certainly, as outlined in the previous chapter, the penetration of the market into service provision has continued apace under the New Labour government. An economistic model has infiltrated in more subtle ways too, in the quantification inherent in school league tables, and the explicit gearing of education to the requirements of the economy, for example. But even this does not sufficiently capture Tam's concerns.

The economisation of social life gives a particular definition to concepts like fairness and equality. Equality, understood as equality of opportunity, is represented as a 'level playing field', with everyone playing according to the same rules, but the fact that everyone is bound by the same rules does not ensure fairness if the rules favour a particular group (most likely the group that was in the position to draw them up), and the rules of the market favour those who are good at market transactions. 'Those who might otherwise score highly in non-economic terms are simply told that their game does not count any longer.'[98] This state of affairs can only be reinforced by the emphasis on economic participation in New Labour employment and inclusion policy: those who cannot or will not get a job and thus play by the rules of the economic 'game' are by definition (on New Labour's understanding of inclusion) excluded from the whole spectrum of society.

Tam's communitarianism is drawn from the three principles of cooperative enquiry, mutual responsibility, and citizen participation.[99] If a community, or 'community' in general, is to defend its interests, or the 'public interest', then this implies a shared set of values on the basis of which to evaluate and establish what that common interest consists in. The concept of shared values is central to communitarian thought from Etzioni to MacIntyre and is often used to differentiate a community from a collection of individuals. For many communitarians, not least those just mentioned, such shared values can be drawn from a stock of religious, cultural and social traditions, and are frequently accepted unquestioningly. As a result they are often perceived, at least by critics of communitarianism, as potentially oppressive of individuals or minority subsets within a community.

Tam seeks to circumvent this objection by setting down strict criteria for the conditions in which shared values must be arrived at if they are to be acceptable to his conception of 'inclusive community'. These criteria constitute his principle of *cooperative enquiry*. This is the process by which all those with an interest can participate on an equal footing to test knowledge claims, and to decide how to proceed, as a community, in the light of the knowledge thus arrived at.

On the face of it, New Labour would seem to endorse the idea of giving people more say in the way their communities are run, and in the formulation of policy both nationally and locally – for example, their 1997 manifesto was famously endorsed by ordinary party members. However, the various forms of consultation employed by them – including all those set out on the Civil Renewal Unit website[100] – fall far short of the criteria of Tam's cooperative enquiry. This is primarily because 'consultation' is generally on a range of predetermined options offered by the government – or, in the extreme case of the manifesto, an invitation to either acclaim the document in its entirety or not be heard at all. In the first place, then, it is very much a top-down process, dominated by those already in a position of power.

Secondly, such processes are only open to those who are willing and able to participate on certain terms, and the structures of consultation – formal or semi-formal meetings, written submissions – will favour the views of those who are skilled and experienced at (in Tam's terms) that 'game'. The whole process is carried out within the terms of the accepted dominant (free market) paradigm; it never sets out to question or offer an alternative to it. Small-scale communities' attempts to do that (for example, travellers' communities and those living 'alternative' lifestyles) are excluded from the formal process. The New Labour government has certainly done much to encourage and require community consultation on a range of issues and in a variety of contexts, but these processes do not approximate to the standards of participation demanded by Tam.

New Labour tend to view citizen participation not so much as an end in itself, as it is for Tam, but as a means towards a range of other outcomes: more effective use of funds; the legitimation of policies through the nominal transfer of the responsibility of decision-making to those affected, sidelining the alternative power base of local government in the process, and the development of 'community spirit' and individual character, as well as practical employment-orientated skills. Overall, then, formal consultation processes fail to meet the demands of Tam's ideal of cooperative enquiry, both in terms of their aims and of their outcomes.

There are, however, other forms of participation which New Labour has experimented with or considered which might approximate more closely to Tam's ideal: focus groups and 'citizen juries'. The first of these, made famous by the party's use of them in the run-up to the 1997 General Election and beyond, is a non-starter in Tam's terms because participants are very carefully selected to be representative of particular groups; participation is not open to all, and, of course, any outcome is entirely at the discretion of the body who paid for the research. Citizen juries, on the other hand, in which a group of people – who may be randomly selected – hear evidence about an issue over a period of time before discussing it and reaching a decision, are more akin to the circumstances of cooperative enquiry. However, although the idea was floated in a 1995 local government policy paper as one of a range of ways by which councils 'could seek to make themselves more responsive'[101] the idea has not been developed as an aspect of New Labour policy.

The role of 'values'

In an inclusive community, cooperative enquiry would yield a set of shared values which the community would unite to defend and promote. The fact that New Labour talk about 'values'[102] to a greater extent than political parties have done previously, and Blair in particular invokes the concept to a noticeably greater degree than previous prime ministers or other members of the government, lends credence to the idea that they are communitarian. It is also important to be aware, however, that in some if not all of the contexts in which he uses the term, the idea of values is not only being understood differently, but is being used to perform different functions.

One of the main functions performed by the concept of values in Blairite rhetoric is as a contrast with means, methods and even 'ideology' in the discourse of modernisation. What this means is that the process of modernising firstly the Labour Party (for example with the replacement of Clause IV), and once in government, reforming institutions like local government, is that 'values' can be held up as unchanging, while large-scale changes are being made in approaches and institutions. The idea of values provides a sense of continuity to reassure in a time of radical change.

This usage is clearly seen in the context of internal Labour Party reform. For example, in his speech to the 1995 Party Conference, Blair sets out what he explicitly refers to as the values of 'my socialism': 'I am worth no more than anyone else. I am my brother's keeper. I will not walk by on the other side. We aren't simply people set in isolation from each other ... but members of the same family, the same community, the same human race'.[103] Here Blair claims that socialism is 'a moral purpose ... A set of values ...' rather than being 'about nationalisation or the power of the State ... economics or politics ...'[104] These values are 'great and timeless' but require new structures and even ideologies in order to be realisable. However, in the same speech Blair also lays claim to values not traditionally associated with the left: 'I believe in the family. I believe in being tough on crime.' Although '[s]ome would say that these are the moral values of the right and of the old fashioned' Blair is adamant that 'they are our values'.[105]

Thus we see Blair setting out what he perceives as fundamental values of the Labour Party, in order to contrast these, which endure, with methods and ideologies which are about to undergo radical change; the concept of values is used to provide a reassuring sense of continuity. In a Fabian Society pamphlet on *Socialism*[106] Blair makes similar points and calls upon the concept of values to perform the same role, but here the actual values which he sets out are different ones — at least in name. They are the 'notions' of 'social justice, cohesion, equality of opportunity and community'.[107] More significant here though is the fundamental claim of the pamphlet: that socialism must seek its roots in values such as these (ethical socialism) rather than in economic relations (dismissed as outdated Marxist socialism).[108] For Blair, a basis in values defines socialism even before the content of those values is established. The mere existence of values is more important than what those values actually are. While the latter changes, the former continues to define Blair's socialism.

In a speech toward the end of Labour's long period in opposition, Blair refers to the same set of values which ground the Labour Party, but as 'radical' rather than traditional.[109] (It may be significant that this speech is not to an exclusively Labour audience.) Here he sets out an ambition for the Labour Party to be a 'broad movement for progress and justice, with appeal across the classes, where people from all walks of life feel at home, because they share the same values and priorities'.[110] Here the presumed values of the nation are to be adopted as those of the party. A clear contrast between values and political ideology is made in this speech, when Blair notes that all over Europe parties of the left are abandoning standard socialist ideology and in its place 'putting in the correct order the values on which their politics are based', followed by a list of examples of this.[111]

This is, then, no longer just about rediscovering the values that underlie the politics of the left and putting them into practice via new means (here, values are at one point contrasted with 'a final goal' but elsewhere identified with 'goals' in contrast to 'how we implement them'), but about re-ordering and reprioritising those values too. Some of the 'old' values cited here are: the worth of every individual; strong families; strong communities; hatred of squalor and idleness (no doubt conscious echoes of Beveridge); the breaking down of barriers of class, race and sex; bonds of tolerance and respect, the curbing of unaccountable power; cherishing the environment (however worthy, hardly a traditional Labour value); a strong and just society, and the empowerment 'of the many not the few'.[112] It is interesting as well as confusing to note the way in which adjectives like 'strong' are attached, and the values themselves are related in various combinations.[113] Also, whereas for Tam, values and principles are two different concepts, with the latter derived from the former, in Blair's usage they tend to be used interchangeably.

Towards the end of his 1995 conference speech, Blair shifts from talking about the values of the party to those of the nation: 'One Britain. The people united by shared values and shared aims.'[114] As, over the course of the late 1990s, Blair's emphasis moves from the reform of the Labour Party to the government of the country, it is increasingly in this context that values are invoked. Two later speeches provide examples of this. In his speech to their Triennial General Meeting in 2000, Blair tells the Women's Institute that they 'take the best of British values and traditions but are as relevant to our national life today as when … founded in 1915'.[115] The thrust of this speech is that a decent society requires strong communities, and the values invoked here (twice on one page) are the 'traditional British values of responsibility and respect for others' (lest

this be ambiguous, it is rendered the second time as 'the values of responsibility *to* and respect for others').[116]

Again (but in a different context) Blair uses this speech to differentiate
between values and other factors, suggesting that it is possible to 'distinguish between the genuine values that underpinned the best of Britain
and the attitudes we can safely and rightly leave behind. Old-fashioned
values are good values. Old-fashioned attitudes or practices may simply
be barriers that hold our values back.'[117] And again, as for the internal
party reforms, this is laying the foundation for change while stressing
continuity, but this time in the context of justifying national government policy: 'we can rebuild these core values of community; but only
by renewing them for the modern world; the old and the new together'.[118]
Later, he says that the 'values we hold dear, responsibility, respect for
others – must be rigorously re-asserted' if opportunities are to be provided to people. In practice, as Blair goes on to make clear, this means
tougher criminal penalties, measures to prevent truancy etc.

This is Blair's new meaning for the old values of responsibility and
respect which might once have rendered such measures unnecessary (and
surely would again if it were indeed possible to revive them). In this
speech, values are again separated from and contrasted with other factors,
but this time with attitudes (something qualitatively similar) rather than
with means (qualitatively different). It seems as if values are actually defined by their endurance, while the things from which they are distin-
guished, like goals, ideology, means and attitude, are by definition
transitory – a definition which is arbitrary and circular. The specific values repeatedly mentioned are respect and responsibility, the latter generally understood as responsibility to, rather than for, others.

A speech from the previous week, again explicitly about values, offers a
different emphasis.[119] Here, 'the ethical values that should guide us in an
era of globalisation' include 'the belief in community, and in the equal
worth of all'; 'mutual responsibility';[120] 'equal worth' meaning 'our equal
right to dignity, liberty, freedom from discrimination', and solidarity.
Again, however, these values are translated into tough law and order measures (including the infamous and quickly ditched proposal for on the
spot fines for drunk and disorderly behaviour), and there is the familiar
aim of 'applying traditional values to the modern world'.

There are therefore, very crudely, two consistent factors in New Labour
values rhetoric: the idea of constant values in a changing context, and the
policy measures/party reforms that these issue in; and one factor which
changes from speech to speech: what those values actually are. They seem
to be many and various and are combined and modified to provide a

greater range still. We can identify some New Labour values which crop up frequently if not consistently in Blair's speeches, Labour documents, and commentaries, but must conclude that the concept of 'values' does not perform the same function for the Labour Party as it does for Tam, for whom specific values, rather than the idea of values as a concept, provide the foundation for principles, action and moral judgement.

Citizenship and education

Tam's final principle of inclusive communitarianism is citizen participation. This is drawn from his understanding of citizenship, which in turn is inseparable from education. The remainder of this chapter will consider these concepts and compare Tam's communitarian understanding with that of New Labour, beginning with their respective views of education; its function and how it should fulfil this.

Tam equates the idea of citizenship with the fulfilment of one's role as a member of an inclusive community; and he sees the primary purpose of education as being the preparation of young people for that role. This is not necessarily a narrow vision, as the importance of inclusive communities permeates every aspect of life. New Labour have set great store by 'education for citizenship'. (David Blunkett, as Education Secretary, Home Secretary and Work and Pensions Minister has been a forceful advocate of firstly, citizenship education and later, active citizenship.) There is, then, a (by now familiar) superficial similarity between the government's position and the communitarian view.

In Tam's ideal view of education, people will have to learn how to 'formulate co-operative solutions to common problems'.[121] Learning to participate in this process is more important than any specific outcomes, in contrast to New Labour's clear 'focus ... on standards, not structures'.[122] More interesting, from the point of view of drawing comparisons with New Labour policies and attitudes, are Tam's ideas about what education *should not* be. For a start, it should not be about equipping people to fulfil different positions in post-school life, but should be 'at best a general preparation for coping with life, with job-related skills being just one element'.[123] He draws on the ideas of both philosopher Mary Warnock and management guru Peter Drucker to claim that the most important consideration is not the range of subjects and knowledge imparted, but a high quality education which exercises the imagination and develops attention to detail. As well as enhancing empathy and compassion, imagination can be applied to solving communities' problems, strengthening community solidarity and developing members. Such an educational grounding would 'allow individuals to use their own initiative in a framework that best guarantees the good of all'.[124] Knowledge is viewed not as a collection of facts, but as being what is 'derived from the intelligent conclusions of co-operative enquiries'.[125]

The emphasis on transmitting 'basic facts' (as promoted by the government via its literacy and numeracy hours) is deemed by Tam to be misguided, revealing 'not only a serious lack of appreciation of the nature of knowledge, but also virtual blindness to contemporary organizational behaviour'.[126] By this he is referring to organisation theory, which holds that knowledge is embodied in organisations, through their members' making their own enquiries, rather than being drawn from 'definitive sources'. This is, then, a practical as well as a principled argument: by adopting his form of communitarian education rather than one based on traditional knowledge, Tam is saying, we will equip people better for the modern world as it is, as well as preparing them for the world as it should be – citizenship in inclusive communities. This chapter has so far shown how Tam's view of the role and purpose of education is derived from the principles and values of his particular communitarian vision. This section will consider some specific recommendations which he makes regarding policy and practice and will compare these to New Labour's policies for citizenship education, before going on to contrast their views on citizenship more generally.

For Tam, education for citizenship cannot be separated out from education considered more generally. Unsurprisingly, the key to both is to apply the approach of cooperative enquiry across the curriculum. It is, he says, 'the development of such an approach which should form the focus of what is often described as "citizenship education"'.[127] This already marks out an approach different from the 'traditional' schooling – for example, a stress on literacy and numeracy, facts and figures, and whole-class teaching, in contrast to some of the more 'child-centred' methods experimented with in the 1970s – advocated by the government (and advocated very strongly by Chris Woodhead, who was Chief Inspector of Education both under John Major's Conservative government and for most of Labour's first term, having been re-appointed by Labour despite his links with the previous government and known conservative views on education).

The approach Tam advocates is a far more 'child-centred' one, insofar as it envisages children actively learning through cooperative enquiry – 'developing young people's confidence and competence in searching for the basis of ideas'[128] – rather than being taught a prescribed set of received 'facts'. He refers to this as 'enquiry-led education',[129] and it is the antithesis of the more traditional methods and approaches (for example, whole-class teaching, regular testing and a stress on the 'basics' of and within literacy and numeracy). Citizenship education must, for Tam, take place right across the curriculum, by encouraging and developing the capacity for democratic participation through the methods just described.

He is scathing about ideas of citizenship education in which '[y]oung people may be encouraged to do a little voluntary work, find out about the availability of public services of interest to them, donate money to charities, and hold mock political debates which mirror outmoded political systems'[130] – yet this model is what is suggested by the National Curriculum guidance for citizenship education, which is primarily about learning facts about how Britain's democracy and economy function and in which 'developing skills of enquiry and communication' is understood as being taught to 'research a[n] … issue, problem or event by analysing information from different sources, including ICT-based sources'.[131] Tam calls this 'a superficial form of introduction to citizenship' which is a 'safe substitute' preferred by educators who fear being tagged authoritarian if they try to develop 'the "right kind" of citizens'.[132] Although Tam does not make the point here, such a model also serves as a safe substitute for a form of citizenship education, such as he advocates, which calls upon citizens to question the way things are done and the bases of all kinds of claims made by those in authority.

This model of citizenship education is inadequate, in Tam's eyes, on a number of counts. In order to have any conception of democratic citizenship, young people 'need to know not only that it is important to help those less fortunate than oneself' – something which itself is not universally accepted – 'but also that there are issues concerning power structures which must be addressed if that help is to be really effective in the long run'.[133] This idea also runs directly counter to the doctrine that people are responsible for their own position and situation. Returning to the conventional model of citizenship education, Tam notes that while debating skills are useful, what is really needed is the ability to question, as well as to defend, one's beliefs. Tam's vision of citizenship education, then, is one which pervades the entire curriculum, puts the focus on children and young people discovering and deciding for themselves, and encourages questioning of the existing system as well as working to alleviate problems within it.

Citizenship education became a statutory part of the National Curriculum for secondary schools in 2002. While it is currently not statutory in primary schools, guidelines for teaching it have been drawn up. The guidelines, both statutory and non-statutory, are based upon the

Citizenship Order 2000, which in turn was based upon the report of the Advisory Group on Citizenship, chaired by Professor Bernard Crick[134] – a former politics tutor to David Blunkett. The Advisory Group interpreted their remit, 'To provide advice on effective education for citizenship in schools – to include the nature and practices of participation in democracy; the duties, responsibilities and rights of individuals as citizens; and the value to individuals and society of community activity'[135] to encompass a broad conception of citizenship, covering 'social and moral responsibility, community involvement and political literacy'.[136]

These aims are reproduced in the DfEE document *Citizenship Education*, but have not found their way into the curriculum guidance. Other recommendations in the Advisory Group's report did not even get as far as *Citizenship Education*; for example, the idea that 'education must also help future citizens distinguish between law and justice'[137] and the aspiration that school pupils should be able to participate as 'active, informed, *critical* and responsible citizens'.[138] Responsibility is also given a wider meaning in the Report, where it is understood as implying '(a) care for others; (b) premeditation and calculation about what effect actions are likely to have on others; and (c) understanding and care for the consequences'[139] in contrast to New Labour's usual understanding of the term as meaning specific, often contractual, duties.

The general tone of the Report, with its stress on pupils' *entitlement* to citizenship education (suggesting that it is for the benefit of the pupils themselves) and its interpretation of what this means, may also be contrasted with that of the New Labour government's first White Paper, *Excellence in Schools*, which says that 'children and young people' need to 'develop the strength of character and attitudes to life and work, such as responsibility, determination, care and generosity, which will enable them to become citizens of a successful democratic society'[140] (for the benefit of society). The emphasis in this latter document is on the economic need for educated citizens.

The content of citizenship education is not prescribed – deliberately, according to the Chair of the Advisory Group, for two reasons: 'it would not be appropriate for ... the government ... to give precise prescriptions on some politically or morally sensitive matters' and 'in the very nature of citizenship (somewhat concerned with enhancing freedom, after all) there must be local discretion'.[141] This means that the provisions of the Order are what Crick calls 'strong, bare bones', intended to be fleshed out with material and approaches from a number of sources and independent organisations promoting citizenship.[142] However, in the National Curriculum guidance, these bare bones begin to look as if they in themselves are considered complete and sufficient citizenship education. The introduction to the subject in the National Curriculum states that 'The programmes of study set out what pupils should be taught, and the attainment target sets out the expected standards of pupils' performance ... the programmes of study set out what pupils should be taught in citizenship and provide the basis for planning schemes of work.'[143]

Rather than stressing how other subjects can contribute to the development of citizenship, as Tam insists they should, the National Curriculum guidance suggests how 'the teaching of citizenship can contribute to learning across the curriculum', including 'promoting key skills' such as 'communication ... application of number ... I[nformation] T[echnology] ... working with others [and] problem solving.'[144] The guidance for older secondary school pupils (Key Stage 4) looks both narrow and prescriptive.[145] Even if it is intended as 'bare bones' onto which teachers can build at their discretion, there is no requirement to do this, and in the curriculum guidance itself (as opposed to in the Report or the Order) not even any suggestion of it. It is possible therefore that citizenship will be taught as these bare bones alone, which relate to specific skills and knowledge, and do not convey anything of the spirit of *Education for Citizenship and the Teaching of Democracy in Schools.*

Thus, although the Report of the Advisory Group on Citizenship favours a conception of citizenship education which has some similarities to Tam's ideal, by the time its proposals have been filtered into statutory guidelines, these have been lost, and citizenship education under New Labour is likely to reflect the narrow view which Tam deplores. The final narrowing of New Labour's attitude to and aims for citizenship education is revealed in their 'selling' of the policy in the 2001 General Election manifesto: '... *so that all young people are aware that the rights they have reflect the duties they owe,* we will introduce citizenship education into the National Curriculum in 2002'[146] – a far cry from the Advisory Group's aspirations, and even further from Tam's communitarian demands.

Tam identifies a number of specific policy implications which arise from his ideal. Classes would have to be smaller, at all age levels, to make possible the discussions required by enquiry-led learning. Teachers would require special training to equip them to facilitate the process, and must be given the necessary support, particularly a sustained increase in pay to 'levels comparable to those of doctors, lawyers and accountants'.[147] Teacher training should be stringent, and based around the idea that '[j]ust as the commitment to save lives is fundamental to the medical profession, teachers need to be trained to devote their careers to the development of young people into citizens who understand how to pursue common values through co-operation'.[148]

A new approach to the curriculum would be required, placing facts in the context of the ways in which knowledge is derived and validated, with less reliance on the 'crude measure' of exams and more on measuring other factors, such as how well the children cooperate and participate with others.[149] Teaching citizenship skills in this way must, Tam claims, be given the highest priority – above the teaching of employment skills: 'Skills to gain paid work, or to provide unpaid service to others in the home or in one's community, should be developed in this wider context, and not treated as an end in itself which squeezes out the other skills of democratic citizenship.'[150]

Commercial sponsorship of schools and universities should be avoided. Although some business funding of research might be justified where business benefits directly, any greater degree of dependence of universities on the commercial sector would 'reduce the development of human understanding to nothing more than items that can be sold for a profit'[151] – arguably the very way that people have come to view their education already, a trend that began before 1997, but has continued to gather momentum under New Labour, who explicitly talk of the 'knowledge economy'. Increased commercialisation of research establishments will in Tam's view destroy the spirit of enquiry and lead ultimately to a pre-enlightenment state in which 'the only alternatives are sceptical ignorance or dogmatic pronouncement by those in powerful positions'.[152]

Although education for citizenship is a significant aspect of New Labour policy, and is absolutely key to Tam's communitarianism, and we have already examined the different understandings and approaches to it, this needs to be set in the wider context of how citizenship more generally is understood. Here the differences between Tam and New Labour become even more apparent, and it appears that Tam's later appointment to the Home Office has done little to alter government attitudes and approaches. The websites of the Civil Renewal Unit and the linked Active Citizenship Centre in 2005 express similar sentiments, in similar terms, to speeches and publications of the mid-1990s.[153]

New Labour's – and particularly Blair's – use of the terms 'citizen' and 'citizenship' suggest two main conceptions of what citizenship is: 'active citizenship', very closely associated with voluntary and community work, and citizenship as inclusion, primarily through participation in the labour market.

Often, the word 'citizen' is used as a synonym for, or interchangeably with, 'person', 'individual' or 'resident'. For example, a law and order policy document from 1995 refers to the local authority's 'responsibility for all citizens in its area'[154] (rather than just for its tenants), while a later document, which incorporates large parts of the earlier one word for word has 'local councils exist to serve the interests of all the residents within their boundaries'[155] whether tenants or not. In other documents, 'citizen' means little more than a resident of Britain. Frequently too the term 'citizen' is used in New Labour rhetoric to designate a status which, according to the distinction made by Bernard Crick, would more properly be called 'subject': 'a subject obeys the laws and a citizen plays a part in making and changing them'.[156]

One conception which is notably absent, however, is an overtly political conception of citizenship in the classical mould. The nearest approximation to such a conception to come out of Blair's mouth occurs in his John Smith memorial lecture in 1996, when he talks of wanting to see a 'fundamental shift in the balance of power between the citizen and the state – a shift away from an overpowering state to a citizens' democracy where people have rights and powers and where they are served by an accountable and responsive government'.[157] Such a reference to rights and powers, not immediately countered by one to duties and responsibilities, as well as the political conception of citizenship, sounds most unBlairlike, and, indeed, in this part of the speech he is quoting the words of John Smith. This anomaly serves above all to highlight a conception of citizenship left behind by New Labour.

Another, rare allusion to a political conception also comes in the form of a quotation, this time from G.D.H. Cole, to the effect that 'a socialist society that is to be true to its egalitarian principles of human brotherhood must rest on the widest possible distribution of power and responsibility, so as to enlist the active participation of as many of its citizens [sic] in the tasks of democratic self government'. However, this isolated paragraph is not picked up on, and Blair continues, using other quotations, to talk about the more familiar rights and duties, and covenants.[158] In the fairly typical New Labour statement (from later in the same speech) that 'there is a covenant between society and each of its citizens within which duty must be set', the term 'citizen' designates a member of a society – rather than of a polity. This is also a common usage in New Labour rhetoric.

Finally, though, what is worth noting is how infrequently the terms are used in New Labour rhetoric, compared to terms such as 'community', 'society' and 'individual'. Their 1997 manifesto uses the term only twice, once fairly insignificantly ('The Tories talk of older citizens as a burden …')[159] and once in the context of an introduction which strongly emphasises rights and responsibilities, to claim that 'a strong society means common values shared by all its citizens'.[160] This might be taken to mean that citizens by definition are those people who share society's values (with those who don't being excluded from citizenship), or the term could be understood more broadly as standing for 'inhabitants' who ought, in the interests of a strong society, to share the same common values. (The significance of values has been discussed above.) This is the only potentially significant mention of citizens or citizenship in the 1997 manifesto.

Most tellingly, there is no reference to the concept in the relatively heavy coverage given in the document to education. Rather than the key role of education being to develop future citizens, as it is for Tam, for New Labour, '[e]ducational reform is our number one priority because it will lay the foundations of the strong economy and fair society we seek'.[161] The claim, quoted above, that citizenship education will be introduced to ensure that 'young people are aware that the rights they have reflect the duties they owe' is one of only three uses of the concept of citizenship in the 2001 manifesto. In the other two examples, the term 'citizen' is again being used to denote 'inhabitant' or possibly 'subject': firstly, in relation to the incorporation of the European Convention on Human Rights, 'for the first time, British citizens can access their rights in British courts',[162] and second, 'We have done much to make Britain a forward-looking democracy that respects its citizens.'[163] The 2005 manifesto is similar. There is again a reference to the fact that British citizens no longer need to go to Strasbourg to bring human rights cases, and a section headed 'Democracy: Power devolved, citizens empowered' which makes no further use of the term.[164]

The conception of citizenship as inclusion through participation in the labour market has been noted by a number of authors.[165] Raymond Plant suggests that New Labour, at least in regard to welfare policy, have adopted 'an obligation-based view of citizenship, [with] particular stress on the idea that work is a major component of citizenship'.[166] The Labour government, he says, 'wants welfare to be replaced by welfare-to-work and status citizenship to be replaced by supply-side or contribution-based citizenship'.[167] Ruth Levitas also draws on welfare policy to conclude that New Labour have adopted a combination of 'social integrationist' and 'moral underclass' discourses of inclusion at the expense of the 'redistributive egalitarian' discourse traditionally associated with social democracy. It is worth noting that such conditional conceptions of citizenship are not new, and nor are they exclusive to New Labour. The claim that 'In a free society the equation that has "rights" on one side must have "responsibilities" on the other ... For more than a quarter of a century public focus has been on the citizen's "rights" and it is now past time to redress the balance' was made in 1988, by a Conservative Secretary of State for Social Security.[168]

In any case, we have already seen how New Labour actually use the terms 'citizen' and 'citizenship' quite casually, sometimes but not invariably denoting a conditional relationship to the state or stressing obligations. The stress on obligation and in particular the obligation to work is more clearly situated in their discourses of social inclusion rather than what they specifically say about citizenship. Having said that, there are some clear examples – albeit a minority of their uses of the term – of New Labour equating citizenship with paid work and paid work in turn with the discharging of responsibilities. One such is Blair's announcement to his party conference that once given the 'chance' to work (in the labour market), single parents, 'no longer the butt of Tory propaganda [...] will be the citizens of New Britain who can earn a wage and look after the children they love'.[169]

Tam addresses the issue of paid employment from a somewhat different perspective. 'Citizens need work', he says, in order 'to convert resources into goods and services' which they themselves seek, to increase autonomy through the generation of income and thus enable people 'to participate in collective deliberations without being dependent on others'[170] and as a direct means of personal fulfilment.[171] This leads Tam to advocate a redistribution of employment opportunities and a recognition of the 'support' provided by other members of the community who are not directly paid for their efforts.[172] In addition, it is not only dependency on the state which undermines autonomy, but insecure employment – by making people fear to offend those on whom they depend and thus curbing their ability to participate in deliberations on equal terms.[173] Whereas Tam sees the problem of unemployment and job insecurity as a structural one, perpetuated by the interest groups who benefit from the free market, New Labour paints unemployment as a matter of individual responsibility, and insecurity as 'flexibility'.

The other key conception of citizenship highlighted by commentators, and more frequently associated with the term by New Labour, is that of 'active citizenship'. As discussed in Chapter 2, this essentially refers to unpaid 'voluntary' and community work, often referred to as 'voluntary activity'. This is one of the three key aspects of citizenship education as set out in *Education for Citizenship and the Teaching of Democracy in Schools*, although Crick makes it plain that it is in no way sufficient in itself – 'Voluntary service ... is a necessary condition of civil society and democracy ... but it is not a sufficient condition for full citizenship in our tradition.'[174] The Report expresses the wish that 'people should think of themselves as active citizens, willing, able and equipped to have an influence in public life'[175] whereas 'active citizenship' as 'voluntary activity' is a vision of citizenship situated firmly in the community rather than the polity; these 'active citizens' are not active in making or changing the law, or in influencing public life, at least beyond very local boundaries. The model of 'active citizenship' as voluntary service is, again, a direct inheritance from the Conservative government whose Commission on Citizenship in 1990 stressed this aspect while sidelining political activity.[176]

This examination of what citizenship, and in particular citizenship education, mean to New Labour have taken us some way from Henry Tam's vision of 'communitarian citizenship [which] requires all members of inclusive communities to develop the understanding and abilities to participate as equals in determining how decisions affecting them are to be made'[177] to a conception of citizenship as obligation and citizenship education as stressing duties. The latter, which characterises the popular perception of New Labour's communitarianism, is very different from the communitarianism of Tam, as well as that of all the other communitarian authors considered.

Part III

The myth of New Labour's communitarianism

Community by contract and the myth of New Labour's communitarianism

Community by contract: Blair's uncommunitarian vision

The idea and rhetoric of community have played a key role in the development of 'New' Labour, and the term has been used in a range of, sometimes contradictory, ways. This has been associated by commentators with a number of communitarian thinkers, the most important of whom have been considered in the preceding chapters. However, where the idea of community is actually translated into policy, or where it is articulated in greater detail, a particular conception emerges; one which is at odds with traditional ideas of community, which flatly contradicts Macmurray's conception and, more surprisingly, is incompatible with Etzioni's position too. While traditional conceptions of community may not go as far as Macmurray does in differentiating community from 'mere society',[1] there is a general core conception of community as embodying voluntary, non-coercive, ends-based relationships in which mutual obligations – if that is not too strong a term – are unstated, unforced and unregulated.

The idea of community presented through New Labour policy and rhetoric is, however, appreciably different from this. Where it is not being used in a very vague and saccharine way (as it frequently is) but actual substance is given to the term, this suggests – and sometimes explicitly states – that Blair and his party view community primarily as a contractual relationship. The term is also frequently used to refer to the nation as a whole and even the government itself. For example, Blair asserts that 'a covenant of opportunities and responsibilities' is a prerequisite of the government 'acting as a community' – here explicitly understood as synonymous with 'spending taxpayers' money on public services or social exclusion'.[2] David Blunkett has also used the term in this way: interviewed about proposed increases in fines for the parents of truants he was referring to the government when he said: 'as the community, a strong community, we have put support measures in place ...'[3] In this way the term 'community' comes to refer not to the people of the nation and their relationship with each other, but their relationship with the state itself, and duties to others within the community or to the community as a whole become duties to the state.

The idea of rights and responsibilities, and of a particular kind of reciprocal relationship between them, is a key marker of New Labour discourse, and this has been instrumental in their characterisation as communitarian. However, the relationship of rights to responsibilities is conceived in New Labour rhetoric as a fundamentally contractual one, and what is more, as a contract between very unequal parties. Duties are from individuals to the state or the government, while 'rights' are portrayed as being in the gift of the state, in contrast to the traditional conception of rights as being absolute and inhering in the individual. This is summed up in Blair's claim that 'a young country gives rights, but demands responsibilities'.[4]

This contractual articulation of rights and responsibilities has become increasingly explicit, and increasingly conditional. 'For every new opportunity we offer, we demand responsibility in return';[5] 'If we invest so as to give an unemployed person the chance of a job, they have a responsibility to take it or lose benefit'[6] (what is given in return for fulfilment of the duty becomes ever less concrete and certain). 'You only take out if you put in. That's the bargain.'[7]

Not only is New Labour's view of community a very contractual one, but the contract they envisage is a highly unequal one, describing the relationship between the individual – frequently, in the case of benefits claimants, the most vulnerable individuals – and the state. It is debatable whether so unequal a relationship could actually even be called a contract – particularly as the involvement of one of the parties – the individual – is not voluntary. Historically, the idea of contract has been used, in political theory, to embody the ideas of equality and consent. 'Social contract' theories can thus reconcile individual freedom with submission to government through the mechanism of a voluntary agreement between free individuals. Used in this way, the contract denotes fairness and this, coupled with its nominally voluntary nature, gives it its binding force. On an everyday level, we are all used to the language of contracts, agreements and deals, which we enter into willingly for mutual benefit, often following a period of bargaining. But New Labour's contract is between two parties – the individual and the state – with very unequal bargaining power. The state has all the power and the citizen-as-claimant none at all when it comes to setting the terms of the welfare contract. All the writers considered in this book are clear that community can not be based upon a contract. New Labour policy does not even represent a contract as generally understood, let alone one which could be compatible with community relationships.

The myth of New Labour's communitarianism

'New' Labour 'officially' came into being on 4 October 1994, when Tony Blair, who had been leader of the party for three months, ended his address to the annual conference with the slogan 'New Labour, New Britain'. This rebranding was primarily about shaking off the associations of 'old' Labour and the image which was widely perceived to have made the party unelectable since 1979. Despite a modernisation process begun in the 1980s it was only now, under Blair, that the image really began to change.

If the product was new and, implicitly, improved, it must somehow differ significantly from 'old' Labour. 'Old' Labour stood – retrospectively, at least – for public ownership, powerful trade unions, high taxes and a bloated public sector (but also after 1979, public sector cuts and the ensuing 'Winter of Discontent'). It also came to be identified by New Labour with things it had never approved of: 'anything goes' social liberalism; unconditional welfare benefits. 'Old' Labour, as a coherent idea, was a creation of the modernisers; enabling them to define themselves in opposition to it by encapsulating all that they were not.

But what was the new ingredient in New Labour? Many were suggested, in terms of ideology, philosophy and political influence; some even suggested that there was nothing new. But many commentators, both journalists and academics, settled upon the doctrine of communitarianism as the miracle ingredient in the new improved product.

This conclusion was generally drawn on one of two bases. The first was that leading members of the party had, in the early 1990s, been mixing with, and therefore were probably influenced directly by, known communitarian thinkers; almost exclusively, Amitai Etzioni. Or perhaps they had picked it up along with other lessons learnt from Bill Clinton's campaign team, who in turn had also been associated with Etzioni. Other commentators found (increasing) evidence of communitarianism in New Labour's rhetoric – a prime example being the wording of the new Clause IV to include references to community and to 'the rights we enjoy reflect[ing] the duties we owe' – and in the party's policy. This took the form of either reference to and practical reliance on the idea of community, or of the party's, and in particular Blair's, heavy stress on the importance of duty and its relationship, as one of (contractual) exchange, with rights.

Either way, the idea that New Labour was significantly communitarian in its outlook became widely accepted in both popular and academic accounts of the party's modernisation. However, this meant different things to different observers. For some it was not only indicated by, but also indicative of, a stress on community (but very often taken as synonymous with society rather than as distinct from it); for others it was characterised by a positive stress on duties and corresponding disparagement of rights, with even the most passing reference to the importance of duties taken as evidence of a communitarian turn.

If the nature of the transformative ingredient was hazy, its provenance was less clear still. This is where matters became yet more confusing, and claims became (unintentionally) misleading. While commentators were not necessarily agreed upon what communitarianism consisted in, at least, individually, each had some understanding of what it stood for. What muddied the waters was the coming to public attention of already existing communitarian writers, each of whom, while not necessarily adopting the term themselves to describe their work, set out distinctive communitarian positions. The fact that they were all described as 'communitarian' despite the fact that on many levels they held very different positions and priorities contributed greatly to the lack of clarity which was already settling around the topic. These 'communitarians' ranged from four academic philosophers whose work developed as a response in the 1980s to liberal (particularly Rawlsian) political theory, to an American sociologist, concerned about the moral degeneration of American society and the over-reliance on the exercise of rights which in his view aggravated it, who founded a 'Communitarian Movement'. A Scottish philosopher, occasionally mentioned by Tony Blair, much of whose work, in the 1930s to early 1960s concerned the idea of community, was drawn posthumously into the communitarian fold on the basis of those two factors. Furthermore, almost unnoticed by New Labour and their chroniclers, two other British academics had developed their own explicit versions of communitarianism.

New Labour had been characterised as communitarian on one set of bases; these writers, frequently, on another. But because they were both called 'communitarian', similarities and lines of influence came to be assumed. New Labour became identified with the whole range of a communitarian writer's output on the basis of a slight and not necessarily significant overlap in their views, which, where it existed, was sometimes more apparent than real. The links drawn between New Labour and the works of various communitarian writers were as numerous as they were tenuous, but through their frequent repetition and circulation became mutually reinforcing.

The myth of New Labour's communitarianism arose in part because commentators latched onto certain aspects of New Labour which had parallels with existing communitarianisms, but failed to note how these concepts were understood differently.

That synecdoche led in turn back to confused and incomplete understandings, among journalists at least, of what the communitarian writers really were saying, which became, in the absence of reading their texts, identified more and more with what New Labour were saying, making it look ever more as if there was a closer resemblance. Confused and incomplete understandings of the positions of the communitarian philosophers, Etzioni, and, above all, Macmurray, abounded in the press and some even found their way into academic accounts. In this way a communitarianism was custom made to fit with what New Labour was saying and doing, but still bore the names of designers who had little or nothing to do with its development.

Various attempts were made to classify these communitarian works, ranging from the political/philosophical distinction which has also been employed in this book, to the detailed typography developed by Driver and Martell. In a way though, this only serves to make things more complicated. Once 'types' have been defined, then any potentially communitarian utterance is fitted into one of them, sometimes being taken out of its context to do so, and as communitarianisms are fitted into existing 'types', new directions (or the potentially radical implications of existing works) may go unnoticed. The use of typographies also tends to reinforce the belief that ideas are shared across the communitarian board, rather than seeing each writer's work as a discrete approach to a particular issue.

Rather than try to fit each of the writers considered into a 'form' of communitarianism, the approach here has been to treat each as *sui generis*; they are so different and distinct as to make this the only realistic approach. As well as avoiding the problems outlined above, this provides a further advantage: there are then clearly attributable primary texts available upon which to base research, analysis and comparison.

If New Labour were found to exhibit similarities with any of the communitarianisms considered, then that, and the relevant aspects, could be clearly delineated and pointed to. If, on the other hand, the party did not exhibit significant similarities with any of this very broad range of communitarianisms, it would be reasonable to conclude that – in the absence of a previously unconsidered communitarianism with which there are significant similarities – there are no grounds for calling New Labour communitarian at all.

The first communitarians to be considered, the four political philosophers Alasdair MacIntyre, Michael Sandel, Charles Taylor and Michael
Walzer, were on the whole working at a very different level from the political communitarians considered subsequently, making direct comparisons between their work and New Labour difficult. This did not, however,
stop some commentators suggesting that their work had been at least
partly responsible for the party's policy changes. Where a communitarian
philosopher did refer directly to issues of policy, as Taylor and Walzer
did, these tended to oppose the positions that New Labour adopted, on
issues like welfare and privatisation, meritocracy and mobility. The practical and political implications of their work, where this could be directly
related to New Labour again tended to run counter to the party's stance.

More often than not these four philosophers were casually treated by
commentators as if they constituted a homogeneous group. In fact, there
are many differences between their positions, both in terms of the level of
abstraction at which they operate, and their diagnosis of and prescriptions (where such are made) for the perceived ills of modern society. One
thing their respective communitarianisms do prove to have in common is
a lack of resemblance to New Labour's.

MacIntyre's main concern is the loss of traditional morality; a loss
which goes back to the Enlightenment and is characterised by liberalism
and modernity, both of which, in the broad sense MacIntyre laments,
New Labour embraces. For MacIntyre, citizenship and the role of the
state is about discovering and promoting what is good for humans *as
such*; for New Labour it is about promoting specific, essentially practical
capacities (such as employability) for the good of the nation. People's
fulfilment as humans is left, in line with post-Enlightenment liberalism,
to the private sphere and the realm of individual choice. Although there
is a superficial similarity between MacIntyre and New Labour in that
both stress the importance of tradition, closer examination shows that
the term is understood very differently by them. For Blair, traditions may
be selected or rejected; maintained or left to wither, while for MacIntyre
the defining feature and point of a tradition is its apparent inevitability
and inescapability.

Michael Sandel, like Michael Walzer, while rejecting significant aspects of Rawls's liberalism as set out in *A Theory of Justice*, shares Rawls's
own rejection of the idea of meritocracy as a basis for the distribution of
goods. Tony Blair, on the other hand, endorses meritocracy. Where Sandel
criticises Rawls's individualism for positing an incoherent idea of a person, Blair erroneously holds that Rawls advocates selfish individualism in
social arrangements. While both Blair and Sandel are critical of Rawls,

their objections are entirely different.

As New Labour has different ideas from Sandel of what individualism means, so their idea of what community is differs from Charles Taylor's, again leading to superficial similarities, artificial comparisons and confusion. For Taylor, community is not a local network or web of interdependent people, but a stock of history, culture and language. The maintenance of strong and stable communities of this kind, particularly at the all important national political level, is undermined by policies which endorse meritocracy and encourage social and geographical mobility and short-term commitment, as New Labour policies arguably do. Furthermore, while citizenship is a central concept for both Taylor and New Labour, their respective understandings of the concept conflict; Taylor's conception reflects the classical ideal of citizenship as public participation, as opposed to what he calls 'ordinary life': the life of work and family. For New Labour, on the other hand, it is precisely with these aspects of 'ordinary life' that citizenship is most closely identified.

For Michael Walzer, inequality and injustice arise when goods are not distributed according to the criteria considered appropriate to their particular spheres; what criteria are considered appropriate is established through the shared understandings of particular societies. By not distributing goods in accordance with the shared understandings of society, for example, by allowing prisons to be run for profit, or by allowing money to give access to better education or healthcare (whether directly or indirectly), New Labour is violating the shared understandings of British society – at least, so John Gray argues – and thus is not communitarian in terms of Walzer's 'radical particularism'.

Daniel Bell attempts to derive a political communitarianism directly from the work of communitarian philosophers. While his work provides by no means the only possible interpretation of those writers' views, neither does it offer sustainable parallels with New Labour, despite some apparent ones. Bell's interpretation of the politics required by communitarianism is a hardline and authoritarian one, and in some ways – for example, the interference of the state in private life, exemplified by limitations on divorce – goes further than the government would want to. Moreover, and more importantly, Bell's communitarianism embraces an essentially collective model, in which people, or rather groups, are rewarded and punished collectively, in an attempt to foster collective identity. New Labour, on the other hand, stress individual responsibility, and, through meritocracy, individual effort and reward. This may be at odds with a stated aim of fostering community identity, but it is certainly the opposite of what Bell's communitarianism advocates.

A large proportion of communitarian philosophy is not directly relevant to policy or amenable to policy comparison. Therefore to suggest,
as a few commentators have done, that their work, as a body, has been an
influence on New Labour, is highly contestable. Not only does their work
coincide with policy at very few points, but communitarian philosophy
is far from being one undifferentiated body of work. Even where
communitarian philosophy does touch upon issues relevant to direct comparison with policy, it offers criticisms rather than endorsement of New
Labour positions, and it is not possible on close examination to discern
anything that might be construed as influence.

The idea that 'political' communitarians, on the other hand, might
have been a significant influence on New Labour, is at first glance more
credible, and was far more widely suggested, particularly with regard to
Amitai Etzioni and the philosopher John Macmurray. While Macmurray
was a philosopher, rather than a political activist, he was acutely keen to
stress the importance of addressing issues of everyday life through his
work; in particular, that of relations between people. He was picked up as
a potential influence on New Labour because Blair himself had expressed
admiration for his work, and as a communitarian influence in particular
because his work stresses the importance of community.

However, as argued in Chapter 4, there are major differences between
Macmurray and New Labour in the understanding of these important
concepts, and a closer reading of Macmurray's work revealed the writer to
be critical rather than supportive of the positions New Labour currently
adopts and the ideas the party espouses. Central among these are the
ideas of community (and society), duty and responsibility, and of interdependence and service to others. While Macmurray understands – and
venerates – community as the highest form of interpersonal relationship,
this is very narrowly defined as a form of relationship which has no end
other than itself; mere pleasure in the other's company and joy in their
existence characterises community. It is thus distinct from society, which
comprises those relationships necessary to achieve common ends and is
characterised by interdependence and shared purpose. For New Labour,
there is no distinction: the latter form of relationship is interchangeably
described as community and society; the former does not appear to have
political importance. For Macmurray interdependence and external ends
undermine and destroy community; for New Labour they characterise it.
While Macmurray spoke very highly of community as a form of interpersonal relationship, his work does not similarly endorse New Labour's
conception of it. Relations between people are undermined still further
on Macmurray's view by the introduction of any kind of contractual

relationship, which is how New Labour has frequently attempted to present even communal relationships. While for New Labour the idea of duty is central to the functioning of community, for Macmurray it is a 'wicked' idea; while service to others is at the heart of New Labour's proposals for restoring community, for Macmurray it degrades people, reducing them to the status of machines, and the dependency so created destroys the possibility of community. And while New Labour view individualism as arising from selfish individuals, Macmurray viewed it as a symptom of insecurity and fear (such as insecure employment and the fear of losing one's job), which would not be an issue if these were addressed. Despite having been frequently cited as an influence on New Labour, Macmurray's work provides trenchant criticism, rather than endorsement, of the party's positions.

Amitai Etzioni, on the other hand, seemed a far more likely candidate as an influence on New Labour. Instrumental in popularising his own ideas of the causes and potential remedies for the ills of modern society – particularly in the US but also adapted to British circumstances and concerns, he addressed and mixed with leading members of all three main British parties in the early 1990s, as well as with influential American and European politicians. His work is generally presented as populist and potentially authoritarian, and on that basis alone seemed to strike a chord with New Labour, whose policies were often similarly perceived, frequently by the same commentators.

What a closer examination showed, however, was that much of Etzioni's work, even his explicitly communitarian output, had been ignored by commentators, and that aspects of what was considered were misinterpreted. Furthermore, uniquely of the communitarians considered in this book, Etzioni had been explicitly critical of New Labour policies (on benefit cuts, for example), as well as implicitly criticising others, including attempts to legislate against anti-social behaviour. Etzioni's work is not entirely consistent, and his views, especially as they relate to New Labour, develop through his communitarian output from 1993–2000. But his most recent work, and that most explicitly related to New Labour and to British policy, was critical of and suggested alternatives to New Labour's approach. Even his earlier work had been read selectively by commentators (the most part of *The Spirit of Community*, Etzioni's definitive communitarian statement, is ignored). Etzioni was at odds, either implicitly or explicitly, with New Labour on a range of issues, including those positions adopted by the party which are widely assumed most directly to reflect his views: the relationship of duties to rights (while Etzioni thinks there are too many rights, at least in the US, he is adamant that any right that does exist must be unconditional, whereas for New Labour the granting of rights is dependent upon the performance of duties. Furthermore, for Etzioni duties should not be given priority over rights, whereas for New Labour they explicitly are) and curbing anti-social behaviour by legislation (for Etzioni while this may in the end be necessary, it represents the failure of communitarianism, which would control such behaviour through informal sanctions, rather than its realisation). He also criticised New Labour welfare policy for being too concerned with fraud, and criticised the implementation of cuts in lone-parent benefit and the proposal to sanction the benefits of people who failed to abide by the terms of community sentences. As well as making these specific points, Etzioni criticised New Labour generally for being insufficiently communitarian; for seeking a 'Third Way' between the private and public spheres while neglecting community, which he saw as the third leg which needs lengthening to bring the three-legged stool of society into balance, and in his most explicitly relevant work he actually criticised New Labour, from a communitarian perspective, for being potentially authoritarian – a position often associated with Etzioni himself.

Furthermore, Etzioni was implicitly critical of New Labour in his criticism of the drive to get parents into the labour market through the provision of childcare (central to New Labour's social inclusion strategy) and the culture of working long hours, of a political funding structure that involves large private or business donations to election campaigns funding, of the contractualisation of mutual support in the community and of the insufficient control by governments of the free market forces which Etzioni viewed as threatening communities.

While there were similarities between Etzioni's language and that of New Labour, these, as Chapter 5 showed, did not reflect the degree of underlying agreement proposed by many commentators. Some suggested that New Labour have deliberately adopted the language to facilitate a move away from social democratic positions. This may well be the case. Nonetheless, when the best known proponent of political communitarianism explicitly criticises New Labour for being insufficiently communitarian, it is worth taking notice.

But if New Labour was not communitarian in the way the term is understood by those who were cited as communitarian influences on the party, perhaps it was nonetheless communitarian in some other, previously unconsidered way (leaving aside those communitarianisms, outlined earlier, which were explicitly fashioned to fit New Labour). Perhaps insights could be gained by looking at the work of communitarians who not only recognised themselves as such, but were concerned specifically with contemporary Britain. Two such writers are Jonathan Boswell and Henry Tam.

Boswell's communitarianism is characterised by the belief that the ideal of community must be given priority over all other aims, in particular over the aim of economic growth and competitiveness which currently dominates it. Community must, in terms of Boswell's 'democratic communitarianism', be considered as an end in itself, not as a means to other ends as it is for New Labour. It is characterised by spontaneous fraternity and participation; participation which may be neither commandeered nor contractual. There are some steps, Boswell suggests, that governments can take to enable community to develop. These involve radical changes to economic policy and industrial relations, reflecting a European rather than Anglo-Saxon model; such reforms have been firmly rejected by New Labour as unworkable and undesirable. Boswell believes that economies can, at least to an extent, be controlled or managed by governments; New Labour subscribes to a globalisation thesis in which markets and economies are forces beyond anyone's control. Like Macmurray, Boswell holds that interdependence is inimical to rather than constitutive of community; it will in his view lead ultimately to conflict and exploitation rather than the desired cooperation. A lack of security and continuity in both the workplace and the wider economy is also, in Boswell's view, a hindrance to the development of community. This is not a problem which New Labour recognises. For Boswell, 'society' cannot be separated from the economy, hence any attempt to encourage the development of community values in the social sphere but not in the economic – arguably exactly what New Labour sets out to do – is doomed to failure.

Boswell's communitarianism is clearly, ultimately, too demanding for New Labour or any other British government to take on. Anything more than a very limited approximation of community in the economic sphere is not possible under capitalism. However, other European countries have done more to achieve what is possible than Britain under New Labour which has explicitly rejected their approach in favour of a more free-market, American model. New Labour policies do not act on the structural factors that Boswell highlights because they simply do not recognise them as problems. Boswell's democratic communitarianism is in fact almost as far removed from the realm of everyday politics as Alasdair MacIntyre's. Nonetheless, it is significant that this is a form of communitarianism not even considered by New Labour or commentators, and the requirement that communitarianism must involve raising the value of community above all others, including liberty and equality as well as economic success, sheds a further, different, light on the idea that New Labour are communitarian.

Henry Tam, finally, writing more recently than Boswell about British politics and society, offers a further, different, vision of communitarianism; one which again differs greatly from that displayed by New Labour. Tam focuses on education, citizenship and the economisation of social life. This last – the imposition of an economic paradigm on social and communal relations – he sees as typifying the actions of an interest group who seek to defend the free market (from the potential rise of community as an opposing interest group) by fostering competitive individualism. He is therefore very scathing of ideas like New Labour's endorsement of business practices in the public and community sectors. Furthermore, his concept of citizenship differs vastly from that promoted by New Labour, and his views on education and its purposes, in general as well as with specific reference to citizenship, are markedly at odds with New Labour's. Finally, the very concept of values is employed in a completely different way (as well as having a different meaning) by New Labour from Tam (as well as from some of the other communitarians considered, and the same also applies to other concepts).

Overall then, a detailed analysis and comparison of party policy and rhetoric and communitarian texts, shows that New Labour's communitarianism, widely accepted and promoted by both academic and popular commentators from the early 1990s onwards, was a myth, which arose from a combination of the perceived need to attribute some philosophy or ideology to the party's new direction, and a process by which poorly or partially understood ideas, by repetition and (re)circulation, develop their own credibility, almost independent of the evidence – often no more than a passing resemblance of language – upon which they were originally based. Communitarianism, both political and philosophical, is an important factor in understanding and analysing New Labour's approaches. However, what such an analysis ultimately demonstrates is not that New Labour were communitarian, but that they were not.

Notes

Introduction

1   In what follows, I use the term 'rhetoric' to refer to politicians' speeches, articles published in their names, pamphlets etc; 'policy' refers to government White and Green papers and, pre-1997, Labour Party policy documents.

2   *Hansard*, House of Commons Debates for 27.02.2002, column 698. The backbencher in question was Tony Walter, MP for Hemel Hempstead.

3   This tendency is examined in detail in Chapter 6.

4   But see Sarah Hale, Will Leggett and Luke Martell, *The Third Way: Criticisms, Futures, Alternatives*, Manchester University Press, 2004.

5   See, for example, Gordon Hughes and Adrian Little, 'The Contradictions of New Labour's Communitarianism', *Imprints* 4:1, 1999, pp. 42, 45; Ruth Lister, 'Political Struggle and Social Justice: New Labour and Citizenship', Interview in *Imprints* 4:1, 1999, p. 11. (Lister refers to New Labour's 'espousal' of these views); Brian Lund, '"Ask Not What Your Community Can Do For You": Obligations, New Labour and Welfare Reform', *Critical Social Policy* 19:4, 1999, pp. 449–50.

6   See, for example, Ruth Lister, 'Vocabularies of Citizenship and Gender: the UK', *Critical Social Policy* 18:3, 1998, p. 313.

7   See Joan Smith, 'The Ideology of "Family and Community": New Labour Abandons the Welfare State', in Leo Panitch (ed.), *The Socialist Register 1997*, London, Merlin Press, 1997, p. 180; Lister, 'Vocabularies of Citizenship and Gender', p. 315.

8   See, for example, Peter Dwyer, 'Conditional Citizens? Welfare Rights and Responsibilities in the Late 1990s', *Critical Social Policy* 18:4, 1998, p. 497.

9   See, for example, Stephen Driver and Luke Martell, *New Labour: Politics After Thatcherism*, Cambridge, Polity Press, 1998.

10 See, for example, Lister 'Vocabularies of Citizenship and Gender', pp. 315, 317; Dwyer, 'Conditional Citizens', pp. 499–501.

11 See, for example, Lister, 'Political Struggle and Social Justice', p. 12; Lister 'Vocabularies of Citizenship and Gender', p. 312.

12 See, for example, Hughes and Little, 'The Contradictions of New Labour's Communitarianism', pp. 52–4; also see Ruth Levitas, *The Inclusive Society? Social Exclusion and New Labour*, Basingstoke, Macmillan, 1998.

13 See, for example, Lund '"Ask Not What Your Community Can Do For You"'.

14 See, for example, Lister, 'Vocabularies of citizenship and gender', p. 313; Lund, '"Ask Not What Your Community Can Do For You"', p. 450.

15 See, for example, Lund, '"Ask Not What Your Community Can Do For You"', p. 459 (this shows that some commentators identify a range of influences and/or parallels; it is

not the case that each commentator claims to identify only one influence); Bernard Crick 'Still Missing: A Public Philosophy', *Political Quarterly* 68:4, 1997, p. 345.

16 Again, see Lund, '"Ask Not What Your Community Can Do For You"', p. 450; Crick, 'Still Missing', p. 346.

17 See, for example, Michael Cockerell, 'The secret world of Tony Blair' *New Statesman* 14.2.2000, p. 14. Cockerell refers to Peter Thomson, the Australian Christian widely credited with introducing Blair to Macmurray's work. Further examples are given in Chapter 4.

18 Although as Stephen Driver and Luke Martell note in 'Left, Right and the Third Way', *Policy and Politics* 28:2, 2000, p. 158, there are also key departures in policy from Giddens' recommendations; the very fact that it is felt necessary to point this out indicates that Giddens is (elsewhere) widely considered to be an influence on New Labour. In the particular case of the Third Way (although not specifically Giddens' version) there is a likelihood that New Labour has influenced the theory, rather than the reverse, in an extreme example of theory being used as post hoc justification.

19 See, for example, Hughes and Little, 'The Contradictions of New Labour's Communitarianism', p. 44.

20 See, for example, Crick, 'Still Missing', p. 351 n.2.

21 Elizabeth Frazer, *The Problems of Communitarian Politics: Unity and Conflict*, Oxford, Oxford University Press, 1999, Chapter 1.

22 Stephen Driver and Luke Martell, 'New Labour's Communitarianisms', *Critical Social Policy* 17:3, 1997.

23 Even the term 'community' is given a range of different meanings by different communitarian writers, and furthermore some positions are defined as communitarian – for example, on the basis of a focus on 'rights and duties' – without any reference to 'community' at all.

24 Claims about New Labour's communitarianism do not always entail that the party has been influenced by communitarian thinkers (although this is frequently assumed); some only suggest that the party has ultimately arrived at a communitarian position, without this necessarily being the result of direct influence. It is this bigger question – of whether the party is communitarian for any reason – which is the subject of this book.

Chapter 1

1 Seumas Milne, 'Everybody's talking about', *Guardian* 07.10.1994, p. 5.

2 Stephen Castle and David Usborne, 'Blair's third way leads to New York', *Independent* 19.09.1998, p. 4.

3 Elizabeth Frazer, in *The Problems of Communitarian Politics: Unity and Conflict*, Oxford, Oxford University Press, 1999, p. 30, mentions Owen as the proponent of one of a number of 'experiments in collective living' in a socialist tradition which has been a 'source for political communitarianism'. Emphasis added.

4 Leading article, 'Blair's Utopian vision is not enough', *Independent* 25.05.1994, p. 15.

5 Mary Riddell, 'New election, new gurus', *Observer* 01.04.2001. The new guru referred to here is Robert Putnam, also seen as a communitarian.

6 This is a characterisation of his creed which Etzioni would reject.

7 Leading article, 'Nostalgia: not yet a thing of the past', *Independent* 05.08.1995, p. 14.

8 Leading article, 'An illusion of happy families', *Independent* 27.09.1994, p. 17.

9 Anthony Barnett, 'Blair's fear of the fear factor', *Independent* 20.02.1997, p. 16.

10   'Park life', *Economist* 06.12.1997.

11   Anne McElvoy, 'Not quite so chic to be Labour', *The Times* 08.04.1995, p. 18.

12   Tony Blair, 'Is Labour the true heir to Thatcher?', *The Times* 17.07.1995, p.17.

13   Andrew Marr, 'Why Blair must give power to the people', *Independent* 18.07.1995, p. 15.

14   Leading article, 'A trimmer round the edges', *Sunday Times* 23.07.1995, p. 3.

15   'Love fest: Blair's American visit', *Economist*, 13.04.1996.

16   'The spiel of the covenant', *Economist* 05.10.1996.

17   Nicholas Deakin, 'Voluntary action: Transparent role for the chameleon', *Guardian* 21.06.1995, p. 36.

18   Leading article, 'Anxious, angry and ugly: What Paulsgrove's passion is telling us', *Guardian* 11.08.2000, p. 19.

19   Leading article, 'Mr. Blair gets the bird', *Guardian* 08.06.2000, p. 23.

20   Patrick Wintour, 'Labour looks abroad for ideas', *Guardian* 06.10.1995, p. 6.

21   'Labour's ladder of opportunity: Tony Blair has the chance to redefine Labour as the party of meritocracy', *Economist* 08.10.1994.

22   Ibid.

23   Ibid.

24   John Gray, 'Divide and rule', *Guardian* 02.10.1995, p. 11. Emphasis added.

25   Michael Freeden, 'Community begins at home', letters, *Independent* 12.02.1995, p. 20.

26   John Gray, 'A radical departure', *Guardian* 27.06.1995, p. 15.

27   Patrick Wintour, 'Major to appeal for volunteers', *Guardian* 26.05.1995, p. 6.

28   'The ties that bind', *Economist* 08.10.1994.

29   Alan Duncan and Dominic Hobson, 'Tired old new Labour', *The Times* 01.06.1995, p. 20.

30   Charlotte Raven, 'Tank boys', *Observer* 30.07.1995, p. 18.

31   Diana Coyle, 'Secret lives of the great and the good', *Independent* 01.09.1995, p. 15.

32   'Communitarian conceits: Amitai Etzioni preaches up a storm, but to what effect?', *Economist*, 18.03.1995.

33   Barry Hugill, 'Why can't we live together?', *Observer* 12.11.1995, p. 18.

34   Nick Cohen, 'The -ism now arriving …', *Independent on Sunday* 05.02.1995, p. 6.

35   Nick Cohen, 'Asia crisis fails to cure Blair's Fukuyama fever', *Observer* 18.01.98, p. 26.

36   Sarah Baxter, 'Blair's backroom boffins make strange bedfellows', *Sunday Times* 08.01.1995, p. 8.

37   'University of Downing Street: The new establishment: Tony Blair's favourite academics', *Economist* 04.09.1999.

38   Anthony Giddens, 'Anomie of the people', *Guardian* 31.07.1997, p. 11.

39   Melanie Phillips, 'The race to wake sleeping duty', *Observer* 02.04.1995, p. 25.

40   Ibid.

41   Geoff Mulgan, 'Beyond the lure of off-the-shelf ethics', *Independent* 30.01.1995, p. 13.

42   Ibid. This is not necessarily a more radical vision, as it is quite compatible with MacIntyre's anti-enlightenment position, but it is potentially so in its attitude to the free market.

43   Ibid.

44   Bill Jordan, 'New Labour, New Community?', *Imprints* 3:2, 1999, p. 113.

45   David Gilbert, 'Don't Look Back?', *Renewal* 4:3, July 1996, p. 26.

46   Gordon Hughes, 'Communitarianism and Law and Order', *Critical Social Policy* 49, 1996, p. 18.

47   Ibid., p. 21.

48   Michael Harris, 'New Labour: Government and Opposition', *Political Quarterly* 70:1, 1999, p. 55.

49   Gillian Peele, 'Political Parties', in Patrick Dunleavy, Andrew Gamble, Ian Holliday and

Gillian Peele, *Developments in British Politics 5*, Basingstoke, Macmillan, 1997, p. 92.

50   John Benyon and Adam Edwards, 'Crime and Public Order' in Dunleavy *et al.*, *Developments in British Politics 5*, p. 335.

51   John Dearlove and Peter Saunders, *Introduction to British Politics*, 3rd edition, Cambridge, Polity Press, 2000, p. 249.

52   Ibid., p. 422.

53   Ibid., p. 611.

54   Ibid., p. 431.

55   Ibid., p. 623.

56   Frazer, *The Problems of Communitarian Politics*, p. 12.

57   Ibid., p. 11. This conception of community as the people who inhabit a particular place is most clearly found in law and order policy documents.

58   Although Etzioni has written for *Tikkun*, (e.g. 'Balancing individual rights and the common good' in *Tikkun Magazine* Jan/Feb 1997), Frazer is right to note that its position is a 'rival' one to his, and it has published articles critical of his position.

59   Frazer, *The Problems of Communitarian Politics*, pp. 33–4.

60   Ibid., pp. 34, 35, 37, 41. Also, on p. 12, speeches by Blair and Brown are used to illustrate communitarian ideas more generally.

61   Ibid., p. 12 n.8. As well as the source cited by Frazer, this claim is also made (by the publishers, but presumably with Etzioni's endorsement) on the back cover of the British paperback edition of *The Spirit of Community*.

62   Ibid., p. 25.

63   Ibid., pp. 34, 38.

64   Ibid., p. 41.

65   See Blair's speech to the Women's Institute for good examples of this kind of rhetoric.

66   Frazer, *The Problems of Communitarian Politics*, p. 41.

67   One example of many can be found in *Giving Time, Getting Involved*, the report of the Working Group on the Active Community, London, Cabinet Office, 1999.

68   Frazer, *The Problems of Communitarian Politics*, p. 42.

69   See for example John Macmurray, *Reason and Emotion* [1935], London, Faber and Faber, 1962, pp. 97–8.

70   Tony Blair, *Socialism*, Fabian Pamphlet 565, London, Fabian Society, 1994.

71   Luke Martell, for example, is clear that the presence of communitarianism *can* be deduced from such evidence.

72   Stephen Driver and Luke Martell, 'New Labour's Communitarianisms', *Critical Social Policy* 17:3, 1997, p. 27.

73   Ibid.

74   Ibid., p. 28.

75   Ibid., p. 29.

76   Ibid., p. 28.

77   Ibid., p. 34.

78   Ibid.

79   Ibid., p. 36.

80   Ibid., p. 34.

81   Ibid., p. 35.

82   See for example these IEA Choice in Welfare Pamphlets: David G. Green, *Community Without Politics: A Market Approach to Welfare Reform* (no. 27, 1996) and *Reinventing Civil Society: The Rediscovery of Welfare Without Politics* (no. 17, 1993), and Robert Whelan, *The Corrosion of Charity: From Moral Renewal to Contract Culture* (no. 29,

1996).

83   Driver and Martell, 'New Labour's Communitarianisms', p. 37.

84   Ibid.

85   This idea is developed by Ruth Levitas in *The Inclusive Society? Social Exclusion and New Labour*, Basingstoke, Macmillan, 1998.

86   An example from Tony Blair, 'Values and the Power of Community', speech to the Global Ethics Foundation, Tübingen University, 30.06.2000.

87   Driver and Martell, 'New Labour's Communitarianisms' p. 37.

88   Ibid., p. 30.

89   Blair, 'Values and the Power of Community' speech.

90   Driver and Martell, 'New Labour's Communitarianisms', p. 38.

91   Ibid., p. 31.

92   Ibid., p. 40.

93   Ibid.

94   Ibid.

95   Ibid., p. 32.

96   Ibid.

97   Ibid.

98   Ibid., p. 32.

99   Ibid. Note the imbalance which has crept in here. Rights in return for duties has at least a ring of fairness about it; it is 1:1. Obligations, responsibilities, rights and duties is 3:1.

100 Ibid., p. 28.

101 Stephen Driver and Luke Martell, *New Labour: Politics After Thatcherism*, Cambridge, Polity Press, 1998, p. 118.

102 Ibid., pp. 29, 181.

Chapter 2

1   Tony Blair, 'Values and the Power of Community', speech to the Global Ethics Foundation, Tübingen University, 30.06.2000.

2   John Lloyd, 'Profile: Amitai Etzioni', *New Statesman* 20.06.1997, p. 28.

3   Amitai Etzioni, *The Spirit of Community: Rights, Responsibilities and the Communitarian Agenda* [1993], London, Fontana, 1995, p. ix.

4   See for example, Amitai Etzioni, *The Third Way to a Good Society*, London, Demos, 2000, p. 29, in which he says: 'It is a grave moral error to argue that "there are no rights without responsibilities" or vice versa.'

5   Margaret Thatcher, interviewed in *Woman's Own* 31.10.87. This part of the interview is much less well known than the earlier assertion that 'There is no such thing as "society" …', which illustrates the dangers of quoting out of context.

6   This 'mission statement' can be found in all Demos' publications.

7   Tony Blair, Speech to the Women's Institutes' Triennial General Meeting, 07.06.2000.

8   Emma Heron and Peter Dwyer, 'Doing the Right Thing: Labour's Attempt to Forge a New Welfare Deal Between the Individual and the State', *Social Policy and Administration* 33:1, March 1999, p. 93.

9   Ibid.

10   Ibid., p. 91.

11   Will Hutton, *The State We're In* [1995], London, Vintage, 1996.

12   Alan Deacon, 'The Green Paper on Welfare Reform: A Case for Enlightened Self-

interest?', *Political Quarterly* 69:3, 1998, pp. 306–11.

13 Department of Social Security, *New Ambitions for our Country: A New Contract for Welfare*, CM3805, 1998.

14 Heron and Dwyer, 'Doing the Right Thing', p. 101, n.1.

15 Ibid., p. 94.

16 Ibid., p. 93.

17 A more detailed examination of Etzioni's position is undertaken in Chapter 5.

18 Heron and Dwyer, 'Doing the Right Thing', p. 95.

19 Deacon, 'The Green Paper on Welfare Reform', p. 306.

20 Ibid.

21 Ibid.

22 Ibid. Deacon cites speeches given in Amsterdam in January 1997 and in South Africa in October 1996.

23 Ibid., p. 307.

24 Charles Murray, *Losing Ground*, New York, BasicBooks, 1984.

25 David Ellwood, *Poor Support*, New York, BasicBooks, 1988.

26 See, for example, Charles Murray, *Underclass: The Crisis Deepens*, London, Institute of Economic Affairs, 1994, and Ruth Lister (ed.), *Charles Murray and the Underclass: The Developing Debate*, London, IEA, 1996.

27 Deacon notes that the new policy 'is remarkable for having eliminated the unemployed … those who are unable to work because no work is available'. He takes this to imply an optimism about economic growth. But in the free market/morally authoritarian dependency culture doctrine, it is welfare which creates unemployment by providing a disincentive to taking low paid work. The logical outcome of pursuing the 'obligation to work' line is that people will be forced to price themselves into low paid work because welfare will no longer provide an alternative.

28 *New Deal for a New Britain: Labour's Proposals to Tackle Youth and Long-term Unemployment*, London, Labour Party, 1997.

29 DSS, *A New Contract for Welfare*, p. v.

30 Field's approach certainly reflects the 'moral underclass' and 'social integrationist' discourses of inclusion identified by Ruth Levitas, but I would contend that these are not intended by Levitas to be understood as forms or aspects of communitarianism. See Ruth Levitas, *The Inclusive Society? Social Exclusion and New Labour*, Basingstoke, Macmillan, 1998. Although this work mentions communitarianism, it actually offers an alternative interpretation of Labour policy change.

31 Frank Field 'Britain's Underclass: Countering the Growth', in Lister (ed.), *Charles Murray and the Underclass*, p. 57.

32 Ruth Lister, 'To Rio via the Third Way: New Labour's "Welfare" Reform Agenda', paper given to the first ESRC Research Seminar Programme on 'New Labour and the Third Way in Public Services', London, 22.04.1999.

33 Fran Bennett, commentary on Alistair Darling, 'Rebuilding the Welfare State: The Moral Case for Reform' in Gavin Kelly (ed.), *Is New Labour Working?*, Fabian Pamphlet 590, London, Fabian Society, 1999, p. 40.

34 DSS, *A New Contract for Welfare*, p. 69.

35 Ibid., pp. 20, 43.

36 Ibid., *A New Contract for Welfare*, p. v.

37 Ibid. These sentiments, like many others, are repeated a number of times, in slightly different forms, throughout the Green Paper. I do not give a reference for every occurrence.

38   Meaning, in this context, not dependent upon the state. The government has no prob-
     lem with, for example, women being dependent on men, or elderly people dependent
     upon their grown-up children. The use of the concept of independence is thus a little
     disingenuous, because the document does not anywhere explicitly recognise this selec-
     tivity.

39   For example Lister, 'To Rio via the Third Way' .

40   Raymond Plant, 'So you want to be a citizen?', *New Statesman* 06.02.1998, pp. 30–2.

41   DSS, *A New Contract for Welfare*, p. 64.

42   Ibid., p. 1.

43   John Pilger 'Mr. Blair's Dubious Moral Purpose', *New Statesman* 25.10.1996, p. 17.

44   DSS, *A New Contract for Welfare*, p. 6. Emphasis and punctuation as original.

45   Ibid., p. 1.

46   Ibid., p. 79.

47   Ibid., p. 81.

48   Ibid., p. 6. On p. 67 the same claim is made, but here it says 'every family *with children*'
     Either this is an inconsistency, or it says something about the government's definition of
     a family.

49   Pilger, 'Mr. Blair's Dubious Moral Purpose', p. 17.

50   DSS, *A New Contract for Welfare*, p. 67.

51   Department for Work and Pensions advertising campaign, 2001/2002.

52   DSS, *A New Contract for Welfare*, p. 3.

53   John Pilger, *Hidden Agendas*, London, Vintage, 1998, p. 84.

54   Alan Deacon, 'The Retreat from State Welfare', in Saul Becker (ed.), *Windows of
     Opportunity: Public Policy and the Poor*, London, Child Poverty Action Group, 1991,
     p. 15.

55   Ibid.

56   Bill Bowring, 'Law and Order in the "New Britain"', in Hall, Massey and Rustin (eds),
     Soundings Special: The Next Ten Years: Key issues for Blair's Britain, London, Soundings/
     Lawrence and Wishart, 1997, p. 105.

57   Ibid., pp. 105–6. (*The Spirit of Community* was published in Britain in 1995 without this
     subtitle, and the date of US publication was actually 1993.)

58   Bowring is not criticising the aims behind community policing, but the way in which it
     has (possibly in unforeseen ways) become a further instrument of social control.

59   Bowring, 'Law and Order', p. 106.

60   Ibid. p. 108. Bowring does not give a reference for the interview in which this claim was
     made, but it appears in the *New Statesman* 20.6.1997.

61   Gordon Hughes, 'Communitarianism and Law and Order', *Critical Social Policy* 49,
     1996.

62   Ibid., p. 18.

63   Ibid., p. 20.

64   Ibid.

65   Ibid., p. 23.

66   These are: *A Quiet Life: Tough Action on Criminal Neighbours*, London, Labour Party,
     1995; *Safer Communities, Safer Britain: Labour's Proposals for Tough Action on Crime*,
     London, Labour Party, 1995; *Protecting Our Communities: Labour's Plans for Tackling
     Criminal, Anti-Social Behaviour in Neighbourhoods*, London, Labour Party, 1996, and
     Tackling the Causes of Crime: Labour's Proposals to Prevent Crime and Criminality, London,
     Labour Party, 1996. This last bears the names of Jack Straw and Alun Michael.

67   *Tackling the Causes of Crime*, Labour Party, p. 6.

68 Ibid.
69 Ibid., p. 6.
70 Amitai Etzioni, *The Parenting Deficit*, London, Demos, 1993.
71 *Tackling the Causes of Crime*, Labour Party, p. 9. This quotation from a 1996 Home Office Research Study, *Young People and Crime*, is given in italics which I have abandoned, and added my own emphasis.
72 Ibid., pp. 9–10.
73 This point is explicitly made by Etzioni in *The Spirit of Community* and is considered in greater detail in Chapter 5.
74 Janet Foster, 'Informal Social Control and Community Crime Prevention', *British Journal of Criminology* 35:4, Autumn 1995.
75 *Safer Communities, Safer Britain*, Labour Party, p. 1.
76 Ibid.
77 Kelly (ed.), *Is New Labour Working?* See especially Jack Straw, 'Freedom From Fear: Building a Safer Britain', p. 29, and Alistair Darling, 'Rebuilding the Welfare State: The Moral Case for Reform', p. 35.
78 Not necessarily self-styled as communitarian.

Chapter 3

1 *Hansard* for 27.02.2002, col. 698
2 Roy Hattersley, 'So what is it that Tony believes in?', *Guardian*, 04.03.2002.
3 I use the former term throughout, to distinguish 'communitarian philosophy' from the 'political communitarianism' of Etzioni, Boswell and Tam. A similar distinction is employed by Elizabeth Frazer (*The Problems of Communitarian Philosophy: Unity and Conflict*, Oxford, Oxford University Press, 1999) and Stephen Kautz (*Liberalism and Community*, Ithaca, Cornell University Press, 1995).
4 Anthony Giddens, 'Anomie of the People', *Guardian* 31.07.1997, p.11.
5 Amitai Etzioni, *The Essential Communitarian Reader*, Lanham, Rowman and Littlefield, 1998, p. x.
6 Philip Collins, 'Community, Morality and Fairness', *Renewal* 4:3, July 1996, p. 32.
7 Stephen Driver and Luke Martell, 'New Labour's Communitarianisms', *Critical Social Policy* 17:3, 1997, p. 28.
8 Geoff Mulgan, 'Beyond the lure of off-the-shelf ethics', *Independent* 30.01.1995, p. 13.
9 Melanie Phillips, 'The race to wake sleeping duty', *Observer* 02.04.1995, p. 25.
10 Some commentators do mention communitarian philosophy while acknowledging its distance from politics – an example is Finn Bowring, 'Communitarianism and Morality: in Search of the Subject', *New Left Review* 222, March/April 1997, p. 96.
11 Amitai Etzioni, *The New Golden Rule: Community and Morality in a Democratic Society* [1996], London, Profile Books, 1997, p. 40.
12 Ibid., p. 9. This description underlines the gulf between political and philosophical concepts; in his utter rejection of post-Enlightenment liberalism and all it stands for, MacIntyre can hardly be called moderate, but his work, perhaps because it is so radical and theoretical, does not present any great threat to the political status quo.
13 Ibid., p. 15.
14 Ibid., pp. 26–7.
15 Charles Taylor, 'Atomism', reproduced in Charles Taylor, *Philosophy and the Human Sciences*, Cambridge, Cambridge University Press, 1985.

16   Ibid., p. 219.

17   Ibid., p. 8.

18   There are other works in which Etzioni discusses the work of communitarian philoso-
     phers, for example, in his 'Introduction' to Amitai Etzioni (ed.), *New Communitarian
     Thinking: Persons, Virtues, Institutions and Communities*, Charlottesville, University Press
     of Virginia, 1995, and his article 'A Moderate Communitarian Proposal' in *Political
     Theory* 24:2, May 1996, pp. 155–71, but this is essentially separate from his 'political
     work' such as 'The Responsive Community: A Communitarian Perspective', Etzioni's
     1995 Presidential Address to the American Sociological Association, published in *American
     Sociological Review* 61, February 1996, pp. 1–11, in which he sets out his own
     communitarian vision which stands independently of the philosophers' work. Indeed,
     he explicitly states that this 'leaves behind' the philosophical debates of the 1980s (p. 6).

19   Henry Tam, *Communitarianism: A New Agenda for Politics and Citizenship*, Basingstoke,
     Macmillan, 1998, p. 224.

20   Jonathan Boswell, *Community and the Economy: The Theory of Public Co-operation*,
     London, Routledge, 1990, pp. 51 and 47 respectively.

21   We can see aspects of it, for example, in British Liberal Party's 'pavement politics' of the
     1970s; in community development work going back to the 1950s, and in recurrent
     laments for lost morality, solidarity and so on.

22   Charles Taylor, 'Atomism', in Taylor, *Philosophy and the Human Sciences*.

23   Stephen Mulhall and Adam Swift, *Liberals and Communitarians*, Oxford, Blackwell,
     1992 (2nd edition).

24   Alasdair MacIntyre, 'The Spectre of Communitarianism', *Radical Philosophy 70*, March/
     April 1995, p. 34.

25   Michael Sandel, preface, *Liberalism and the Limits of Justice*, Cambridge, Cambridge
     University Press, 1998 (2nd edition), p. ix.

26   Michael Walzer, 'The Communitarian Critique of Liberalism', *Political Theory* 18:1,
     February 1990, p. 6.

27   Ibid., *passim*.

28   Charles Taylor, 'Cross-Purposes: The Liberal-Communitarian Debate', in Charles Tay-
     lor, *Philosophical Arguments*, Cambridge, MA, Harvard University Press, 1995, pp. 181–
     203.

29   The best introductory text for a fuller account is Mulhall and Swift, *Liberals and
     Communitarians*.

30   Mulhall and Swift explicitly do this.

31   See Will Kymlicka, 'Community', in Robert E. Goodin and Philip Pettit (eds), *Blackwell
     Companion to Contemporary Political Philosophy*, p. 367.

32   John Rawls, *A Theory of Justice*, Oxford, Oxford University Press, 1972, p. 3.

33   Will Kymlicka, 'Community', in Goodin and Pettit (eds), *Blackwell Companion to Con-
     temporary Political Philosophy*, p. 367.

34   Tony Blair, 'The Stakeholder Society', from a speech given in Southwark Cathedral
     29.01.1996, reprinted in Tony Blair, *New Britain: My Vision of a Young Country*, London,
     Fourth Estate, 1996, p. 299 (emphasis added).

35   This distinction is made by David Miller ('Communitarianism: Left, Right and Centre'
     in Dan Avnon and Avner de-Shalit (eds), *Liberalism and its Practice*, London, Routledge,
     1999, p. 172), who suggests that any political theory 'contains two analytically separable
     elements': a 'philosophical anthropology', and a set of 'prescriptive principles'. The
     philosophical anthropology, which may be explicit or implicit but is always present, is a
     'general account of the human person, of the conditions of moral agency, of the nature of

human relationships and so forth', while the prescriptive principles 'specify [...] how social relationships are to be ordered, how the state is to be constituted and so on.' The relationship between the two is one of support rather than entailment, so one kind of anthropology could be associated with a number of different sets of principles (and vice versa).

36   Tony Blair, 'My Kind of Britain', foreword to *New Britain: My Vision of a Young Country*, *New Statesman Special Selection*, London, Fourth Estate, 1996, p. v.

37   Michael Sandel, *Liberalism and the Limits of Justice* [1982], Cambridge, Cambridge University Press, 1998, p.11.

38   Kymlicka, 'Community', in Goodin and Pettit (eds), *Blackwell Companion to Contemporary Political Philosophy*, p. 370.

39   Ibid.

40   Will Kymlicka, *Contemporary Political Philosophy: An Introduction*, Oxford, Clarendon Press, 1990, p. 212.

41   Mulhall and Swift, *Liberals and Communitarians*, p. 160.

42   Kymlicka, 'Community', in Goodin and Pettit (eds), *Blackwell Companion to Contemporary Political Philosophy*, p. 370.

43   Tony Blair, *Let Us Face the Future: The 1945 Anniversary Lecture*, Fabian Pamphlet 571, London, Fabian Society, 1995, p. 1.

44   Labour Party, *New Labour: Leading Britain into the Future*, 1997 General Election manifesto.

45   Michael Sandel, *Democracy's Discontent: America in Search of a Public Philosophy*, Cambridge, MA, Belknap/Harvard University Press, 1996, p. 6.

46   DETR, *Modern Local Government: In Touch with the People*, summary leaflet, 1998.

47   Alasdair MacIntyre, *After Virtue: a Study in Moral Theory* [1981] London, Duckworth, 1985.

48   Alasdair MacIntyre, 'A Philosophical Self-portrait', in Thomas Mautner (ed.), *Penguin Dictionary of Philosophy*, London, Penguin, 1997, p.332.

49   Mulhall and Swift, *Liberals and Communitarians*, p. 72.

50   MacIntyre, *After Virtue*, Chapter 15.

51   MacIntyre has 'continued the project initiated in *After Virtue* ... in *Whose Justice? Which Rationality?* (1988) and in *Three Rival Versions of Moral Enquiry* (1990)' (MacIntyre, *Penguin Dictionary of Philosophy*, p. 332).

52   Mulhall and Swift, *Liberals and Communitarians*, p. 86.

53   Ibid., p. 88.

54   MacIntyre, *After Virtue*, p. 156.

55   See for example, Tony Blair, 'The Stakeholder Society' in Tony Blair, *New Britain: My Vision of a Young Country*, London, Fourth Estate, 1996, p. 298: 'To recover national purpose we need to start thinking and acting as one nation, one community again.'

56   Tony Blair, *The Third Way: New Politics for the New Century*, Fabian Pamphlet 588, London, Fabian Society, 1998.

57   MacIntyre, *After Virtue*, p. 263.

58   Tony Blair, speech to the Women's Institutes' Triennial Meeting, 07.06.2000.

59   Ibid.

60   Charles Taylor, *Sources of the Self: The Making of Modern Identity*, Cambridge, Cambridge University Press, 1989, p. x.

61   Taylor, *Sources of the Self*, p. 4.

62   Ibid., p. 3.

63   Ibid., p. 19.

64   Ibid., p. 21.

65   Ibid., p. 27.
66   Ibid., p. 213.
67   Tony Blair, speech to the 1995 Labour Party Annual Conference, 03.10.1995.
68   Taylor, *Sources of the Self,* p. 395.
69   Ibid., p. 502.
70   Tony Blair, Speech to the Women's Institute', 07.06.2000. This is just one of many possible examples.
71   Taylor, *Sources of the Self,* p. 508.
72   Ibid., p. 505.
73   Michael Walzer, *Spheres of Justice: A Defense of Pluralism and Equality,* Oxford, Blackwell, 1983, p. 10.
74   Ibid., Chapter 1.
75   Ibid., p. xiv.
76   Ibid., p. xiv.
77   John Gray, *After Social Democracy: Politics, Capitalism and the Common Life,* London, Demos, 1996, p. 45.
78   For example, a MORI poll for *The Times* in July 2001showed that only 11% of those interviewed believed that privatisation would improve NHS services, while another, in November 2000 for Transport for London, found that 53% of Londoners were opposed to PPP for the London Underground while 23% were in favour. The largest single category, at 36%, comprised those who were 'strongly opposed'. (www.mori.com)
79   Labour Party, *Safer Communities, Safer Britain: Labour's Proposals for Tough Action on Crime,* London, Labour Party, 1995.
80   Daniel Bell, *Communitarianism and its Critics,* Oxford, Oxford University Press, 1993.
81   Alasdair MacIntyre, 'The Spectre of Communitarianism', *Radical Philosophy* 70, March/April 1995, pp. 34–5.
82   Ibid., p. 100. Bell takes this phrase from Taylor's *Sources of the Self,* although he applies it in a much more literal, concrete way than Taylor does.
83   Ibid., p. 1.
84   Ibid., p. 11.
85   Ibid., p. 28. Again, these terms are taken from Taylor, but not explicitly so.
86   Ibid., p. 31.
87   Ibid., p. 14. 'Communities of memory' include language communities and religious communities – large groups to which one can belong without having a face to face relationship with other members, and which may be geographically dispersed. 'Psychological communities' include families and schools, and are characterised by face to face relationships between members.
88   Ibid., p. 156.
89   Ibid., p. 170.
90   Ibid., p. 94.
91   Ibid., p. 1. The danger throughout Bell's work is that in trying to derive practical policy positions from ontological ones he conflates the two, and translates, sometimes misleadingly, from one sphere to the other. While it might be true that A (ontological) entails B (ontological) it doesn't necessarily follow that the same terms, or even the same concepts, will have the same relation to each other in the real world. 'Community', for example, has (many) different meanings in the two spheres.
92   Ibid., p. 93.
93   Ibid., p. 140.
94   Ibid.

95 Ibid., p. 141.
96 Ibid., p. 183. Bell has worded this carefully, as he admits in a footnote that there is in fact little evidence of a causal link between the availability of divorce and family breakdown (p. 204 n.66). He is however prepared to press ahead with policy proposals on the basis of what is 'not implausible' but which tends to be contradicted by what evidence exists.
97 Ibid. There is of course nothing objectionable about the proposal's mildness, but, as Will Kymlicka points out in his critical appendix to *Communitarianism and Its Critics* (Kymlicka is in fact the second critic of the title; in an earlier version there was only one: the fictitious Philip) it is inconsistent with the belief from which Bell ostensibly draws it. If he were consistent, he would call for divorce to be outlawed, according to Kymlicka (Bell, *Communitarianism and Its Critics*, p. 217).
98 See Polly Toynbee and David Walker, *Did Things Get Better? An Audit of Labour's Successes and Failures*, London, Penguin, 2001, p. 34.
99 Quoted in Norman Fairclough, *New Labour, New Language?*, London, Routledge, 2000, p. 43.
100 Tony Blair, speech to the Labour Party Annual Conference, 30.09.1997.
101 Toynbee and Walker, *Did Things Get Better?*, p. 32.
102 Bell, *Communitarianism and Its Critics*, p. 143.
103 Ibid., p. 142.
104 Ibid., p. 143.
105 The degree of autonomy enjoyed by voluntary organisations increasingly dependent for funding on the local, central and European state is debatable, but on this point there is certainly a clear difference between involvement in such organisations – even if it is in some cases effectively coerced – and the national service Bell advocates.
106 Bell, *Communitarianism and Its Critics*, p. 174.
107 Ibid., p. 175.
108 Ibid., p. 217.
109 It may be of course that understandings on some matters are not shared across a whole society. Most Britons are probably not fundamentally sympathetic to liberal ideals, although significant communities within that society – for example, the academic community – might be. See Andy Beckett, 'Me? A member of the liberal elite?', *Guardian* 17.08.2001.
110 Tony Blair, speech to the Labour Party Annual Conference, 04.10.1994.
111 While one aim of such policies is the promotion of social inclusion, New Labour's vision of inclusion through economic participation is very different from Bell's ties of social and communal loyalty.

Chapter 4

1 John Macmurray in a letter to his sister, 1931, quoted in John E. Costello, *John Macmurray: A Biography*, Edinburgh, Floris Books, 2002, p. 192.
2 A version of this chapter has been published as 'Professor Macmurray and Mr. Blair: The Strange Case of the Communitarian Guru that Never Was', *Political Quarterly* 73:2, April–June 2002.
3 Gabriel Channon, *Searching for Solid Foundations: Community Involvement and Urban Policy*, London, ODPM, 2003, p. 17.
4 Paul Brickell, *People Before Structures: Engaging Communities Effectively in Regeneration*, London, Demos, 2000, p. 16.

5   Working Group on the Active Community, *Giving Time, Getting Involved*, London, Cabinet Office, 2000. My emphasis. The impression given by this is that such opposi- tional community activity is rare (which it isn't) and undesirable, but something to be borne as inevitable in a democracy.

6   Ibid.

7   See www.homeoffice.gov.uk/inside/org/dob/direct/cru.html, accessed 23.05.2005.

8   The term 'voluntary sector' is fraught with problems and there is a growing literature pointing these out and suggesting alternative terms such as 'not for profit sector' and 'third sector'. It can even be suggested that the term 'sector' is misleading, suggesting as it does clear boundaries to these activities. However, for the time being at least I shall ignore these valid and justified criticisms and continue to use the term 'voluntary sector' which is the most widely used and understood outside of the specialist field.

9   See, for example, Marilyn Taylor, *Unleashing the Potential: Bringing Residents to the Centre of Regeneration*, York, Joseph Rowntree Foundation, 1995, p. 12; Hazel Blears, fore- word to Ben Rogers (ed.), *Lonely Citizens: Report of the Working Party on Active Citizen- ship*, London, IPPR, 2004.

10 Working group on the Active Community, *Giving Time, Getting Involved*, p. 10.

11 Gabriel Channon and Alison West, *Regeneration and Sustainable Communities*, London, Community Development Foundation, 1999, p. 29.

12 Ibid.

13 Ibid., p. 8.

14 See, for example, Hazel Blears, foreword to Rogers (ed.), *Lonely Citizens*.

15 Ibid., p. 9.

16 David G. Green, *Community Without Politics: A Market Approach to Welfare Reform*, London, IEA, 1996; Robert Whelan, *The Corrosion of Charity: From Moral Renewal to Contract Culture*, London, IEA, 1996.

17 Working Group on the Active Community, *Giving Time, Getting Involved*, p. 10.

18 In this context it cannot honestly be called voluntary.

19 See Working Group on the Active Community, *Giving Time, Getting Involved*, p. 12.

20 Ibid., p. 13. Note that community activity is to be taken into account *particularly* – not *exclusively*, when deciding between similarly qualified candidates; community involve- ment may be used as a criterion even when candidates are not of equivalent academic ability, so it might promote a less able candidate over a more able one who has not undertaken such 'approved' activity.

21 Ibid., p. 14.

22 Ibid.

23 Tony Blair, 'Values and the power of Community', speech to the Global Ethics Founda- tion, Tübingen University, 30.06.2000. My emphasis.

24 Gordon Brown, 'The Politics of Potential: a New Agenda for Labour' in David Miliband (ed.), *Reinventing the Left*, Cambridge, Polity, 1994.

25 Tony Blair, Speech to the 1994 Labour Party Conference.

26 John Rentoul, *Tony Blair* [1995], London, Warner Books, revised edition 1996, p. 479.

27 Ibid., p. 42.

28 Stephen Driver and Luke Martell, *New Labour: Politics After Thatcherism*, Cambridge, Polity Press, 1998, p. 27.

29 Stephen Driver and Luke Martell 'New Labour's Communitarianisms', *Critical Social Policy* 17:3, August 1997.

30 Jon Sopel, *Tony Blair: The Moderniser*, London, Bantam, 1995, p. 34.

31 Ibid., p. 144.

32   Elizabeth Frazer, *The Problems of Communitarian Politics: Unity and Conflict*, Oxford, Oxford University Press, 1999, p. 25.
33   Norman Fairclough, *New Labour, New Language?*, London, Routledge, 2000, p. 38.
34   Kamal Ahmed and Denis Staunton, 'Whose side is God on?', *Observer* 25.06.2000, p. 17.
35   Stephen Bates, 'Peace of the action', *Guardian Society* 22.05.2002.
36   This is reported by Rentoul, *Tony Blair*, who has Thomson going in alone (p. 51); Sopel, *Tony Blair: The Moderniser* says that 'a group' of Thomson's friends 'travelled to Scotland ... and met John Macmurray' (p. 34).
37   Ian Hargreaves, 'Tony's best mate is back', *New Statesman and Society* 31.05.96, p. 18.
38   Sopel, *Tony Blair: The Moderniser*, p. 34.
39   Quoted by Paul Anderson and Nyta Mann in *Safety First: The Making of New Labour*, London, Granta Books, 1997, p. 10, who give the source as Robert Crampton, 'Labour Exchange', in *The Times* 30.09.1995; and by Rentoul, *Tony Blair* (p. 42) who sources it to *Scotland on Sunday* 24.07.1994.
40   Rentoul, *Tony Blair* p. 44, again, sourced to *Scotland on Sunday* as above.
41   For example, David Remnick, 'The Real Mr. Blair', *Observer* 01.05.2005.
42   Tony Blair, 'Why I am a Christian', *Sunday Telegraph* 07.04.1996, reprinted in Tony Blair, *New Britain: My Vision of a Young Country*, London, Fourth Estate, 1996, pp. 59–60.
43   Andy McSmith, *Faces of Labour: The Inside Story* (1996), London, Verso, 2nd edition 1997, p. 26. My emphasis. When Blair first became Prime Minister, Thomson was apparently enthusiastic about the potential of his leadership, but in an interview in 2002 he expressed serious doubts about the direction of Labour policy, and said '"I don't think Tony's ever tried to use Macmurray as a source of social policy ..."' (Nick Cohen, 'The Lesson the Prime Minister Forgot', *New Statesman* 01.07.2002, p. 21).
44   Tony Blair, Speech to the Women's Institutes' Triennial General Meeting 07.06.2000. This paragraph alone covers community as location, as synonymous with society, as a means to individual fulfilment, as renewable, and as the solution to the problems of modernity.
45   For example, see Driver and Martell, notes 28 and 29 above.
46   Sopel, *Tony Blair: The Moderniser*, p. 34.
47   Ibid., p. 144.
48   It is not my aim here to 'rehabilitate' Macmurray, nor to defend him in particular against traduction. It may well be that his current obscurity is deserved; some of his ideas are decidedly eccentric, and others – for example, his belief in the inevitability of Socialism – outdated. But he writes eloquently and, throughout his career and across his popular and academic work, consistently; and what he says on his main theme, the nature of human relations, bears re-reading in an age which barely acknowledges the possibility of non-instrumental relationships.
49   These include: Ruth Levitas, *The Inclusive Society? Social Exclusion and New Labour*, Basingstoke, Macmillan, 1998, pp. 105–10, and Samuel Brittan, 'Tony Blair's Real Guru', *New Statesman* 07.02.1997, pp. 18–20.
50   The one area in which Blair's views might be compatible with his supposed mentor's relates to their shared view that Christianity is best expressed through action – Macmurray's view being that that is religion's only worthwhile manifestation. It is through this understanding, Blair has claimed (see Michael Cockerell, 'The Secret World of Tony Blair', *New Statesman* 14.02.2000, p. 13), that his Oxford Christianity led him into politics and specifically into the Labour Party. It is certainly well documented that Blair did not show much interest in politics while an undergraduate, preferring to divide his spare time between religion and rock music. On the other hand,

the claim that his involvement in politics is no more than an expression of his Christianity and a desire to put Christian principles into action sits a little uneasily with the clear ambition and calculation with which he secured both his Sedgefield seat and the leadership of his party (see in particular McSmith, *Faces of Labour*, Chapter 1).

51 His writing on education continues to enjoy some currency in that field. A new biography, Costello, *John Macmurray: A Biography* was published in February 2002.

52 Collections of lectures include *Freedom in the Modern World*, [1932] London, Faber, 1968; and *Reason and Emotion*, [1935] London, Faber, revised edition 1962.

53 Including *A Challenge to the Churches: Religion and Democracy*, London, Kegan Paul, 1941; and *Conditions of Freedom*, Toronto, Ryerson Press, 1949.

54 Including *The Self as Agent*, London, Faber and Faber, 1957 and *Persons in Relation*, London, Faber and Faber, 1961. These are also lecture series, but as the Glasgow Gifford Lectures, of a more academic nature.

55 *Freedom in the Modern World*, London, Faber, 1968 edition, inside front cover.

56 *Reason and Emotion*, p. 97.

57 Ibid., pp. 96–7.

58 Ibid., p. 97.

59 Ibid., p. 94.

60 Ibid., p. 98.

61 *Challenge to the Churches*, pp. 23–4.

62 *Freedom in the Modern World*, pp. 160–2.

63 Tony Blair, 'The Rights we Enjoy Reflect the Duties we Owe', *Spectator* Lecture, 22.03.1995.

64 Blair, 'Values and the Power of Community' speech, 30.06.2000.

65 Gordon Brown, Speech by the Chancellor of the Exchequer at the National Council for Voluntary Organisations' Annual Conference, 09.02.2000.

66 Although in fairness it should be pointed out that Macmurray appears to accept that a functioning society is a prerequisite of community.

67 Tony Blair, speech to the Women's Institutes' Triennial General Meeting, 07.06.2000. The terms are used interchangeably throughout this speech, and are also confused in Gordon Brown's speech to the National Council for Voluntary Organisations, 09.02.2000.

68 The same distinction is made by Macmurray in his *Creative Society*, p. 97. A feature of Macmurray's work is its consistency on key themes.

69 Tony Blair, Speech to the Women's Institutes' Triennial General Meeting, 07.06.2000.

70 See for example, Tony Blair, *The Third Way: New Politics for the New Century*, London, Fabian Society, 1998, p. 4; Gordon Brown, speech to the NCVO, 09.02.2000. Blair's speech to the Women's Institute, 07.06.2000, provides particularly good examples.

71 Driver and Martell, *New Labour: Politics After Thatcherism*, pp. 28–9.

72 Rentoul, *Tony Blair*, pp. 42–3. Original emphasis.

73 In fact Macmurray did strongly object to the philosophy that was 'modern' when he was writing, this being linguistic philosophy, which he saw as sterile and irrelevant to the more important questions of human and social relations. He would probably have greatly welcomed the revival of normative political philosophy which is usually attributed to Rawls.

74 Driver and Martell, *New Labour: Politics After Thatcherism*, p. 27.

75 Macmurray, *The Self as Agent*, p. 30.

76 For example, by Gordon Brown in his speech to the NCVO, 09.02.2000.

77 This claim, of course, was never in fact made so explicitly as its inevitably incomplete quotation suggests.

78   Macmurray, *Freedom in the Modern World*, p. 59.
79   Blair, 'Values and the Power of Community' speech, 30.06.2000.
80   Blair, Speech to the Women's Institutes' Triennial General Meeting, 07.06.2000. Both these examples in fact demonstrate a shift in which responsibilities are no longer exchanged for rights, but for mere 'opportunities'.
81   Tony Blair, speech to the Labour Party Annual Conference, 30.09.1997.
82   Macmurray, *Freedom in the Modern World*, pp. 215–16.
83   Rentoul, *Tony Blair*, p. 42. A similar, although not identical, version of this quotation is given by Peter Mandelson and Roger Liddle, *The Blair Revolution: Can New Labour Deliver?*, London, Faber and Faber, 1996, p. 33.
84   For example, in his 'Values and the Power of Community' speech, 30.06.2000 Blair says that a 'covenant of opportunities and responsibilities' is a necessary condition of 'spending taxpayers' money on public services or social exclusion'.
85   Macmurray, *Challenge to the Churches*, p. 9.
86   This point is made in his *Freedom in the Modern World*, p. 48.
87   Working Group on the Active Community, *Giving Time, Getting Involved*, p. 9.
88   See for example, Labour Party, *Building the Future Together: Labour's Policies for Partnership between Government and the Voluntary Sector*, London, Labour Party, March 1997, pp. 1, 4 and 6.
89   Working Group on the Active Community, *Giving Time, Getting Involved*, p. 13.
90   Amitai Etzioni, *The Spirit of Community* (1993), London, Fontana, 1995, pp. 113–15.
91   Daniel Bell, *Communitarianism and its Critics*, Oxford, Clarendon, 1993, pp. 141–2.
92   Macmurray, *Freedom in the Modern World*, Chapter 9.
93   Ibid., pp. 195–6.
94   Ibid., p. 196.
95   Ibid., p. 198.
96   Ibid., p. 199.
97   Ibid.
98   Ibid., pp. 200–1. Emphasis added.
99   Quoted in Blair, *New Britain: My Vision of a Young Country*, p. 11.

Chapter 5

1   Amitai Etzioni, *The Spirit of Community: Rights, Responsibilities and the Communitarian Agenda*, London, Fontana, 1995, p. ix.
2   Etzioni, *Spirit of Community*, p. ix.
3   Polly Toynbee, 'How liberal is New Labour?', *Independent* 23.04.1996, p. 15. This is also of course another example of the assumption that Labour is indeed so infatuated.
4   Etzioni, *Spirit of Community*, p. ix
5   Amitai Etzioni, *The New Golden Rule: Community and Morality in a Democratic Society* [1996], London, Profile Books, 1997, back cover. Clearly, very little credence should be attached to such claims by publishers. Nonetheless, categorical statements like this do much to fuel the belief that Etzioni has been a significant influence on New Labour.
6   Ruth Levitas, *The Inclusive Society? Social Exclusion and New Labour*, Basingstoke, Macmillan, 1998.
7   Ibid., Chapter 1.
8   Etzioni, *Spirit of Community*, p. 11.
9   Levitas, *The Inclusive Society*, p. 178.

10 Ibid., p. 179.

11 Simon Prideaux, 'From Organisational Theory to the Third Way: Continuities and Contradictions Underpinning Amitai Etzioni's Communitarian Influence on New Labour', in Sarah Hale, Will Leggett and Luke Martell (eds), *The Third Way: Criticisms, Futures, Alternatives*, Manchester, Manchester University Press, 2004.

12 Joan Smith, 'The Ideology of "Family and Community": New Labour Abandons the Welfare State', in Leo Panitch (ed.), *The Socialist Register 1997: Ruthless Criticism of All That Exists*, London, Merlin Press, 1997, p. 180.

13 Ibid. Etzioni's own comment on Murray is worth noting. When asked by Beatrix Campbell 'What do you think about the work of … Murray who has been very influential in Britain?' Etzioni replies 'I think he should wash his mouth with soap because he's a racist. Some people began to feel slightly shocked that they had adopted his view on the underclass and then were embarrassed by his view on race. They are indefensible. Not only from an ethical viewpoint, they are also scientifically indefensible. That's the worst of both worlds.' (Beatrix Campbell, 'So what's the Big Idea Mr. Etzioni?', *Independent* 16.03.1995. p. 15.)

14 Ibid., p. 181.

15 Ibid., p. 184.

16 While Blair has explicitly distanced New Labour from 'old' Labour activists and trade unions, the party still seeks to appeal to 'old' Labour voters.

17 Campbell, 'So What's the Big Idea', p. 185.

18 Ibid., p. 191.

19 Adam Crawford, 'Review Article: The Spirit of Community: Rights, Responsibilities and the Communitarian Agenda', *Journal of Law and Society* 23:2, June 1996, p. 247. Emphasis added.

20 Ibid.

21 Ibid.

22 Ibid., p. 249.

23 Ibid., p. 251.

24 Paul Anderson and Nyta Mann, *Safety First: the Making of New Labour*, London, Granta Books, 1997, p. 245.

25 Amitai Etzioni, *The Third Way to a Good Society*, London, Demos, 2000.

26 Peter Wilby, 'Blair's warm blanket looks threadbare', *Observer* 11.06.2000, p. 29.

27 Polly Toynbee and David Walker, *Did Things Get Better? An Audit of Labour's Successes and Failures*, London, Penguin, 2001, p. 37.

28 Seumas Milne, 'Everybody's talking about', *Guardian* 07.10.1994, p. 5.

29 'The man with the big idea?', *Sunday Times* 09.10.1994, p. 3.

30 'Information technology can be a builder of communities', leading article, *The Times* 13.03.1995, p. 19.

31 'Write compassion into the new faith', leading article, *Independent* 18.03.1995, p. 12.

32 'Communitarian conceits: Amitai Etzioni preaches up a storm, but to what effect?', *Economist*, 18.03.1995.

33 'Freedom and community', *Economist* 24.12.1994.

34 Oliver James, 'The guru with a message of repression', *Independent* 06.10.1998.

35 'Write compassion into the new faith', leading article, *Independent* 18.03.1995, p. 12.

36 John Lloyd, 'Profile: Amitai Etzioni', *New Statesman* 20.06.1997, p. 28.

37 Martin Walker, 'Community Spirit', *Guardian* 13.03.1995, p. 10.

38 Paul Anderson and Kevin Davey, 'Tough on Crime', *New Statesman* 03.03.1995.

39 Amitai Etzioni, 'A mad scramble for the centre', *Sunday Times* 09.10.1994, p. 3.

40		Clearly, not all these examples are explicit claims that Etzioni has directly influenced New Labour (although some are), but they do all illustrate the prevailing view that New Labour had some sort of communitarian link with the writer.

41		Roger Scruton, 'Why Mr Clinton's guru neglects posterity', *The Times* 07.12.1995, p. 40.

42		Anna Coote, 'A bit too much of a prig and a prude', *Independent* 03.07.1995, p. 14.

43		Andrew Marr, 'Ruling Britannia: Gloom will Bring us Together', *Independent* 08.09.1995, p. 15.

44		Bernard Crick, 'Prophets, creeps and publishers', *Independent* 05.07.1997, p. 7.

45		Tony Blair, speech at Wellingborough 19.02.1993, quoted in John Rentoul, 'Learning from Clinton, Stealing from Thatcher', *Independent* 18.01.1995, p. 19.

46		Margaret Thatcher, interview in *Woman's Own*, 31.10.1987. However, Thatcher undoubtedly saw 'society' differently from Blair, and quite possibly the relationship between entitlements and obligations too – the impression here is that she is referring to a strictly logical relationship, rather than one of exchange, and merely pointing out the impossibility of someone having an entitlement unless someone *else* has an obligation *to them*.

47		Rentoul, 'Learning from Clinton'. Rentoul suggests that the DLC's ideas in America came in part from 'a new school of political philosophy called "communitarianism"', but he also suggests that the American communitarians had 'rediscovered the work of, among others … John Macmurray' – a claim for which I can find no evidence. Certainly Etzioni never refers to Macmurray, and his ideas have little in common with those of the Communitarian Movement.

48		Tony Blair, speech in Alloa, June 1993, in Rentoul, 'Learning from Clinton'.

49		See Etzioni, *The Spirit of Community*, pp. 60–2. When asked whether he was 'implying that single parents *cannot* bring up a child properly', Etzioni, on his account, answered '"As I read the social science findings, it would be preferable to have *three* parents per child … parenting is a heavy-duty load for single parents to carry out entirely on their own, especially if they are employed full-time outside the household."' Like Blair's statement, this focuses on the practical rather than the moral aspects of the issue.

50		Elizabeth Frazer, for example, notes that '[t]here is no reason, given Tony Blair's intellectual history, to accept' the claim that the wording of the new Clause IV was inspired by Etzioni. (*The Problems of Communitarian Politics: Unity and Conflict*, Oxford, Oxford University Press, 1999, p. 12 n.8.)

51		Martin Walker, 'Community Spirit', p. 10.

52		A recent paper has suggested that Etzioni's communitarianism is in fact little more than a rehash of functionalist organisation theory, applied to the broader and therefore inappropriate model of society as a whole. (Simon Prideaux, 'From Organisational Theory to the Third Way: The Continuities Underpinning the New Communitarianism of Amitai Etzioni', paper given at 'The Third Way and Beyond: Criticisms, Futures, Alternatives', conference held at the University of Sussex, 02.11.2000.)

53		Sarah Baxter, 'I am the way and I am the truth', interview with Etzioni, *Sunday Times* 19.03.1995, p. 3.

54		John Lloyd, 'Profile: Amitai Etzioni', *New Statesman* 20.06.1997, p. 28.

55		For example, *The Moral Dimension: Toward a New Economics* (1988), *Capitol Corruption: the Attack on American Democracy* (1984) and *A Responsive Society* (1991).

56		Also published during this period but not considered here is *The Limits of Privacy* (1999).

57		Amitai Etzioni, *The New Golden Rule: Community and Morality in a Democratic Society* [1996], London, Profile Books, 1997, back cover.

58   Ibid., p. xvii.
59   Ibid., p. 12.
60   Ibid., p. 13. Etzioni does not appear to consider here the argument that coercion has a role in reinforcing shared values, by reassuring those who would comply voluntarily that others will not be allowed to free-ride on their compliance.
61   Ibid., p. 12.
62   Amitai Etzioni, 'The Responsive Community: A Communitarian Perspective', *American Sociological Review* 61, February 1996, p. 6. Original emphasis.
63   Ibid., p. 6.
64   Ibid.
65   Ibid., p. 7. It strikes me that this in fact would be the case in a conventional understanding of a symbiotic relationship. It is certainly true, for example, of the example that Etzioni gives of the symbiotic relationship between the crocodile and the plover bird which sits in its mouth and cleans its teeth, to the benefit of both parties. It is possible to conceive hypothetically of one or other of these creatures 'gaining too much strength' e.g. if the crocodile were suddenly to eat the bird, or if the bird got over-enthusiastic and began to eat the crocodile's gums, the relationship would then have become antagonistic. So I cannot see the difference between ordinary symbiosis and Etzioni's inverting kind. If a symbiotic relationship ceases, for whatever reason, to work as such, then it simply no longer exists.
66   Ibid., p. 10.
67   Etzioni, *The New Golden Rule*, p. 35.
68   Ibid., p. 56.
69   John Lloyd, 'Profile: Amitai Etzioni', *New Statesman* 20.06.1997, p. 29.
70   Amitai Etzioni, 'Nation in Need of Community Values' (Second *Times*/Demos Lecture), *The Times* 20.02.1995, p. 9. Almost exactly the same wording is used in the preface to the British edition of *The Spirit of Community*, p. x.
71   Amitai Etzioni, 'Common Values', *New Statesman and Society* 12.05.1994, p. 24.
72   Etzioni, *The Spirit of Community*, Chapters 8 and 9.
73   Ibid., Chapter 6.
74   Ibid., Chapter 7.
75   In an email to the author (July 2005) Etzioni confirms that the views expressed in *The Spirit of Community* apply to the proposed laws.
76   Etzioni, *The Spirit of Community*, p. 236.
77   Ibid., p. 33.
78   Ibid., p. 32. An alternative, rational individualist, interpretation might be that locals realised that it was in everybody's interest, including their own, to wait in turn as it resulted in a more efficient traffic flow, whereas outsiders would have been ignorant of this.
79   For example, see the opening paragraphs of Blair's Labour Party Conference speech, 03.10.1995.
80   Etzioni, *The Spirit of Community*, p. ix. Also, almost word for word, in Amitai Etzioni, 'Nation in need of Community Values', *Times* 20.02.1995, p. 9.
81   Tony Blair, *The Third Way: New Politics for the New Century*, Fabian Pamphlet 588, London, Fabian Society, 1998.
82   Etzioni, *The Spirit of Community*, p. 54.
83   This is considered in greater detail in Chapter 7.
84   Etzioni, *The Spirit of Community*, p. 59.
85   Ibid., p. 66.

86   Ibid., p. 136.
87   Etzioni, *The New Golden Rule*, p. 7. 'I support the claim that communitarian thinking leapfrogs the old debate between left-wing and right-wing thinking and suggests a third social philosophy'.
88   See Anthony Giddens, *The Third Way: The Renewal of Social Democracy*, London, Polity Press, 1998, and *The Third Way and Its Critics*, Cambridge, Polity Press, 2000, and Tony Blair, *The Third Way*.
89   Etzioni, *The Third Way to a Good Society*, p. 17 for example.
90   See, for example, the reference to tower blocks, ibid., p. 25.
91   For example, Etzioni suggests that in order reduce class distinctions and further fairness, one symbolic 'place to start may be to bring back Harold Wilson's beer and sandwiches with working class people, rather than leaders limiting their outings to posh yuppie restaurants' (ibid., p. 33). In British popular understanding, Harold Wilson's 'beer and sandwiches at number 10' does not, of course, symbolise solidarity with the working class, but rather a too-cosy relationship with overly powerful trade union leaders.
92   *Independent*, 06.07.1995, p.16.
93   Etzioni, *The Third Way to a Good Society*, p. 15 and Chapter 2 passim.
94   Ibid., p. 27.
95   Ibid., pp. 53–6.
96   Ibid., p. 32.
97   Ibid., pp. 28–9.
98   Ibid., p. 33.
99   Ibid., p. 12.
100 Ibid., p. 11.
101 Ibid., p. 13.
102 Ibid., p. 59 n. 6.
103 Ibid., p. 14.
104 Blair, *The Third Way: New Politics for the New Century*.
105 Ibid., p. 3.
106 Ibid., p. 12.
107 Ibid., p. 4.
108 Etzioni, *The Third Way to a Good Society*, p. 27.
109 Ibid.
110 Blair, *The Third Way: New Politics for the New Century*. Emphasis added.
111 See for example Coote, 'A bit too much of a prig and a prude', p. 13. While Coote's criticisms of New Labour are valid, her attribution of their ideas to Etzioni is less so.
112 However, any similarity to Macmurray should not be overstated. Etzioni views community and communal relationships in a far more instrumental way than Macmurray would countenance.
113 Etzioni, *The Third Way to a Good Society*, p. 19.
114 See Kirsty Milne, 'Doing it for real', *New Statesman* 03.03.1995, p. 22. It's ironic that Etzioni focuses on this controversial aspect of the Balsall Heath scheme, as Milne's article details many other mutual ventures, including a school, local history archive and urban farm.
115 Etzioni, *The Third Way to a Good Society*, p. 19.
116 Ibid., p. 20 – although this would not seem a very realistic basis on which to run a credit union, which Etzioni has just cited as an example of mutuality.
117 Ibid.
118 Gordon Brown, speech to the National Council for Voluntary Organisations' Annual

Conference, 09.02.2000. In this speech, Gordon Brown, as Chancellor of the Exchequer, announced a number of policy measures to make charitable giving easier and more tax-effective, and introduced the concept of 'civic patriotism' to describe this new spirit of giving, of both time and money.

119 Blair, speech to the Women's Institutes' Triennial General Meeting, 07.07.2000.

120 Blair, 'Values and the Power of Community' speech, 30.06.2000. Emphasis added.

121 See Lloyd, 'Profile: Amitai Etzioni', p. 29; Etzioni, *The Third Way to a Good Society*, p. 29.

122 These examples are taken from Amitai Etzioni, 'Common Values', *New Statesman and Society*, 12.05.1995. More are provided in his *The New Golden Rule*. In both cases Etzioni recognises that attitudes in the UK are different, but perhaps not the extent to which this is so.

123 Etzioni, 'Common Values', p. 24.

124 Tony Blair, speech to the Labour Party Annual Conference, 30.09.1997.

125 Blair, 'Values and the Power of Community' speech, 30.06.2000.

126 Tony Blair, speech to the Labour Party Annual Conference, 04.10.1994.

127 David Blunkett, interviewed on the *Today* programme, BBC Radio 4, 29.09.1999.

128 Blair, speech to the Labour Party Annual Conference, 03.10.1995.

129 Blair, speech to the Women's Institutes' Triennial General Meeting, 07.06.2000. It is of course extremely disingenuous to suggest that benefits ever have been handed out without conditions.

130 Etzioni, *The Third Way to a Good Society*. In a footnote here (p. 61 n.32) Etzioni states that this is a point on which he is in fundamental disagreement with Giddens, although this seems to represent a rather selective reading of Giddens. (The argument referred to is in Giddens, *The Third Way: The Renewal of Social Democracy*, pp. 65–6.)

131 Etzioni, *The Third Way to a Good Society*, pp. 29–30.

132 Blair, 'Values and the Power of Community' speech, 30.06.2000.

133 *Guardian* 24.06.2000, p. 21. This, incidentally, illustrates an interesting variation on the idea of a contract (and here, even, an 'agreement') as an agreement freely made between two consenting parties; a variation which is prevalent in government rhetoric.

134 Seminar on communitarian policy, London School of Economics, 07.07.2000.

135 For example, in an article in the *Observer* in early 2001, concerning the extension of the New Deal to all unemployed people, David Blunkett (then Secretary of State for Education and Employment) wrote of 'fraudsters' who are 'quite simply thieving from everyone else' by working while claiming benefit, with whom the government was 'getting tough' and who would find that there was 'no hiding place'. (David Blunkett, 'No hiding place for fraudsters', *Observer* 14.01.2001, p. 31.)

136 Tony Blair, speech at the Aylesbury Estate, Southwark, 02.06.1997.

137 Etzioni, *The Third Way to a Good Society*, p. 32.

138 Ibid., p. 30.

139 Ibid., p. 31.

140 Tony Blair, *Spectator* Lecture, 22.03.1995.

141 Tony Blair, speech to the Labour Party Annual Conference, 01.10.1996.

142 Tony Blair, speech to the Women's Institutes' Triennial General Meeting, 07.06.2000.

143 Blair, *The Third Way: New Politics for the New Century*, p. 3.

144 Etzioni, *The Third Way to a Good Society*, p. 12.

145 Blair, 'Values and the Power of Community' speech, 30.06.2000. Emphasis added.

146 Lloyd, 'Profile: Amitai Etzioni', p. 28.

147 Etzioni, *The Third Way to a Good Society*, p. 12.

148 Ibid., p. 43.
149 Ibid. Original italics removed.
150 Ibid., p. 44.
151 See Toynbee and Walker, *Did Things Get Better?*, pp. 112–13.
152 *Observer* 03.03.2002.
153 Fran Abrams, 'Labour attacked by guru', *Independent* 27.12.1997, p. 2.
154 Etzioni, *The Third Way to a Good Society*, p. 45.
155 Ibid., p. 46.
156 Toynbee and Walker, *Did Things Get Better?*

Chapter 6

1   Of all the other writers considered in this book, only MacIntyre is even technically British, but the bulk of his work has been undertaken in the US and Canada. Interestingly both he and Macmurray are Scottish.
2   Tam has been mentioned on a few occasions; for example by Paul Anderson and Kevin Davey ('Import Duties', *New Statesman* 03.03.1995, p. 21), who mention him only to suggest that he is a UK disciple of Etzioni, and by Elizabeth Frazer (*The Problems of Communitarian Politics: Unity and Conflict* p. 5, n.8), who lists him as an example of a political communitarian but does not examine his work in detail.
3   Boswell's other published work includes *Capitalism in Contention: Business Leaders and Political Economy in Modern Britain* (with James Peters, Cambridge, Cambridge University Press, 1997), an examination of the roles and attitudes of business leaders in understanding economic policy change; *Business Policies in the Making: Three Steel Companies Compared* (1983), and *The Rise and Decline of Small Firms* (1973).
4   Jonathan Boswell, *Community and the Economy: The Theory of Public Co-operation*, London, Routledge, 1990. Chapter 1 is entitled 'The Recovery of Community'.
5   Ibid., Chapter 1.
6   Blair, speech to the Women's Institutes' Triennial General Meeting, 07.06.2000.
7   Tony Blair, 'Values and the Power of Community', speech to the Global Ethics Foundation, Tübingen, 30.06.2000.
8   Tony Blair, speech to the Women's Institutes' Triennial General Meeting, 07.06.2000.
9   Tony Blair, 'Values and the Power of Community' speech, 30.06.2000.
10 Boswell, *Community and the Economy*, pp. 3 and 31.
11 Ibid. p. 3.
12 Ibid., p. 5. This claim is debatable, on two grounds. Firstly, I am not aware that 'prosperity' forms the basis of any political ideology; certainly not on the same level as freedom and equality, and secondly, a more appropriate comparison would be between liberty, equality etc. and *community*, rather than those secondary values which, for Boswell, characterise the last. Secondly, community *has* been endlessly debated and it may be argued that it has formed the basis of ideologies including, obviously, communitarianism and, more controversially, Nazism and related doctrines.
13 Ibid.
14 Ibid. Boswell is quoting Durkheim. Emphasis added.
15 For example, Daniel Bell's communitarianism includes compulsory citizen service; Amitai Etzioni also suggests a year of national service in the community in *The Spirit of Community: Rights, Responsibilities and the Communitarian Agenda* [1993], London, Fontana, 1995, p. 112. The New Labour proposal to encourage community activity by making it

a factor in allocating university places looks like a step – albeit a small one – towards de facto compulsion (Working Group on the Active Community, *Giving Time, Getting Involved*, London, Cabinet Office, 1999, p. 13), as does the inclusion of voluntary work as the fourth and final option under the New Deal for unemployed people.

16 Boswell, *Community and the Economy*, p. 22.

17 Ibid., p. 17. This is of course a gross exaggeration, implying as it does that contractual relationships, rather than being an invaluable theoretical and practical device, are the *only* sort of relationship that liberals, or people as liberals conceive of them, are capable of having.

18 Ibid.

19 It is important to note that this is Boswell's point, and does not represent a complete picture of Durkheim's position.

20 Tony Blair, 'The Rights we Enjoy Reflect the Duties we Owe', *Spectator* Lecture, 22.03.1995.

21 Boswell, *Community and the Economy*, p. 18.

22 Ibid., p. 19.

23 Ibid., p. 20.

24 Ibid.

25 Ibid., p. 22.

26 Ibid.

27 Ibid., p. 23.

28 Ibid., p. 26.

29 Ibid.

30 Blair, *Spectator* Lecture, 22.03.1995. Emphasis added.

31 Ibid.

32 Ibid.

33 See note 15 for examples.

34 Boswell, *Community and the Economy*, p. 28.

35 Ibid., p. 31.

36 Ibid.

37 Cf. Macmurray's distinction between 'community' and 'mere society'.

38 Boswell, *Community and the Economy*, p. 31.

39 Ibid., p. 32.

40 Ibid.

41 Ibid., p. 33.

42 Ibid., p. 37.

43 Ibid., p. 38.

44 Ibid.

45 Social Exclusion Leaflet, London, Cabinet Office, 2000. In fact, the SEU has focused on particular single issues, such as truancy, teenage pregnancy and rough sleepers, and its role has been to work across government departments and produce reports and recommendations.

46 See Tony Blair, *Socialism*, Fabian Pamphlet 565, London, Fabian Society, 1994, p. 2.

47 Tony Blair, speech at the Aylesbury Estate, Southwark, 02.06.1997. This was Blair's first official speech as Prime Minister.

48 Polly Toynbee and David Walker, *Did Things Get Better? An Audit of New Labour's Successes and Failures*, London, Penguin, 2001, p. 113.

49 Ibid.

50 In spring 2002 the trade union Amicus won a ruling from the European Commission

that Britain was 'unlawfully and inadequately' implementing the directive. (Jackie Ashley, 'A foot in the door, and a finger on the pulse', *Guardian* 27.05.2002, p. 10.)

51 Boswell, *Community and the Economy*, p. 42.
52 Ibid., p. 46.
53 Ibid., p. 52.
54 Ibid., p. 47.
55 Ibid., p. 43.
56 Tony Blair, *Spectator* Lecture, 22.03.1995.
57 Blair, speech to the Women's Institutes' Triennial General Meeting, 07.06.2000.
58 Blair, *Spectator* Lecture, 22.03.1995.
59 Gordon Brown, speech by the Chancellor of the Exchequer to the NCVO Annual Conference, 09.02.2000.
60 Active Community Unit, *Giving Time, Getting Involved*, p. 9.
61 Boswell, *Community and the Economy*, p. 45.
62 Ibid.
63 Tony Blair, speech to the Labour Party Annual Conference, 04.10.1994.
64 Boswell, *Community and the* Economy, p. 45.
65 Ibid., p. 52.
66 Ibid.
67 Ibid., p. 53. Emphasis added.
68 Stephen Driver and Luke Martell, *New Labour: Politics After Thatcherism*, Cambridge, Polity Press, 1998, p. 46.
69 Boswell, *Community and the Economy*, p. 58.
70 Toynbee and Walker, *Did Things Get Better?*, p. 119.
71 Tony Blair, speech to the Labour Party Annual Conference, 03.10.1995.
72 Boswell, *Community and the* Economy, p. 66.
73 Ibid., p. 141.
74 Although it can equally be counter argued that the minimum wage is set at a level low enough to be compatible with exploitation, and that its main effect is to save on the bill for 'in work' benefits while not benefiting the worker overall. See for example Fran Abrams, 'The Breadline: A month on the minimum wage', *Guardian* 28.01.2002 and 29.01.2002, *G2* p. 2.
75 For example, the introduction of citizenship education in primary and secondary schools, which includes elements on the importance of democracy, and various campaigns encouraging young people to use their vote.
76 Boswell, *Community and the Economy*, p. 151.
77 Ibid., p. 152.
78 Ibid., p. 153.
79 Ibid., p. 154.
80 See for example Blair's speech to the Women's Institutes' Triennial General Meeting, 07.06.2000, in which he says that 'the renewal of community is the answer to the challenges of a changing world'.
81 While it is no doubt true that such behaviour makes people's lives a misery and curbing it is a good thing, it is only certain kinds of anti-social behaviour that come under the New Labour spotlight – the vandalism, swearing and intimidation of the young poor and unemployed, but not (for example) the arguably equally socially destructive withdrawal of services by shops and banks from the poorest areas.
82 Other policies are also divisive – albeit arguably in a good cause. Schemes which encourage people to 'shop' their neighbour for benefit fraud surely represent the antithesis of

fraternal values, suggesting that for the government community is far more a means than an end.

83 Boswell, *Community and the Economy*.

84 This is the sort of thing voluntary and community organisations have to do in order to access the government funding available for partnership working. Boswell wants to see the private sector developing more of the attributes of community; New Labour's vision of partnership involves the exact reverse.

85 Boswell, *Community and the Economy* p. 183.

86 See Labour Party, *Building the Future Together: Labour's policies for partnership between Government and the Voluntary Sector*, London, Labour Party, 1997, especially p. 6.

87 Ibid., p. 3

88 Tony Blair, 'Faith in the City – Ten Years On', speech at Southwark Cathedral 29.01.1996, reproduced in *New Britain, New Statesman Special Selection*, p. 63.

89 Tony Blair, speech at the Aylesbury Estate, Southwark, 02.06.1997.

90 Henry Tam, *Communitarianism: A New Agenda for Politics and Citizenship*, Basingstoke, Macmillan, 1998, p. 3. This also clearly echoes Macmurray's views on individualism, as a result rather than a cause of social inequality and injustice.

91 Ibid.

92 Ibid., p.4. It is worth remembering that this book was published in 1998 – too soon for any changes made by the Labour government to be taken into account, but certainly not at the height of Thatcherism.

93 Ibid.

94 Ibid., pp. 4–5. Tam (p. 6) points out that the defenders of the market have no objection to authoritarianism when it acts in their interests; this may be unfair to a writer like Hayek, who sees the free market as a bulwark against totalitarian politics, but is generally the case in day to day life.

95 Tony Blair, speech at the Aylesbury Estate, Southwark, 02.06.1997.

96 Tam, *Communitarianism*, p. 4.

97 Ibid., p. 5.

98 Ibid.

99 There may be some overlap with Boswell's respective values of associativeness in liberty, fraternity, and participation, but in general Tam is heading in a different direction.

100 www.active-citizen.org.uk

101 Labour Party, *Renewing Democracy, Rebuilding Communities*, London, Labour Party, 1995, p. 15.

102 Meaning references to the *concept* of values; previous governments and politicians have of course referred to and espoused specific values, perhaps even to a greater extent than New Labour do.

103 Tony Blair, Speech to the Labour Party Annual Conference, Brighton, 03.10.1995.

104 Ibid.

105 Ibid.

106 Blair, *Socialism*.

107 Ibid., p. 2.

108 Ibid.

109 Tony Blair, speech to the *Guardian*/Nexus Conference, London School of Economics, 01.03.1997.

110 Ibid.

111 Ibid.

112 Ibid.

113 Norman Fairclough, in *New Labour, New Language* , London, Routledge, 2000, pp. 47–8, traces the changing use of the term 'values' in Labour rhetoric, but does not really convey the subtle effects of this combination.

114 Tony Blair, Speech to the Labour Party Annual Conference, Brighton, 03.10.1995.

115 Tony Blair, Speech to the Women's Institutes' Triennial General Meeting, 07.06.2000.

116 Ibid. Emphasis added.

117 Ibid. The question raised here is just *how* that distinction can be made. It looks as though it is that values are *by definition* what we keep, while 'attitudes' are by definition that which is left behind. It is hard to see on what independent basis this distinction is being made. It is harder still in the next few paragraphs to understand the basis on which Blair decides what to keep from the past and what to leave behind. Nowhere here does he give any indication of fundamental values informing that choice.

118 Ibid.

119 Blair, 'Values and the Power of Community' speech, 30.06.2000.

120 Ibid. Note the different emphasis.

121 Ibid.

122 *Excellence in Schools* White Paper Cm3681, 1997, p.5.

123 Tam, *Communitarianism*, p. 57.

124 Ibid., p. 59.

125 Ibid., p. 60.

126 Ibid.

127 Ibid., p. 63.

128 Ibid., p. 64.

129 Ibid.

130 Ibid., p. 63.

131 http://www.nc.uk.net/servlets/NCParserPhase1?Section=PoS&Subject=Ci&Key Stage=4, accessed 13.02.2002, p. 1.

132 Tam, *Communitarianism*, p. 63.

133 Ibid.

134 *Education for Citizenship and the Teaching of Democracy in Schools*, Final Report of the Advisory Group on Citizenship, London, Qualifications and Curriculum Authority, 1998.

135 Ibid., p. 4.

136 Ibid., p. 11.

137 Ibid., p. 10.

138 Ibid., p. 9. Emphasis added.

139 Ibid., p. 13.

140 *Excellence in Schools* Cm 3681, July 1997.

141 Bernard Crick, 'In Defence of the Citizenship Order 2000' in Bernard Crick, *Essays on Citizenship*, London, Continuum, 2000, p. 118.

142 Ibid.

143 http://www.nc.uk.net/about_citizenship.html, accessed 13.02.2002, p. 1.

144 Ibid., p. 2.

145 www.nc.uk.net/servlets/NCParserPhase1?Section=PoS&Subject=Ci&KeyStage=4, accessed 13.02.2002, p. 1.

146 *The Choices for Britain*, General Election manifesto, London, Labour Party, 2001, p. 23, emphasis added.

147 Tam, *Communitarianism*, p. 76.

148 Ibid., p. 77.

149 Ibid., p. 67.

150 Ibid., p. 68.

151 Ibid., p. 79.

152 Ibid.

153 www.homeoffice.gov.uk/inside/org/dob/direct/cru.html and www.active-citizen.org.uk both accessed 27.07.2005.

154 Labour Party, *A Quiet Life: Tough Action on Criminal Neighbours*, London, Labour Party, 1995, p. 8.

155 Labour Party, *Protecting our Communities: Labour's Plans for Tackling Criminal, Anti-social Behaviour in Neighbourhoods*, London, Labour Party, 1996, p. 11.

156 Bernard Crick, 'A Subject at Last!' in Crick, *Essays on Citizenship*, London, Continuum, 2000, p. 4.

157 Tony Blair, John Smith Memorial Lecture 07.02.1996, reproduced in Tony Blair, *New Britain: My Vision of a Young Country*, New Statesman Special Selection, London, Fourth Estate, 1996, p. 58.

158 Blair, *Spectator* Lecture 22.03.1995, p. 6. The same quote was used eight years later by a then junior Home Office minister in the context of community participation (Hazel Blears, *Communities in Control: Public Services and Local Socialism* Fabian Ideas no. 607, London, Fabian Society, 2003, p. 1.)

159 Labour Party, *New Labour: Leading Britain into the Future*, General Election manifesto, London, Labour Party, 1997, p. 12.

160 Ibid., p. 2.

161 Ibid., p. 7.

162 Labour Party, *The Choices for Britain*, General Election manifesto, London, Labour party, 2001, p. 22.

163 Ibid., p. 23.

164 Labour Party, *Forward not Back*, General Election Manifesto, London, Labour Party, 2005.

165 Most notably, Ruth Levitas, *The Inclusive Society? Social Exclusion and New Labour*, London, Macmillan, 1998; Raymond Plant, 'So You Want to be a Citizen?', *New Statesman* 06.02.1998, p. 30.

166 Plant, 'So You Want to be a Citizen?', *New Statesman* 06.02.1998, p. 31.

167 Ibid.

168 John Moore, speech to the 1988 Conservative Party Conference, quoted in Ruth Lister (ed.), *The Exclusive Society: Citizenship and the Poor*, London, Child Poverty Action Group, 1990, p. 7.

169 Blair, speech to the Labour Party Annual Conference, 03.10.1995.

170 This is a somewhat dubious point, as it can be argued that employment creates as great a dependency as benefits. One of the arguments deployed against the extension of the franchise to employees in seventeenth-century Britain ran on these lines.

171 Tam, *Communitarianism*, p. 85.

172 Ibid., p. 86.

173 Ibid., p. 87.

174 Bernard Crick, 'A Subject at Last!', in Crick, *Essays on Citizenship*, pp. 7–8.

175 *Education for Citizenship and the Teaching of Democracy in Schools*, p. 7.

176 See Crick, 'A Subject at Last!', in Crick, *Essays on Citizenship*, p. 7.

177 Tam, *Communitarianism*, p. 57.

Chapter 7

1   See Chapter 4.
2   Tony Blair, 'Values and the Power of Community', speech to the Global Ethics Foundation, 30.06.2000.
3   David Blunkett, interviewed on the *Today* programme, BBC Radio 4, 29.09.1999.
4   Tony Blair, speech to the Labour Party Annual Conference, 03.10.1995.
5   Tony Blair, speech to the Women's Institutes' Triennial General Meeting, 07.06.2000.
6   Tony Blair, 'Values and the Power of Community', speech, 30.06.2000.
7   Tony Blair, speech at Aylesbury Estate, Southwark, 02.06.1997.

Bibliography

Abrams, Fran, 'Labour attacked by guru', *Independent* 27.12.1997, p. 2.

Abrams, Fran, 'The breadline: a month on the minimum wage', *Guardian G2* 28.01.2002 and 29.01.2002.

Advisory Group on Citizenship, *Education for Citizenship and the Teaching of Democracy in Schools: Final Report of the Advisory Group on Citizenship*, London, Qualifications and Curriculum Authority, 1998.

Ahmed, Kamal, and Denis Staunton, 'Whose side is God on?', *Observer* 25.06.2000.

Anderson, Paul, and Kevin Davey, 'Import Duties', *New Statesman and Society* 03.03.1995.

Anderson, Paul, and Kevin Davey, 'Tough on Crime' (interview with Amitai Etzioni), *New Statesman and Society* 03.03.1995.

Anderson, Paul, and Nyta Mann, *Safety First: The Making of New Labour*, London, Granta Books, 1997.

Ashley, Jackie, 'A foot in the door, and a finger on the pulse', *Guardian* 27.05.2002, p. 10.

Atkinson, Dick, *The Common Sense of Community*, London, Demos, 1994.

Audi, Robert (ed.), *The Cambridge Dictionary of Philosophy*, Cambridge, Cambridge University Press, 1995.

Avineri S., and A. de-Shalit, *Communitarianism and Individualism*, Oxford, Oxford University Press, 1992.

Avnon, Dan, and Avner de-Shalit (eds), *Liberalism and its Practice*, London, Routledge, 1999.

Backhurst, David, and Christine Sypnowich (eds), *The Social Self*, London, Sage, 1999.

Barnes, Marian, 'Users as Citizens: Collective Action and the Local Governance of Welfare', *Social Policy and Administration* 33:1, March 1999.

Barnett, Anthony, 'Blair's fear of the fear factor', *Independent* 20.02.1997, p. 16.

Bates, Stephen, 'Taking orders from God', *Guardian* 30.03.2001.

Bates, Stephen, 'Peace of the action', *Guardian Society* 22.05.2002.

Baxter, Sarah, 'Blair's backroom boffins make strange bedfellows', *Sunday Times* 08.01.1995, p. 8.

Baxter, Sarah, 'I am the way and I am the truth', *Sunday Times* 19.03.1995, p. 3.

Becker, Saul (ed.), *Windows of Opportunity: Public Policy and the Poor*, London, Child Poverty Action Group, 1991.

Beckett, Andy, 'Me? A member of the liberal elite?', *Guardian* 17.08.2001.

Bell, Daniel, *Communitarianism and its Critics*, Oxford, Oxford University Press, 1993.

Bell, Daniel, 'Communitarianism' in *Stanford Encyclopedia of Philosophy*, http//plato.stanford. edo/entries/communitarianism/, accessed 22.02.2002.

Bellah, Robert *et al.*, *Habits of the Heart: Individualism and Commitment in American Life*, Berkeley, University of California Press, 1985.

Bellamy, R., and J. Greenaway, 'The New Right Conception of Citizenship and the Citizen's Charter', *Government and Opposition* 30:4, 1995.

Bennett, Fran, 'Rebuilding the Welfare State: The Moral Case for Reform' in Gavin Kelly (ed.), *Is New Labour Working?*

Benyon, John, and Adam Edwards, 'Crime and public order' in Dunleavy *et al.*, *Developments in British Politics 5*, 1997.

Bethke Elshtain, Jean, 'When Privacy Goes Too Far', *Times Literary Supplement* 24.09.1999.

Bird, John, 'Stop the rot before it sets in', *Guardian* 15.08.1997.

Blair, Tony, *Socialism*, Fabian Pamphlet 565, London, Fabian Society, 1994.

Blair, Tony, Speech to the Labour Party Annual Conference, 04.10.1994.

Blair, Tony, *Let Us Face the Future: the 1945 Anniversary Lecture*, Fabian Pamphlet 571, London, Fabian Society, 1995.

Blair, Tony, 'The Rights we Enjoy Reflect the Duties we Owe', *Spectator* Lecture, 22.03.1995.

Blair, Tony, 'Valuing families', *Sun* 31.03.1995, reproduced in Blair, *New Britain*.

Blair, Tony, Mais Lecture, 22.05.1995.

Blair, Tony, 'Is Labour the true heir to Thatcher?', *The Times* 17.07.1995, p. 17.

Blair, Tony, Speech to the Labour Party Annual Conference, 03.10.1995.

Blair, Tony, *New Britain: My Vision of a Young Country*, New Statesman Special Selection, London, Fourth Estate, 1996.

Blair, Tony, Speech to the Singapore Business Community, 08.01.1996, reproduced in Blair, *New Britain*.

Blair, Tony, Speech at the Assembly Rooms, Derby, 18.01.1996, reproduced in Blair, *New Britain*.

Blair, Tony, 'Faith in the City – Ten Years On', speech given in Southwark Cathedral 29.01.1996, reproduced in Blair, *New Britain* as 'The Stakeholder Society'.

Blair, Tony, John Smith Memorial Lecture, 07.03.1996, reproduced in Blair, *New Britain*.

Blair, Tony, 'Why I am a Christian', *Sunday Telegraph* 07.04.1996, reproduced in Blair, *New Britain*.

Blair, Tony, Speech to the Labour Party Annual Conference, 01.10.1996.

Blair, Tony, *New Britain: My Vision of a Young Country*, London, Fourth Estate, 1996.

Blair, Tony, Speech to the *Guardian*/Nexus Conference, London School of Economics, 01.03.1997.

Blair, Tony, Speech at the Aylesbury Estate, Southwark, 02.06.1997.

Blair, Tony, Speech to the Party of European Socialists' Congress, Malmo, 06.06.1997.

Blair, Tony, Speech to the Labour Party Annual Conference, 30.09.1997.

Blair, Tony, Speech launching the Social Exclusion Unit, Stockwell Park School, Lambeth, 08.12.1997.

Blair, Tony, *Leading the Way: A New Vision for Local Government*, London, Institute for Public Policy Research, 1998.

Blair, Tony, *The Third Way: New Politics for the New Century*, Fabian Pamphlet 588, London, Fabian Society, 1998.

Blair, Tony, 'The new givers: supporting volunteering and community involvement', *Guardian* 01.03.2000.

Blair, Tony, Speech to the Women's Institutes' Triennial General Meeting, 07.06.2000.

Blair, Tony, 'Values and the Power of Community', speech to the Global Ethics Foundation, Tübingen University, 30.06.2000.

Blair, Tony, Prime Minister's speech on the launch of the Employment Green Paper, 14.03.2001, www.primeminister.gov.uk/news.asp?NewsId=1895&SectionId=32, accessed 28.02.2002.

Blears, Hazel, *Communities in Control: Public Services and Local Socialism*, Fabian Ideas no. 607, London, Fabian Society, 2003.

Blunkett, David, interview, *Today* programme, BBC Radio 4, 29.09.1999.

Blunkett, David, 'No hiding place for fraudsters', *Observer* 14.01.2001, p. 31.

Boswell, Jonathan, *Community and the Economy: The Theory of Public Co-operation*, London, Routledge, 1990.

Bowring, Bill, 'Law and Order in the "New" Britain', in Hall, Massey and Rustin (eds), *Soundings Special.*

Bowring, Finn, 'Communitarianism and Morality: In Search of the Subject', *New Left Review* 222, March/April 1997.

Brickell, Paul, *People Before Structures: Engaging Communities Effectively in Regeneration*, London, Demos, 2000

Bright, Martin, and Vikram Dodd, 'Pupils face "good citizen" class', *Observer* 15.03.1997.

Brittan, Samuel, 'Blair's Real Guru', *New Statesman* 07.12.1997.

Brivati, Brian, and Tim Bale, *New Labour in Power: Precedents and Prospects*, London, Routledge, 1997

Brown, Gordon, *Fair is Efficient: A Socialist Agenda for Fairness*, Fabian Pamphlet 563, London, Fabian Society, 1994.

Brown, Gordon, 'The Politics of Potential: A New Agenda for Labour' in David Miliband (ed.), *Reinventing the Left.*

Brown, Gordon, Speech by the Chancellor of the Exchequer at the National Council for Voluntary Organisations' Annual Conference, 09.02.2000.

Burchardt, Tania, Julian LeGrand and David Piachaud, 'Social Exclusion in Britain 1991– 1995', *Social Policy and Administration* 33:3, September 1999.

Burkitt, Brian, and Frances Ashton, 'The Birth of the Stakeholder Society', *Critical Social Policy* 49, 1996.

Burnham, Peter, 'New Labour and the Politics of Depoliticisation', *British Journal of Politics and International Relations* 3:2, June 2001.

Burns, Danny and Marilyn Taylor, *Mutual Aid and Self-Help: Coping Strategies for Excluded Communities*, Bristol, Joseph Rowntree Foundation/Policy Press, 1998.

Butcher, Hugh, Andrew Glen, Paul Henderson and Jenny Smith (eds), *Community and Public Policy*, London, Pluto Press, 1993.

Cabinet Office, *Citizen's Charter: Raising the Standard*, CM1599, London, HMSO, 1991.

Campbell, Beatrix, 'So what's the big idea Mr. Etzioni?', *Independent* 16.03.1995, p.15.

Campbell, Beatrix, 'Granddaddy of the backlash', *Guardian* 01.04.1995, p. 31.

Caney, Simon, 'Liberalism and Communitarianism: A Misconceived Debate', *Political Studies* 45, 1992.

Carling, Alan, 'New Labour's Polity: Tony Giddens and the "Third Way"', *Imprints* 3:3, 1999.

Castle, Stephen, and David Usborne, 'Blair's third way leads to New York', *Independent* 19.09.1998, p. 4.

Channon, Gabriel, *Searching for Solid Foundations: Community Involvement and Urban Policy*, London, ODPM, 2003.

Channon, Gabriel and Alison West, *Regeneration and Sustainable Communities*, London, Community Development Foundation, 1999.

Chaudhary, Vivek, 'Appeal for lessons in citizenship', *Guardian* 27.03.1998, p. 8.

Cockerell, Michael, 'The Secret World of Tony Blair', *New Statesman* 14.02.2000.

Cohen, Nick, 'The -ism now arriving …', *Independent on Sunday* 05.12.1995, p. 6.

Cohen, Nick, 'Asia crisis fails to cure Blair's Fukuyama fever', *Observer* 18.01.1998, p. 26.

Cohen, Nick, 'The Lesson the Prime Minister Forgot', *New Statesman* 01.07.2002.

Collins, Philip, 'Community, Morality and Fairness', *Renewal* 4:3, July 1996.

Commission on Social Justice, *Social Justice: Strategies for National Renewal*, London, Vintage, 1995.

Coote, Anna, 'A bit too much of a prig and a prude', *Independent* 03.07.1995, p. 14.

Costello, John E., *John Macmurray: A Biography*, Edinburgh, Floris Books, 2002.

Coyle, Diana, 'Secret lives of the great and the good', *Independent* 01.09.1995, p. 15.

Craig, Gary, and Jill Manthorpe, 'Unequal Partners? Local Government Reorganisation and the Voluntary Sector', *Social Policy and Administration* 33:1, March 1999.

Crampton, Robert, 'Labour exchange', *The Times* 30.09.1995, p. 8.

Crawford, Adam, 'Review Article: The Spirit of Community: Rights, Responsibilities and the Communitarian Agenda', *Journal of Law and Society* 23:2, June 1996.

Crick, Bernard, *Socialism*, Milton Keynes, Open University Press, 1987.

Crick, Bernard, 'Prophets, creeps and publishers', *Independent* 05.07.1997, p. 7.

Crick, Bernard, 'Still Missing: A Public Philosophy', *Political Quarterly* 68:4, Oct/Dec 1997.

Crick, Bernard, *Essays on Citizenship*, London, Continuum, 2000.

Crick, Bernard, 'A Subject at Last!', in Crick, *Essays on Citizenship*.

Crick, Bernard, 'In Defence of the Citizenship Order 2000', in Crick, *Essays on Citizenship*.

Darling, Alastair, 'Rebuilding the Welfare State: The Moral Case for Reform', in Kelly (ed.), *Is New Labour Working?*

Darling, Alastair, letter, *Guardian* 24.06.2000, p. 21.

Deacon, Alan, 'The Retreat from State Welfare', in Becker (ed.), *Windows of Opportunity: Public Policy and the Poor.*

Deacon, Alan, 'The Green Paper on Welfare Reform: A Case for Enlightened Self-Interest?', *Political Quarterly* 69:3, 1998.

Deacon, Alan, 'Learning From the US? The Influence of American Ideas Upon "New Labour" Thinking on Welfare Reform', *Policy and Politics* 28:1, 2000.

Deakin, Nicholas, 'Voluntary action: transparent role for the chameleon', *Guardian* 21.06.1995, p. 36.

Dearlove, John, and Peter Saunders, *Introduction to British Politics*, 3rd edition, Cambridge, Polity Press, 2000.

Department for Education and Employment, *Excellence in Schools*, White Paper Cm3681, London, HMSO, 1997.

Department of the Environment, Transport and the Regions, *Modern Local Government: In Touch With the People*, summary of White Paper, London, DETR, 1998.

Department of Social Security, *New Ambitions for Our Country: A New Contract for Welfare*, CM3805, 1998.

Driver, Stephen, and Luke Martell, 'Beyond Equality and Liberty: New Labour's Liberal Conservatism', *Renewal* 4:3, July 1996.

Driver, Stephen, and Luke Martell, 'New Labour's Communitarianisms', *Critical Social Policy* 17:3, August 1997.

Driver, Stephen, and Luke Martell, *New Labour: Politics After Thatcherism*, Cambridge, Polity Press, 1998.

Driver, Stephen, and Luke Martell, 'New Labour, Work and the Family: Communitarianisms in Conflict?', paper given at the Sociology and Social Psychology Graduate/Faculty Seminar, University of Sussex, 18.10.1999.

Driver, Stephen, and Luke Martell, 'Left, Right and the Third Way', *Policy and Politics* 28:2, 2000.

Duncan, Alan, and Dominic Hobson, 'Tired old New Labour', *The Times* 01.06.1995, p. 20.

Dunleavy, Patrick, Andrew Gamble, Ian Holliday, and Gillian Peale, *Developments in British*

Politics 5, Basingstoke, Macmillan, 1997.

Dwyer, Peter, 'Conditional Citizens? Welfare Rights and Responsibilities in the Late 1990s', *Critical Social Policy* 18:4, 1998.

Economist, 'Labour's ladder of opportunity: Tony Blair has the chance to redefine Labour as the party of meritocracy', leading article, 08.10.1994.

Economist, 'The ties that bind', leading article, 08.10.1994.

Economist, 'Freedom and community', leading article, 24.12.1994.

Economist, Communitarian conceits: Amitai Etzioni preaches up a storm, but to what effect?', leading article, 18.03.1995.

Economist, 'Down with rights', leading article, 18.03.1995.

Economist, 'Love fest: Blair's American visit', leading article, 13.04.1996.

Economist, 'The spiel of the covenant', leading article, 05.10.1996.

Economist, 'Park Life', leading article, 06.12.1997.

Economist, 'The strangest Tory ever sold', leading article, 02.05.1998.

Economist, 'University of Downing Street: the new establishment: Tony Blair's favourite academics', leading article, 04.09.1999.

Ellwood, David, *Poor Support*, New York, BasicBooks, 1988.

Etzioni, Amitai, *Capitol Corruption: The New Attack on American Democracy*, New Brunswick, NJ, Transaction Books, 1988.

Etzioni, Amitai, *The Parenting Deficit*, London, Demos, 1993.

Etzioni, Amitai, 'A mad scramble for the centre', *Sunday Times* 09.10.1994, p. 3.

Etzioni, Amitai, 'Nation in Need of Community Values', (Second *Times*/Demos Lecture), *The Times* 20.02.1995, p. 9.

Etzioni, Amitai, 'Common Values', *New Statesman and Society* 12.05.1995, p. 24.

Etzioni, Amitai, *The Spirit of Community: Rights, Responsibilities and the Communitarian Agenda* [1993], London, Fontana, 1995.

Etzioni, Amitai (ed.), *New Communitarian Thinking: Persons, Virtues, Institutions and Communities*, Charlottesville, University of Virginia Press, 1995.

Etzioni, Amitai, 'The Responsive Community: A Communitarian Perspective', (Presidential Address to the American Sociological Association), *American Sociological Review* 61, February 1996, pp. 1–11.

Etzioni, Amitai, 'A Moderate Communitarian Proposal', *Political Theory* 24:2, May 1996, pp. 155–71.

Etzioni, Amitai, *The New Golden Rule: Community and Morality in a Democratic Society* (1996), London, Profile Books, 1997.

Etzioni, Amitai, 'Balancing individual rights and the common good', *Tikkun Magazine*, Jan/Feb 1997.

Etzioni, Amitai, 'Tony Blair: a communitarian in the making?', *The Times* 21.06.1997, p. 20.

Etzioni, Amitai, 'What should Jack Straw do about crime?', *Guardian* 28.06.1997, p. 21.

Etzioni, Amitai (ed.), *The Essential Communitarian Reader*, Lanham, Rowman and Littlefield, 1998.

Etzioni, Amitai, *The Third Way to a Good Society*, London, Demos, 2000.

Fairclough, Norman, *New Labour, New Language?*, London, Routledge, 2000.

Field, Frank, *Losing Out: The Emergence of Britain's Underclass*, London, Blackwell, 1989.

Field, Frank, 'Britain's Underclass: Countering the Growth', in Lister (ed.), *Charles Murray and the Underclass*.

Foster, Janet, 'Informal Social Control and Community Crime Prevention', *British Journal of Criminology* 35:4, Autumn 1995.

Frazer, Elizabeth, *The Problems of Communitarian Politics: Unity and Conflict*, Oxford, Oxford

University Press, 1999.

Freeden, Michael, 'Community begins at home', letters, *Independent* 12.02.1995, p. 20.

Giddens, Anthony, *Beyond Left and Right: The Future of Radical Politics*, Cambridge, Polity Press, 1994.

Giddens, Anthony, letter, *Independent* 06.07.1995, p. 16.

Giddens, Anthony, 'Anomie of the people', *Guardian* 31.07.1997, p. 11.

Giddens, Anthony, *The Third Way: The Renewal of Social Democracy*, Cambridge, Polity Press, 1998.

Giddens, Anthony, 'Beyond Left and Right', *Observer* 13.09.1998, p. 27.

Giddens, Anthony, *The Third Way and its Critics*, Cambridge, Polity Press, 2000.

Gilbert, David, 'Don't Look Back?', *Renewal* 4:3, July 1996.

Goodin, Robert E., and Philip Pettit (eds), *Blackwell Companion to Contemporary Political Philosophy*, Oxford, Blackwell, 1993.

Gray, John, 'A radical departure', *Guardian* 27.06.1995, p. 15.

Gray, John, 'Divide and rule', *Guardian* 02.10.1995, p. 11.

Gray, John, *After Social Democracy: Politics, Capitalism and the Common Life*, London, Demos, 1996.

Gray, John, 'What Community Is Not', *Renewal* 4:3, July 1996.

Green, David G., *Reinventing Civil Society: The Rediscovery of Welfare Without Politics*, IEA Choice in Welfare Series no. 17, London, Institute of Economic Affairs, 1993

Green, David G., *Community Without Politics: A Market Approach to Welfare Reform*, IEA Choice in Welfare Series no. 27, London, Institute of Economic Affairs, 1996.

Guardian, 'Mr. Blair gets the bird', leading article, 08.06.2000, p. 23.

Guardian, 'Anxious, angry and ugly: What Paulsgrove's passion is telling us', leading article, 11.08.2000, p. 19.

Gutmann, Amy, 'Communitarian Critics of Liberalism', *Philosophy and Public Affairs* 14, 1985.

Hale, Sarah, 'Professor Macmurray and Mr. Blair: The Strange Case of the Communitarian Guru that Never Was', *Political Quarterly* 73:2, 2002.

Hale, Sarah, Will Leggett and Luke Martell, *The Third Way: Criticisms, Futures, Alternatives*, Manchester University Press, 2004.

Hall, Stuart, Doreen B. Massey, and Michael Rustin (eds), *Soundings Special: The Next Ten Years: Key Issues for Blair's Britain*, London, Soundings/Lawrence and Wishart, 1997.

Hansard, House of Commons Debates for 27.02.2002.

Hargreaves, Ian, 'Tony's Best Mate is Back', *New Statesman and Society* 31.05.1996, p. 18.

Hargreaves, Ian, and Stewart Fleming, 'Labour's Most Fertile Policy Thinker Outside the Shadow Cabinet is Willing to Think the Unthinkable About the Welfare State', interview with Frank Field, *New Statesman* 18.10.1996.

Harris, Michael, 'New Labour: Government and Opposition', *Political Quarterly* 70:1, 1999, p. 55.

Hattersley, Roy, 'In the lingerie shop', *Guardian* 15.04.2000 (review of Giddens, *The Third Way and its Critics*).

Hattersley, Roy, 'So what is it that Tony believes in?', *Guardian* 04.03.2002.

Hay, Colin, *The Political Economy of New Labour*, Manchester, Manchester University Press, 1999.

Heron, Emma, and Peter Dwyer, 'Doing the Right Thing: Labour's Attempt to Forge a New Welfare Deal Between the Individual and the State', *Social Policy and Administration* 33:1, March 1999.

Hoggart, Simon, 'Blair bamboozled when asked about his beliefs', *Guardian* 28.02.2002.

Holmes, Stephen, *The Anatomy of Antiliberalism*, Cambridge, MA, Harvard University Press, 1993.

Horton, John, and Susan Mendus (eds), *After MacIntyre: Critical Perspectives on the Work of Alasdair MacIntyre*, London, Polity Press, 1994.

Hoyle, Caroline, and David Rose, 'Labour, Law and Order', *Political Quarterly* 72:1, 2001.

Hughes, Gordon, 'Communitarianism and Law and Order', *Critical Social Policy* 49, 1996, p. 18.

Hughes, Gordon, and Adrian Little, 'The Contradictions of New Labour's Communitarianism', *Imprints* 4:1, 1999.

Hugill, Barry, 'Why can't we live together?', *Observer* 12.11.1995, p.18.

Hurd, Douglas, 'Citizenship in the Tory Democracy', *New Statesman* 29.04.1988.

Hutton, Will, *The State We're In* [1995], London, Vintage, 1996.

Imrie, Rob, and Mike Raco (eds), *Urban Renaissance? New Labour, Community and Urban Policy*, Bristol, Policy Press, 2003.

Imrie, Rob, and Mike Raco, 'Community and the changing nature of urban policy' in Imrie and Raco (eds), *Urban Renaissance? New Labour, Community and Urban Policy*, Bristol, Policy Press, 2003.

Independent, 'Blair's Utopian vision is not enough', leading article, 25.05.1994, p. 15.

Independent, 'An illusion of happy families', leading article, 27.09.1994, p. 17.

Independent, 'Write compassion into the new faith', leading article, 18.03.1995, p. 12.

Independent, 'Nostalgia: not yet a thing of the past', leading article, 05.08.1995, p. 14.

James, Oliver, 'The guru with a message of repression', *Independent* 06.10.1998.

Jordan, Bill, 'New Labour, New Community?', *Imprints* 3:2, 1999.

Kandiah, Michael David, and Anthony Selsdon (eds), *Ideas and Think Tanks in Contemporary Britain*, London, Frank Cass, 1996.

Kautz, Stephen, *Liberalism and Community*, Ithaca, Cornell University Press, 1995.

Kellner, Peter, 'A New "ism" for our Times', *New Statesman* 22.05.1998.

Kelly, Gavin (ed.), *Is New Labour Working?*, Fabian Pamphlet 590, London, Fabian Society, 1999.

Kennedy, Helena, 'An enemy of justice', *Guardian* 20.01.2000, p. 21.

Kukathas, Chandran, 'Liberalism, Communitarianism, and Political Community', *Social Philosophy and Policy* 13:1, 1996.

Kymlicka, Will, *Contemporary Political Philosophy: An Introduction*, Oxford, Clarendon Press, 1990.

Kymlicka, Will, 'Community', in Goodin and Pettit (eds), *Blackwell Companion*.

Labour Party, *A Quiet Life: Tough Action on Criminal Neighbours*, London, Labour Party, 1995.

Labour Party, *Renewing Democracy, Rebuilding Communities*, London, Labour Party, 1995.

Labour Party, *Safer Communities, Safer Britain: Labour's Proposals for Tough Action on Crime*, London, Labour Party, 1995.

Labour Party, *Protecting Our Communities: Labour's Plans for Tackling Criminal, Anti-Social Behaviour in Neighbourhoods*, London, Labour Party, 1996.

Labour Party, *Tackling the Causes of Crime: Labour's Proposals to Prevent Crime and Criminality*, London, Labour Party, 1996.

Labour Party, *Building the Future Together: Labour's Policies for Partnership between Government and the Voluntary Sector*, London, Labour Party, 1997.

Labour Party, *New Deal for a New Britain: Labour's Proposals to Tackle Youth and Long-Term Unemployment*, London, Labour Party, 1997.

Labour Party, *New Labour: Leading Britain into the Future*, London, Labour Party, 1997.

Labour Party, *Labour in Government: Delivering our Contract to the People*, NEC Statement to the Labour Party Annual Conference, London, Labour Party, 1997.

Labour Party, *The Choices for Britain*, General Election Manifesto, London, Labour Party, 2001.

Labour Party, *Forward not Back*, General Election Manifesto, London, Labour Party, 2005.

Le Grand, Julian, 'The Third Way Begins With Cora', *New Statesman* 06.03.1998.

Leadbeater, Charles, *The Rise of the Social Entrepreneur*, London, Demos, 1997.

Leadbeater, Charles, 'Inside the wonkathon: what the wonk told the PM', *Observer* 10.05.1998, p. 23.

Levitas, Ruth, 'The Concept of Social Exclusion and the New Durkheimian Hegemony', *Critical Social Policy* 16, 1996.

Levitas, Ruth, *The Inclusive Society? Social Exclusion and New Labour*, Basingstoke, Macmillan, 1998.

Lister, Ruth (ed.), *The Exclusive Society: Citizenship and the Poor*, London, Child Poverty Action Group, 1990.

Lister, Ruth (ed.), *Charles Murray and the Underclass: The Developing Debate*, London, Institute of Economic Affairs, 1996.

Lister, Ruth, 'From Equality to Social Inclusion: New Labour and the Welfare State', *Critical Social Policy* 18:2, 1998.

Lister, Ruth, 'Vocabularies of Citizenship and Gender: the UK', *Critical Social Policy* 18:3, 1998.

Lister, Ruth, 'To Rio via the Third Way: New Labour's "Welfare" Reform Agenda', paper given to the first ESRC Research Seminar Programme on 'New Labour and the Third Way in Public Services', London, 22.04.1999.

Lister, Ruth, 'Political Struggle and Social Justice: New Labour and Citizenship', *Imprints* 4:1, 1999.

Lloyd, John, 'Profile: Amitai Etzioni', *New Statesman* 20.06.1997, pp. 28–30.

Ludlam, Steve, and Martin J. Smith (eds), *New Labour in Government*, London, Macmillan, 2001.

Ludlam, Steve, and Martin J. Smith (eds), *Governing as New Labour: Policy and Politics under Blair*, Basingstoke, Palgrave Macmillan, 2004.

Lund, Brian, '"Ask Not What Your Community Can Do For You": Obligations, New Labour and Welfare Reform', *Critical Social Policy* 19:4, 1999.

MacIntyre, Alasdair, *After Virtue: A Study in Moral Theory* [1981], London, Duckworth, 1985.

MacIntyre, Alasdair, 'The Spectre of Communitarianism', *Radical Philosophy* 70, March/April 1995.

MacIntyre, Alasdair, 'A Philosophical Self-Portrait', in Mautner (ed.), *Penguin Dictionary of Philosophy*, p. 332.

Macmurray, John, *Freedom in the Modern World* [1932], London, Faber and Faber, 1968.

Macmurray, John, *Creative Society: A Study of the Relation of Christianity to Communism*, London, Student Christian Movement Press, 1935.

Macmurray, John, *Reason and Emotion* [1935], London, Faber and Faber, 1962.

Macmurray, John, *A Challenge to the Churches: Religion and Democracy*, London, Kegan Paul, 1941.

Macmurray, John, *Conditions of Freedom*, Toronto, Ryerson Press, 1949.

Macmurray, John, *The Self as Agent*, London, Faber and Faber, 1957.

Macmurray, John, *Persons in Relation*, London, Faber and Faber, 1961.

McElvoy, Anne, 'Not quite so chic to be Labour', *The Times* 08.04.1995, p. 18.

McSmith, Andy, *Faces of Labour: The Inside Story*, London, Verso, 2nd edition, 1996.

Malik, Kenan, 'Creating a sense of Us and Them', *Independent* 08.08.1994, p. 15.

Mandelson, Peter, *Labour's Next Steps: Tackling Social Exclusion*, Fabian Pamphlet 581, London, Fabian Society, 1997.

Mandelson, Peter, and Roger Liddle, *The Blair Revolution: Can New Labour Deliver?*, London, Faber and Faber, 1996.

Marquand, David, *The Unprincipled Society: New Demands and Old Politics*, London, Fontana, 1988.

Marquand, David, 'The Blair Paradox', *Prospect*, May 1998.

Marr, Andrew, 'Why Blair must give power to the people', *Independent* 18.07.1995, p. 15.

Marr, Andrew, 'Ruling Britannia: gloom will bring us together', *Independent* 08.09.1995, p. 15.

Marr, Andrew, 'Where sheep may safely graze', *Observer* 22.11.1998.

Mautner, Thomas (ed.), *Penguin Dictionary of Philosophy*, London, Penguin, 1997.

Mead, Lawrence, *Beyond Entitlement: The Social Obligations of Citizenship*, New York, The Free Press, 1986.

Miliband, David, *Reinventing the Left*, Cambridge, Polity Press, 1994.

Miller, David, 'Communitarianism: Left, Right and Centre' in Avnon and de-Shalit (eds), *Liberalism and Its Practice*.

Milne, Kirsty, 'Doing it for real', *New Statesman* 03.03.1995.

Milne, Seumas, 'Everybody's talking about', *Guardian* 07.10.1994, p. 5.

Mouffe, Chantal (ed.), *Dimensions of Radical Democracy: Pluralism, Citizenship and Community*, London, Verso, 1992.

Mulgan, Geoff, 'Beyond the lure of off-the-shelf ethics', *Independent* 30.01.1995, p. 13.

Mulgan, Geoff, and Charles Landry, *The Other Invisible Hand: Remaking Charity for the 21st Century*, London, Demos, 1995.

Mulgan, Geoff, *Connexity*, London, Chatto and Windus, 1997.

Mulhall, Stephen, and Adam Swift, *Liberals and Communitarians*, Oxford, Blackwell, 1992.

Mulhall, Stephen, and Adam Swift, 'The Social Self in Political Theory: The Communitarian Critique of the Liberal Subject', in Backhurst and Sypnowich (eds), *The Social Self*.

Murray, Charles, *Losing Ground*, New York, BasicBooks, 1984.

Murray, Charles, *The Emerging British Underclass*, London, Institute of Economic Affairs, 1990.

Murray, Charles, *Underclass: The Crisis Deepens*, London, Institute of Economic Affairs, 1994.

National Curriculum, *About Citizenship in the National Curriculum*, www.nc.uk.net/about/about_citizenship.html, accessed 13.02.2002.

National Curriculum, *The Importance of Citizenship*, www.nc.uk.net/importance/import_citizenship.html, accessed 13.02.2002.

National Curriculum, Key Stage 3, Citizenship, www.nc.uk.net/servlets/NCParserPhase1?Section=PoS&Subject+CI&KeyStage=3, accessed 13.02.2002.

National Curriculum, Key Stage 4, Citizenship, www.nc.uk.net/servlets/NCParserPhase1?Section=PoS&Subject+CI&KeyStage=4, accessed 13.02.2002.

Panitch, Leo (ed.), *The Socialist Register 1997: Ruthless Criticism of All That Exists*, London, Merlin Press, 1997.

Peele, Gillian, 'Political Parties' in Dunleavy, Gamble, Holliday and Peele, *Developments in British Politics 5*.

Pettit, Philip, 'Liberal/Communitarian: MacIntyre's Mesmeric Dichotomy', in Horton and Mendus (eds), *After MacIntyre*.

Phillips, Derek L., *Looking Backward: A Critical Appraisal of Communitarian Thought*, Princeton, Princeton University Press, 1993.

Phillips, Melanie, 'The father of Tony Blair's big idea', *Observer*, 24.07.1994.

Phillips, Melanie, 'Freedom and community reconciled', *Observer*, 25.09.1994.

Phillips, Melanie, 'The race to wake sleeping duty', *Observer* 02.04.1995, p. 25.

Pilger, John, 'Mr. Blair's Dubious Moral Purpose', *New Statesman* 25.10.1996, p. 17.

Pilger, John, *Hidden Agendas*, London, Vintage, 1998.

Plant, Raymond, 'Community: Concept, Conception, and Ideology', *Politics and Society* 8, 1978.

Plant, Raymond, 'So You Want to be a Citizen?', *New Statesman* 06.02.1998.

Pollard, Charles, Commentary on Jack Straw, 'Freedom From Fear: Building a Safer Britain', in Kelly (ed.), *Is New Labour Working?*

Powell, M. (ed.), *New Labour, New Welfare State?*, Bristol, Policy Press, 1999.

Powell, Martin, 'New Labour and the Third Way in the British Welfare State: A New and Distinctive Approach?, *Critical Social Policy* 20:1, 2000.

Prideaux, Simon, 'From Organisational Theory to the Third Way: The Continuities Underpinning the New Communitarianism of Amitai Etzioni', paper given at 'The Third Way and Beyond: Criticisms, Futures, Alternatives', conference held at the University of Sussex, 02.11.2000.

Prideaux, Simon, 'From Organisational Theory to the Third Way: continuities and contradictions underpinning Amitai Etzioni's communitarian influence on New Labour', in Hale, Leggett and Martell (eds), *The Third Way*, pp. 128–45.

Raven, Charlotte, 'Tank boys', *Observer* 30.07.1995, p. 18.

Rawls, John, *A Theory of Justice* [1971], Oxford, Oxford University Press, 1973.

Rawnsley, Andrew, *Servants of the People: The Inside Story of New Labour*, London, Penguin, 2001.

Remnick, David, 'The Real Mr. Blair', *Observer* 01.05.2005.

Rentoul, John, *Tony Blair* [1995], London, Warner Books, revised edition, 1996.

Rentoul, John, 'Learning from Clinton, stealing from Thatcher', *Independent* 18.01.1995, p. 19.

Richards, Paul, *Is the Party Over? New Labour and the Politics of Participation*, London, Demos, 2000.

Riddell, Mary, 'New Election, New Gurus', *Observer* 01.04.2001.

Riddell, Peter, 'I'm a guru, are you one too?', *Times* 07.09.1996.

Rogers, Ben, 'An illiterate philosopher', *Guardian* 30.03.2001.

Rogers, Ben (ed.), *Lonely Citizens: Report of the Working Party on Active Citizenship*, London, IPPR, 2004.

Ross, Kathleen, and Stephen P. Osborne, 'Making a Reality of Community Governance: Structuring Government-Voluntary Sector Relations at the Local Level', *Public Policy and Administration* 14:2, 1999.

Russell, Conrad, 'New Labour: Old Tory Writ Large?', *New Left Review* 219, Sep/Oct 1996.

Salmon, Harry, 'Community, Communitarianism and Local Government', *Local Government Policy Making* 22:3, 1995.

Sandel, Michael, *Liberalism and the Limits of Justice* [1982], Cambridge, Cambridge University Press, 1998.

Sandel, Michael, *Democracy's Discontent: America in Search of a Public Philosophy*, Cambridge, MA, Belknap/Harvard University Press, 1996.

Scruton, Roger, 'Why Mr. Clinton's guru neglects posterity', *The Times* 07.12.1995, p. 40.

Selbourne, David, *The Principle of Duty: An Essay on the Foundations of Civic Order*, London, Sinclair Stevenson, 1994.

Selznick, Philip, 'The Idea of a Communitarian Morality', *California Law Review* 75, 1987.

Smith, Joan, 'The Ideology of "Family and Community": New Labour Abandons the Welfare State', in Panitch (ed.), *The Socialist Register 1997*.

Smith, Joan, 'Should we live this way? Communitarians say we have too much freedom', *Independent on Sunday* 22.06.1997, p. 27.

Social Exclusion Unit, *Bringing Britain Together: A National Strategy for Neighbourhood Renewal* Cm4342, London, Cabinet Office, 1998.

Social Exclusion Unit, www.cabinet-office.gov.uk/seu/index/more.html, accessed 23.03.2000.

Social Exclusion Unit, Introductory Leaflet, www.cabinet-office.gov.uk/seu/index/march_%202000_%20leaflet.htm, accessed 23.03.2000.

Sopel, John, *Tony Blair: The Moderniser*, London, Bantam, 1995.

Steele, Jonathan, 'Clinton policies are caught in communitarian crossfire', *Guardian* 12.04.1995, p. 20.

Stepney, Paul, Richard Lynch, and Bill Jordan, 'Poverty, Exclusion and New Labour', *Critical Social Policy* 19:1, 1999.

Straw, Jack, 'Put the heart back into communities', *The Times* 13.11.1995.

Straw, Jack, 'I have a dream – and I don't want it mugged', *Guardian* 08.06.1996.

Straw, Jack, 'Freedom From Fear: Building a Safer Britain' in Kelly (ed.), *Is New Labour Working?*

Sunday Times, 'The man with the big idea?', leading article, 09.10.1994, p. 3.

Sunday Times, 'A trimmer round the edges', leading article, 23.07.1995, p. 3.

Swanson, Jacinda, 'Self Help: Clinton, Blair, and the Politics of Personal Responsibility', *Radical Philosophy* 101, May/June 2000.

Swift, Adam, 'Politics v. Philosophy', *Prospect*, August/September 2001.

Tam, Henry, *Communitarianism: A New Agenda for Politics and Citizenship*, Basingstoke, Macmillan, 1998.

Taylor, Charles, *Philosophy and the Human Sciences*, Cambridge, Cambridge University Press, 1985.

Taylor, Charles, *Sources of the Self: The Making of Modern Identity*, Cambridge, Cambridge University Press, 1989.

Taylor, Charles, *Philosophical Arguments*, Cambridge, MA, Harvard University Press, 1995.

Taylor, Charles, 'Cross-Purposes: The Liberal-Communitarian Debate', in Taylor, *Philosophical Arguments*.

Taylor, Charles, 'Atomism', in Taylor, *Philosophy and the Human Sciences*.

Taylor, Marilyn, *Unleashing the Potential: Bringing Residents to the Centre of Regeneration*, York, Joseph Rowntree Foundation, 1995

The Times, 'Information technology can be a builder of communities', leading article, 13.05.1995, p. 19.

Tonkin, Boyd, 'Why New Labour is in search of an ideology', *Independent* 25.04.1998, p. 21.

Toynbee, Polly, 'How liberal is New Labour?', *Independent* 23.04.1996, p. 15.

Toynbee, Polly, 'Blair's community spirit needs to find its focus', *Guardian* 28.03.2001.

Toynbee, Polly, and David Walker, *Did Things Get Better? An Audit of Labour's Successes and Failures*, London, Penguin, 2001.

Travis, Alan, 'Labour toes Thatcher line to aid poor', *Guardian* 15.08.1997, p. 4.

Twigg, Stephen, 'Is There a Policy Solution to Morality?', *Fabian Review* 108:6, 1996.

Vallely, Paul, 'Does God Vote Labour or Tory?', *New Statesman* 27.11.1988.

Walker, Martin, 'Community spirit', *Guardian* 13.03.1995, p. 10.

Walzer, Michael, *Spheres of Justice: A Defense of Pluralism and Equality*, New York, BasicBooks, 1983.

Walzer, Michael, 'The Communitarian Critique of Liberalism', *Political Theory* 18:1, February

1990.

Walzer, Michael, 'The Civil Society Argument', in Mouffe (ed.), *Dimensions of Radical Democracy*.

Whelan, Robert, *The Corrosion of Charity: From Moral Renewal to Contract Culture*, IEA Choice in Welfare Series no. 29, London, Institute of Economic Affairs, 1996.

White, Stuart, 'Interpreting the Third Way: Not One Road, But Many', *Renewal* 6:2, 1998.

Wilby, Peter, 'Blair's warm blanket looks threadbare', *Observer* 11.06.2000, p. 29.

Willetts, David, *Blair's Gurus: An Examination of Labour's Rhetoric*, Policy Study no. 145, London, Centre for Policy Studies, 1996.

Wintour, Patrick, 'Labour looks abroad for ideas', *Guardian* 06.10.1995, p. 6.

Wintour, Patrick, 'Major to appeal for volunteers', *Guardian* 26.05.1996, p. 6.

Working Group on the Active Community, *Giving Time, Getting Involved: Report of the Working Group on the Active Community*, London, Cabinet Office, 1999.

Young, Hugo, 'Blair treads lightly between gobbledegook and platitude', *Guardian* 08.06.2000.

Index